HEADWAY

STUDENT'S BOOK   ADVANCED

John & Liz Soars

Oxford University Press

SKILLS DEVELOPMENT

READING	SPEAKING	LISTENING	WRITING
Topic	**Activity**	**Topic**	**Activity**
Quiz – test your aptitude for language learning	Discussion – the characteristics of a good language learner		
An extract from *My Early Life*, by Winston Churchill Extracts from *Summerhill*, by A. S. Neill	Discussion – the organization of state education in England Discussion – the aims of education	Public schools – an interview with Mr Ian Beer, Head Master of Harrow School, and a radio programme (jigsaw listening)	An essay on school life
The opening and closing paragraphs of different kinds of stories Extracts from *The Picture of Dorian Gray*, by Oscar Wilde	Discussion – characters from English literature Devising a horror story	An interview with the writer Graham Greene	A horror story
'A happy landing for the Tarzan of Central Park' – an article from the *Independent*	Discussion – what is normal behaviour? Discussion – culture shock!	An interview with the writer and raconteur, Quentin Crisp	An essay about a strange time in your life
'Bringing up a better baby' – an article from *Harper's and Queen* magazine	Discussion – parents and children Roleplay – parents at the Better Baby Institute	People talking about their childhood The American comedian George Burns on 'How to live to be a hundred or more'	An essay on bringing up children
An extract from *War*, by Gwynne Dyer 'The Responsibility', a poem	Discussion – quotations on the subject of war	The Christmas Truce, 1914 – interviews with men who were there	A description of a historical event
'Exposed! The fine art of artspeak' – an article from the *Mail on Sunday* Extracts from *Pygmalion*, by George Bernard Shaw	Discussion – objective and subjective descriptions Play reading Describing treasured possessions	Extracts from *Pygmalion*, by George Bernard Shaw	Describing a treasured possession, or a favourite room
Newspaper reports of seven court cases 'Meet the burglar', an article from the *Guardian*	Discussion – what sentence should be imposed? Game – Dilemma!	Television censorship – interviews with Kate Adie, a BBC journalist, and Joanna Bogle of the National Viewers' and Listeners' Association (jigsaw listening)	A report on the role of television
'Parson's Pleasure', an abridged short story by Roald Dahl	Discussion – famous stories Poetry reading (pronunciation) – Roald Dahl's version of 'Little Red Riding Hood'	An interview wtih the writer Barbara Cartland	An up-to-date fairy story

LANGUAGE INPUT

SKILLS DEVELOPMENT

READING	SPEAKING	LISTENING	WRITING
Topic	**Activity**	**Topic**	**Activity**
Extracts from three autobiographies (jigsaw reading)	Practising limericks Discussion – Home sweet home	People talking about where they come from	An essay on the sounds and smells of childhood
'The upper class' – an article from the *Guardian*	Discussion – social classes in Britain Making a speech	An interview with the gossip column writer Nigel Dempster	A speech A formal letter
An extract from *Mindwatching*, by Hans and Michael Eysenck	Problem solving Telling a story from a cartoon by Sempé	An interview with the writer Tony Buzan on how to use the brain more effectively	A story from cartoon prompts
'On the brink of tranquillity' – an article on Near Death Experiences from the *Guardian*	Discussion – the world's religions	An interview with the writer and cosmologist Dr Carl Sagan on the creation of the universe	Correcting mistakes

ORIENTATION

What makes a good language learner?

This unit is an introduction to the course you are about to follow. The aims of the unit are for you to:
– think about your language learning strategies
– check that you know what information a dictionary can provide you with
– find out which areas of English grammar you need to revise.

Quiz

TEST YOUR APTITUDE FOR LEARNING A FOREIGN LANGUAGE

Test your aptitude for language learning by doing this quiz, adapted from *The Sunday Times Magazine*. Write your answers on a piece of paper, then add up your scores to find out how good a language learner you are.

I. Learn the following Samoan words (Samoa is in the South Pacific):

toalua	husband
tamaloa	man
tamaitiiti	child
taulealea	youth
loomatua	old woman

Did you find this task
a) easy and fascinating?
b) very difficult?
c) not easy; the words look the same?
d) so boring you didn't even try?

2. Exhausted after swimming the river, Fred decided to get some sleep, but the *boolles* made it impossible, and even the smoke from his camp fire didn't keep them away.

What is a *boolle*?
a) a wild animal   c) a kind of noise
b) a giant mosquito   d) don't know

3. Someone asks you the way in very bad English. When he/she doesn't understand your reply, do you
a) say it again but louder?
b) get irritated and give up?
c) draw him/her a map?
d) find out if he/she speaks another language you know?

4. Here is a new language:
ek kum chuchu – the train is coming
ek namas chuchu – the train is very big
nek kum niva chuchu – the train isn't coming
ek chuchu – it's a train
How would you say 'It's not a train'?
a) nek chuchu niva
b) ek niva chuchu

c) nek niva chuchu
d) don't know

5. How many foreign languages can you greet someone in?

6. Your boss tells you that you have been chosen to go on a six-month course to learn a completely new language. Do you
a) look for another job?
b) say they've chosen the wrong person?
c) worry a bit but reckon you'll cope?
d) long to get started?

7. You go to an evening class to learn a language. The class lasts two hours a week. List the sorts of practice you might do on your own at home.

8. How good are you at expressing yourself in your own language, both in speaking and in writing?
a) I can always put into words exactly what I want to say.
b) I don't know.
c) It depends on the situation.
d) People sometimes say I am not clear.

9. When did you last read a book for pleasure (in any language)?
a) yesterday
b) I can't remember.
c) last week
d) last month

10. Have you got
a) a bilingual dictionary (English into your language)?
b) a monolingual dictionary (English–English)?
c) both a bilingual and a monolingual dictionary?
d) no dictionary at all?

11. Read through this list of words, then write down as many of them as you can without looking.
pin church identify luxury accelerate carefully miscalculate occasional anxious knot daffodil impertinent

12. In one minute write a list of things you could do with a cabbage (apart from cooking or eating it).

13. In one minute write down as many reasons as you can why it might be useful to learn Eskimo.

14. Fill in the blank with one of the words below.
Shakucomespiteare isos wonone ovofef tehe wororolid's grematerest's wririterners. Hehe wasis .... onin Staratarafoorrd-inon-Aravont.
a) borotone   c) shororit
b) born   d) don't know

15. What is your attitude to learning about British culture (arts, institutions, way of life)?
a) I'm not interested in the slightest, I just need to learn the language.
b) I'm interested a little bit, but only out of curiosity.
c) I'm very interested to find out about the people behind the language.

16. What do the following words in Samoan mean?
loomatua tamaitiiti tamaloa taulealea toalua

17. Are you male or female?

ANSWERS

1. a: score 10 points. b: 4 c: 8 d: 0
Good language learners find words fairly easy, and aren't put off by the way they look.

2. a: 5 b: 10 c: 0 d: 0
Good language learners are able to make imaginative guesses about the meaning of words.

3. a: 0 b: 0 c: 10 d: 8
Good language learners make the most of their skills, and manage to communicate in all sorts of unlikely situations.

4. a: 2 b: 2 c: 10 d: 0
Good language learners are quick at seeing patterns in a foreign language. (Negative sentences in this language begin with 'nek'. The last word is always 'chuchu'.)

5. Two points for each language (maximum 10 points).
This question shows how interested you are in languages and communication.

6. a: 0 b: 3 c: 7 d: 10
Being scared stiff is obviously a bad sign.

7. Good language learners practise a lot on their own. Give yourself two points for each different activity you listed (e.g. listening to cassettes while driving, watching foreign language films on TV). Maximum 10 points.

8. a: 4 b: 0 c: 10 d: 7
Good language learners think a lot about how they use language.

9. a: 10 b: 0 c: 5 d: 2
Good language learners seem to read a lot. (It's a good way of increasing your vocabulary.)

10. a: 5 b: 8 c: 10 d: 0
Good language learners have reference books and consult them regularly.

11. Less than 5, score 0. 6–8, score 5. More than 8, score 10. This test measures your short-term memory. Most people can remember 5 or 6 words out of the list.

12. A point for each idea (maximum 10). People who are very rigid in the way they see things tend not to be very good at learning languages. This is probably because they don't like being in situations they can't control.

13. Two points for each idea (maximum 10). An important factor in learning a language is motivation.

14. a: 10 b: 2 c: 7 d: 0
This question assesses how willing you are to take risks in a language you don't know well.

15. a: 0 b: 5 c: 10
It is impossible to separate a language from its culture. Good language learners are open to other cultures and individuals, and this creates more opportunities for progress.

16. Two points for each word you got right. This question tests your memory again.

17. Females score ten. On the whole, women are better at languages.

INTERPRET YOUR SCORE
0–30 You think you are useless at languages, and can't see the point in trying. Don't give up! Keep at it!

30–70 Learning a language is hard work for you, but you get there in the end. You probably had a bad experience at school. Just remember that most people in the world speak at least two languages, and lots speak four or five, so it can't be all that difficult, can it?

70–100 You're an average sort of learner, not brilliant, but you manage. You're always willing to have a go. Surprisingly, it usually works, too! Add some systematic study to this, and a bit of practice, and you'll be able to cope in most situations.

100–140 You can probably get by in one or two languages already, and learning a new language holds no terror for you. Don't give up when you feel you're not making progress. A bit more confidence, and some concentrated practice, and you could easily start feeling really at home in your foreign language.

140–170 You are an outstanding language learner. You enjoy using words, and language is a constant source of delight for you. You don't learn a language to go on holiday – you enjoy going abroad because it gives you an excuse to learn another language!

Adapted from a quiz by Dr Paul Meara of Birkbeck College, London.

Discussion

1 Do you agree with the interpretation?
Is it a good description of *you* as a language learner?

2 The tone of the quiz is quite light-hearted, but the content is serious. Read through the Answers section of the quiz again. Do you agree that the things it suggests are what a 'good learner' does?
For example, is it important to be able to guess the meaning of words? Why/why not?
Is it important to be able to see patterns in a language?
Is it important to have a good memory?

3 The answer to question 3 says that good language learners make the most of their skills, and manage to communicate in all sorts of unlikely situations.
Think of ways in which communication can take place *other than* with words.

4 The quiz contains some surprising ideas. For example, the answer to question 12 suggests that good language learners don't mind being in situations that they can't control, and the answer to question 14 that they are prepared to take risks.
To what extent is this true in your own experience?

5 Research does suggest that women are generally better language learners than men.
Can you think of reasons why this might be so?

6 Researchers also feel that the personality of the learner must affect the way he or she learns, but no-one quite knows how!
Can you think of any qualities that might help or hinder language learning? The following adjectives might help you:

confident shy outgoing extrovert sociable
tolerant patient inquisitive

Vocabulary

Dictionaries not only give help with meaning, but also provide information about pronunciation, grammar, and style.

The vocabulary section in this unit deals with the organization of a dictionary entry, and pronunciation. The other areas are dealt with in Units 2 (Revision), 7 (Language study), and 9 (Vocabulary 1).

1 The organization of a dictionary entry

Look at the order in which a dictionary entry gives information, and answer the questions.

First, definitions are listed in order of frequency.

book¹ /bʊk/ *n* **1** [C] (**a**) number of printed or written sheets of paper bound together in a cover: *a leather-bound book.* (**b**) written work or composition, eg a novel, dictionary, encyclopedia, etc: *writing/reading a book about/on Shakespeare.* **2** [C] number of blank or lined sheets of paper fastened together in a cover and used for writing in: *Write the essay in your (exercise-)books, not on rough paper.* **3 books** [pl] written records of the finances of a business; accounts: *do the books,* ie check the accounts ○ *The company's books are audited every year.* **4** [C] number of similiar items fastened together in the shape of a book: *a book of stamps/tickets/matches.* **5** [C] any of the main divisions of a large written work: *the books of the Bible.* **6** [sing] words of an opera or musical; libretto. **7** [C] record of bets made, eg on a horse race: *keep/make/open a book (on sth),* ie take bets (on a match, race, etc). **8 the book** [sing] telephone directory: *Are you in the book?* **9** (idm) **be in sb's good/bad 'books** (*infml*) have/not have sb's favour or approval: *You'll be in the boss's bad books if you don't work harder.* **bring sb to 'book (for sth)** require sb to give an explanation (of his behaviour): *bring a criminal to book.* **by the 'book** (*infml*) strictly according to the rules: *He's always careful to do things by the book.* **a closed book** ⇨ CLOSE⁴. **cook the books** ⇨ COOK. **every/any trick in the book** ⇨ TRICK. **(be) on the books of sth** (be) employed as a player by a football club; *He's on Everton's books.* ⇨ OPEN¹. **read sb like a book** ⇨ READ. **suit one's/sb's books** ⇨ SUIT. **take a leaf out of sb's book** ⇨ LEAF. **throw the book at sb** (*infml*) remind sb forcefully of the correct procedure to be followed in some task (and perhaps punish him for not following it).
□ **'bookbinder** [C]. **'bookbinding** [U] *ns* (person whose job is) putting covers on books.
'bookcase *n* piece of furniture with shelves for books.
book club club which sells books at a reduced price to members who agree to buy a minimum number.
'book-end *n* (usu *pl*) either of a pair of supports to keep books upright.
'bookkeeper [C], **'bookkeeping** [U] *ns* (person whose job is) recording business transactions.
'bookmaker (also **bookie**) [C], **'bookmaking** [U] *ns* (person whose job is) taking bets on horse races, etc.

'bookmark (also **'bookmarker**) *n* strip placed between the pages of a book to mark the reader's place.
'bookmobile /-məʊbi:l/ *n* (*esp US*) vehicle used as a travelling library.
'book-plate *n* piece of paper, usu with a printed design, pasted in a book to show who owns it.
'bookseller *n* person whose job is selling books.
'bookshop (*US* also **'bookstore**) *n* shop which sells mainly books.
'bookstall *n* (*US* **'news-stand**) stall or stand at which books, newspaper and magazines are sold.
book token voucher that can be exchanged for books of a given value: *a £10 book token.*
'bookworm *n* **1** grub that eats holes in books. **2** (*fig*) person who is very fond of reading books: *She's a bit of a bookworm.*
book² /bʊk/ *v* **1** (**a**) [I, Tn, Tn.p] ~ **sth (up)** reserve (a place, accommodation, etc); buy (a ticket, etc) in advance: *Book early if you want to be sure of a seat.* ○ *book a hotel room, a seat on a plane* ○ *I'd like to book three seats for tonight's concert.* ○ *The hotel/performance is fully booked (up),* ie There are no more rooms/tickets available. (**b**) [Tn.pr] ~ **sb on sth** reserve a place, ticket, etc for sb on (a plane, etc): *We're booked on the next flight.* (**c**) [Tn] engage or hire (sb) in advance: *We've booked a conjuror for our Christmas party.* **2** [Tn] (*infml*) enter the name of (sb) in a book or record, esp when bringing a charge: *The police booked me for speeding.* ○ *He was booked by the referee for foul play.* **3** (phr v) **book in** register at a hotel, an airport, etc. **book sb in** make a reservation for sb (at a hotel, etc): *We've booked you in at the Plaza for two nights.*
▷ **'book-able** *adj* that can be reserved: *All seats are bookable in advance.*
book·ing *n* [C, U] (*esp Brit*) (instance of) reserving seats, etc in advance; reservation; *a block booking* ○ *We can't accept any more bookings.* ○ *She's in charge of booking(s).* **'booking-clerk** *n* (*esp Brit*) person who sells tickets, eg at a railway station. **'booking-office** *n* (*esp Brit*) office where tickets are sold.

feather¹ /'feðə(r)/ *n* **1** any of the many light fringed structures that grow from a bird's skin and cover its body. ⇨illus.

---

idm shows the start of the idioms section. This comes after the main definitions.

What is 'sth' an abbreviation for?

What is 'sb' an abbreviation for?

What does this mean?

Compounds are listed as sub-entries. □ shows the start of the compound section.

What does this mean?

What does this mean?

What does this mean?

What does this mean?

What does this mean?

There is sometimes a separate entry when the word belongs to more than one class (for example, noun and verb) or the meaning is different.

What does this mean?

What is 'infml' an abbreviation for?

(phr v) shows the start of the phrasal verb (multi-word verb) section.

□ shows the start of the derivative section.

What does this mean?

What does this mean?

What does this mean?

What do the following abbreviations stand for?

i e   usu

8

2 Pronunciation

It is very useful to be able to recognize the phonetic symbols. Here is the key from the *Oxford Advanced Learner's Dictionary*.

Vowels and diphthongs

1	iː	as in	**see** /siː/		11	ɜː	as in	**fur** /fɜː(r)/
2	ɪ	as in	**sit** /sɪt/		12	ə	as in	**ago** /əˈgəʊ/
3	e	as in	**ten** /ten/		13	eɪ	as in	**page** /peɪdʒ/
4	æ	as in	**hat** /hæt/		14	əʊ	as in	**home** /həʊm/
5	ɑː	as in	**arm** /ɑːm/		15	aɪ	as in	**five** /faɪv/
6	ɒ	as in	**got** /gɒt/		16	aʊ	as in	**now** /naʊ/
7	ɔː	as in	**saw** /sɔː/		17	ɔɪ	as in	**join** /dʒɔɪn/
8	ʊ	as in	**put** /pʊt/ ·		18	ɪə	as in	**near** /nɪə(r)/
9	uː	as in	**too** /tuː/		19	eə	as in	**hair** /heə(r)/
10	ʌ	as in	**cup** /kʌp/		20	ʊə	as in	**pure** /pjʊə(r)/

Consonants

1	p	as in	**pen** /pen/		13	s	as in	**so** /səʊ/
2	b	as in	**bad** /bæd/		14	z	as in	**zoo** /zuː/
3	t	as in	**tea** /tiː/		15	ʃ	as in	**she** /ʃiː/
4	d	as in	**did** /dɪd/		16	ʒ	as in	**vision** /ˈvɪʒn/
5	k	as in	**cat** /kæt/		17	h	as in	**how** /haʊ/
6	g	as in	**got** /gɒt/		18	m	as in	**man** /mæn/
7	tʃ	as in	**chin** /tʃɪn/		19	n	as in	**no** /nəʊ/
8	dʒ	as in	**June** /dʒuːn/		20	ŋ	as in	**sing** /sɪŋ/
9	f	as in	**fall** /fɔːl/		21	l	as in	**leg** /leg/
10	v	as in	**voice** /vɔɪs/		22	r	as in	**red** /red/
11	θ	as in	**thin** /θɪn/		23	j	as in	**yes** /jes/
12	ð	as in	**then** /ðen/		24	w	as in	**wet** /wet/

/ˈ/ represents *primary stress* as in **about** /əˈbaʊt/
/ˌ/ represents *secondary stress* as in **academic** /ˌækəˈdemɪk/

(r) An 'r' in parentheses is heard in British pronunciation when it is immediately followed by a vowel-sound. Otherwise it is omitted. In American pronunciation no 'r' of the phonetic spelling or of the ordinary spelling is omitted.

1 Work in pairs.
Practise saying the example words.

2 Identify the vowel sound in the following words, and say what number it is according to the key.

bread	fear	wood	noise	cheap	wise
steak	wear	bath	round	ham	bird
suit	hut	rose	chip	more	fox

Practice

There are many words in English that sound like their meaning.

Examples
*The bees **buzzed** around the honey-pot.*
*I couldn't get to sleep last night because my husband was **snoring** so much.*

1 Here is the phonemic script of several such words. Work in three groups. Look at the words in your column, practise saying them, and decide how you think they are spelt. Then find the words in your dictionary to check the spelling and the meaning. Finally, explain them to the other two groups.

Group A	Group B	Group C
/θʌmp/ _____	/ˈmʌmbl/ _____	/ˈgɪgl/ _____
/mʌntʃ/ _____	/skrætʃ/ _____	/smuːð/ _____
/snɪf/ _____	/skreɪp/ _____	/skwiːz/ _____
/ˈskwiːmɪʃ/ _____	/miːˈaʊ/ _____	/slaʊtʃ/ _____
/ˈslaɪmɪ/ _____	/haʊl/ _____	/ˈslʌgɪʃ/ _____
/ˈgrʌmbl/ _____	/ˈgɑːgl/ _____	/ˈwɒbl/ _____

Which words sound like something:
– pleasant/unpleasant?
– short/long-lasting?
– high/low-pitched?

2 Fill in the gaps or answer the questions with one of the above words in its correct form.
  a. 'I refuse to resign!' said the Prime Minister, _____ the table defiantly.
  b. 'I've got a terrible cold. I've been _____ and sneezing all day long.'
  c. It began to rain while we were having a walk. I had to _____ the mud off my shoes when we got back.
  d. Many people think snakes are _____, but it isn't true. Their skins are smooth and dry.
  e. This is what cats do with their claws!
  f. This is what you are if you don't like the sight of blood!
  g. A good sea crossing is this, or a baby's skin!

In pairs, write similar sentences for the other words to test your colleagues. Either write sentences with gaps (as in **a.–d.**) or definitions (as in **e.–g.**), and then read them out loud.

LANGUAGE STUDY

The following two exercises test your ability in different aspects of the language.

1 Tenses and verb forms

In the following sentences, put the verb in brackets in the most appropriate tense or verb form. Be careful with the position of the words in italics.

a. Hello, Paul! How are you? I _____ *not* (see) you for ages! What _____ you (do) since I last _____ (see) you?

b. I _____ (look) forward to spring _____ (arrive). Winter seems _____ (be) with us for months, and I can't stand _____ (get) up when it's still dark outside. Soon some flowers should _____ (come) out. That'll be nice.

c. I _____ (arrive) home last night to find that my house was flooded. Someone _____ (forget) _____ (turn) off the bathroom tap, and water _____ (pour) out the whole day. Before _____ (phone) the plumber, I checked _____ (see) that the electricity supply was turned off, because I didn't want there _____ (be) a fire as well as a flood.

d. I wish you _____ (tell) me that you _____ *not* (like) fruit cake, and I _____ (make) something else. What _____ I (do) with it? I can't eat it all myself!

e. Take your umbrella with you in case it _____ (rain). The weather forecast _____ (say) it _____ (get) colder today as well, so I _____ (wrap) up well, dear. You don't want to catch another cold.

f. I loathed the school I went to. I might _____ (like) it more if the teachers _____ (be) kind, but they were cruel. When my children _____ (be) old enough _____ (go) to school, which is in a few years' time, they _____ (go) to a very nice school just down the road.

g. I'm sorry I _____ *not* (be) in touch for so long. Since we _____ (move) to our new house, we _____ (be) busy _____ (decorate). I _____ (want) to phone you, but I'm afraid I _____ (lose) your number.

h. Yesterday the Azra Trading Company _____ (take) over by an American firm. Azra _____ (lose) nearly £50 million over the past few years. A spokesman for the American firm said he _____ (hope) that Azra _____ *soon* (be) back in business.

i. I intended _____ (finish) _____ (write) the report last night, but then I realized that I _____ *not* (have) all the information I needed.

j. I _____ (go) out to the theatre tonight, but I _____ *just* (hear) that the production _____ (cancel), so I suppose I _____ *just* (stay) at home instead.

2 Correcting mistakes

On the page opposite is a letter from Serge, a French student studying in Edinburgh, to his friend Anna. Unfortunately, he makes a lot of mistakes! There are between forty and fifty. Find the mistakes and rewrite the corrected letter.

Anna Jones
April Cottage
Meadow Lane
Bideford
Devon B123 6X

Edinburgh
6 October

Dear Anna

Thank you for your letter, that came yesterday.
I do like to hear from you. The news of your interview
are very interesting. You didn't say did you get
the work? I hope it. I was sorry hear that
you been burgled again. How much time has this
happen to you? Five hundred pounds are a lot of
money. Does the police know who did do it?

You wanted that I tell you about what am I
doing in Edinburgh, and how is my life here. Well,
I enjoy very much. The course is good, but more hard
that I thought. First I hadn't no friend, but I soon
knew the people who they are in same department
than me. Actually I spend the all time trying to
buy the books, which I need reading for my course,
although it is difficult find. I'm sure I find soon.
When I'll buy them, I'll be very busy!

I finish now. A friend of me must write the
letter in French, and I said to help him. Write or
phone to me soon. If you go to Scotland, you must
visit me, but remember taking a warm clothes! It's
so cold weather here!

Best wishes,
Serge

UNIT 1

The best days of your life?

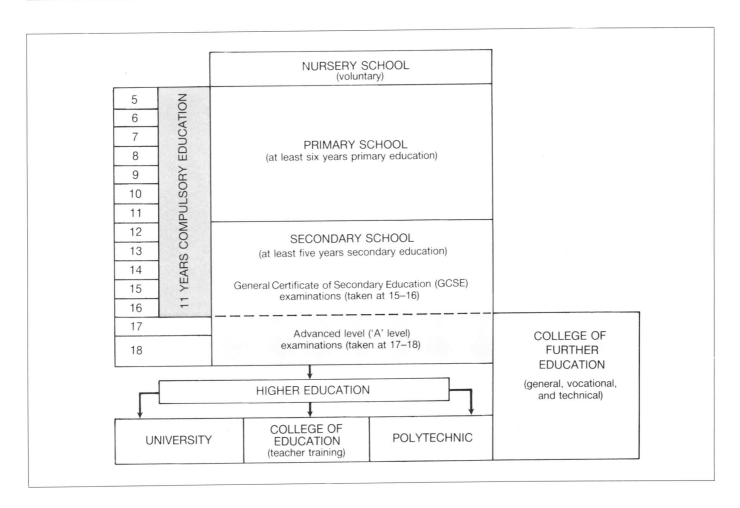

		NURSERY SCHOOL (voluntary)	
5			
6			
7		PRIMARY SCHOOL	
8		(at least six years primary education)	
9			
10			
11	11 YEARS COMPULSORY EDUCATION		
12		SECONDARY SCHOOL	
13		(at least five years secondary education)	
14			
15		General Certificate of Secondary Education (GCSE)	
16		examinations (taken at 15–16)	
17		Advanced level ('A' level)	COLLEGE OF FURTHER EDUCATION
18		examinations (taken at 17–18)	(general, vocational, and technical)

HIGHER EDUCATION

UNIVERSITY	COLLEGE OF EDUCATION (teacher training)	POLYTECHNIC

Discussion

The chart explains how state education is organized in England. In each town or district, the system is decided by the local education authority and so it can vary, but this is the usual system.

1 Ask your teacher questions to find out more about the system in England.

Examples
What does 'comprehensive school' mean?
How many subjects do pupils study for 'A' level exams?
What do you call the qualification you get at university?

2 In what ways does the state education system in your country differ from that in England?

3 Discuss the following questions:
Did you have to wear a uniform?
Were there many rules and regulations?
What forms of punishment were there?
What exams did you have to take?
Could you choose the subjects you studied?

Reading

You will read two texts that describe different kinds of schools.

Before you read, talk with your colleagues about your first school. How old were you when you started? What did you think of it? Can you remember your first day there?

Now read the text. It was written by Winston Churchill (1874–1965), and is from his autobiography *My Early Life*. He describes his first day at school, when he was seven.

WINSTON CHURCHILL'S PREP SCHOOL

The school my parents had selected for my education was one of the most fashionable and expensive in the country. It modelled itself upon Eton and aimed at being preparatory for that Public School above all others. It was
5 supposed to be the very last thing in schools. Only ten boys in a class; electric light (then a wonder); a swimming pond; spacious football and cricket grounds; two or three school treats, or 'expeditions' as they were called, every term; the masters all M.A.'s in gowns and mortar-
10 boards; a chapel of its own; no hampers allowed; everything provided by the authorities. It was a dark November afternoon when we arrived at this establishment. We had tea with the Headmaster, with whom my mother conversed in the most easy manner. I was pre-
15 occupied with the fear of spilling my cup and so making 'a bad start'. I was also miserable at the idea of being left alone among all these strangers in this great, fierce, formidable place. After all I was only seven, and I had been so happy in my nursery with all my toys. I had such
20 wonderful toys: a real steam engine, a magic lantern, and a collection of soldiers already nearly a thousand strong. Now it was to be all lessons. Seven or eight hours of lessons every day except half-holidays, and football or cricket in addition.
25   When the last sound of my mother's departing wheels had died away, the Headmaster invited me to hand over any money I had in my possession. I produced my three half-crowns, which were duly entered in a book, and I was told that from time to time there would be a 'shop' at
30 the school with all sorts of things which one would like to have, and that I could choose what I liked up to the limit of the seven and sixpence. Then we quitted the Headmaster's parlour and the comfortable private side of the house, and entered the more bleak apartments reserved
35 for the instruction and accommodation of the pupils. I was taken into a Form Room and told to sit at a desk. All the other boys were out of doors, and I was alone with the Form Master. He produced a thin greeny-brown covered book filled with words in different types of print.
40   'You have never done any Latin before, have you?' he said.

    'No, sir.'

    'This is a Latin grammar.' He opened it at a well-thumbed page. 'You must learn this,' he said, pointing to

45 a number of words in a frame of lines. 'I will come back in half an hour and see what you know.'

    Behold me then on a gloomy evening, with an aching heart, seated in front of the First Declension.

Mensa	a table
Mensa	O table
Mensam	a table
Mensae	of a table
Mensae	to or for a table
Mensa	by, with or from a table

55 What on earth did it mean? Where was the sense in it? It seemed absolute rigmarole to me. However, there was one thing I could always do: I could learn by heart. And I thereupon proceeded, as far as my private sorrows would allow, to memorize the task which had been set me.
60   In due course the Master returned.

    'Have you learnt it?' he asked.

    'I think I can say it, sir,' I replied; and I gabbled it off.

    He seemed so satisfied with this that I was embol-
65 dened to ask a question.

    'What does it mean, sir?'

    'It means what it says. Mensa, a table. Mensa is a noun of the First Declension. There are five declensions. You have learnt the singular of the First Declension.'
70   'But,' I repeated, 'what does it mean?'

    'Mensa means a table,' he answered.

    'Then why does mensa also mean O table,' I enquired, 'and what does O table mean?'

    'Mensa, O table, is the vocative case,' he replied.
75   'But why O table?' I persisted in genuine curiosity.

    'O table – you would use that in addressing a table, in invoking a table.' And then seeing he was not carrying me with him, 'You would use it in speaking to a table.'

    'But I never do,' I blurted out in honest amazement.
80   'If you are impertinent, you will be punished, and punished, let me tell you, very severely,' was his conclusive rejoinder.

    Such was my first introduction to the classics from which, I have been told, many of our cleverest men have
85 derived so much solace and profit.

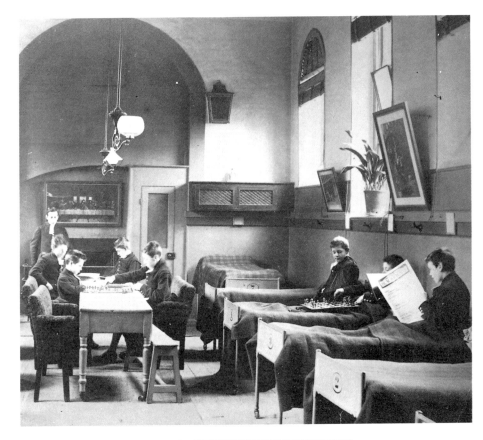

Comprehension check

1 In the first paragraph, what is the contrast that the writer makes between his new school and how he felt on his first day there?
2 What were some of his fears?
3 What did he do with his 'three half-crowns'? Why?
4 Why didn't Churchill understand the task that the Form Master set him?
   Do you think he knew what Latin was?
   Did he know what declensions are?
5 Why did the Form Master threaten to punish Churchill?
6 Churchill obviously felt very miserable on his first day at school. Find the words in the text that describe his negative attitude to the day.

Examples
a dark November afternoon (lines 11–12)
the fear of spilling my cup (line 15)

What do you think?

1 Have you ever learnt Latin or Greek?
   How was it taught?
2 Have you ever learnt a modern language in the way Churchill had to learn Latin?
   What did you think of learning in that way?

▶ Language focus

Read the Language study on *noun phrases* (page 20) and do the practice exercise.

Vocabulary 1

1 Synonyms in context

Good writers try to avoid repeating the same words or phrases, using instead words that have a similar meaning in that particular context.

Here are some examples from the text about Churchill's prep school:

*The **school** my parents had selected* (line 1)
*we arrived at this **establishment*** (lines 12–13)

*the Headmaster invited me to **hand over** any money* (lines 26–7)

*I **produced** my three half-crowns* (lines 27–8)

*I could **learn by heart*** (line 57)
*I thereupon proceeded . . . to **memorize*** (lines 58–9)

*. . . he **asked*** (line 61)
*. . . I **enquired*** (lines 72–3)

In the gap in the following sentences, put one word that has a similar meaning to the word in italics. Notice that sometimes the word-class changes (e.g. adjective to noun).

a. She is not only a *skilled* painter, she is also a(n) _____ piano player.

b. You've managed to *persuade* me! Your argument is most _____.

c. He and his daughter were always writing each other *letters*, and their _____ lasted for over thirty years.

d. She was *crippled* in an accident when she was five, but this _____ didn't stop her from writing poetry and prose.

e. You simply must *control* your finances better. If you don't _____ your spending, you'll go bankrupt.

f. Advertisements are not allowed to *lie*, but they _____ us in many subtle ways.

g. There has been great *progress* in medical research this century. As a result, there have been significant _____ in all aspects of health care.

h. Mr Henderson was an excellent *manager*. Under his _____, the company went from strength to strength.

i. Chess is a game of *tactics*. You have to plan your _____ well in advance.

j. The doctor looked at my notes *carefully*, then gave me a _____ examination.

2 Synonyms and their associations

Find synonyms, or near synonyms, for the following words, and write sentences to explore their associations.

Example
enemy
*Your **enemy** is the person you're fighting against in a war.*
*A **competitor** is someone you're trying to do better than, for example, in business.*
*We talk about a **rival** in love, or a business **rival**.*
*We talk about an **opponent** in a game or sport.*

a. friend	e. love	h. mend
b. talk	f. hate	i. attractive
c. look	g. break	j. mad
d. worried		

Use a lexicon for this activity if you have one.

Listening

Pre-listening task

1 Compare the pictures of modern-day public schools with those of a hundred years ago on page 15.

Divide into two groups.

T.1a   **Group A** You will hear an interview with Mr Ian Beer, the Head Master of Harrow School. This is the public school that Winston Churchill attended.

T.1b   **Group B** You will hear a radio programme on the subject of independent schools today.

Listen to the interview or the radio programme to see if the questions you wrote in Exercise 2 are answered.
Then listen for information on the following questions:
1 What do you learn about the names *independent* school and *public* school?
2 What changes have taken place in public-school life?
3 What is said about the curriculum, especially in relation to classics, sport, science, and computers?
4 Do you get the impression that academic success is important or not?
5 What is said about discipline?
6 To what extent are public schools involved with the local community, and with the rest of the world at large?

When you have answered your questions, find a partner from the other group.
Compare your answers and swap information.

What do you think?

1 If any of the questions you wrote in Exercise 2 were unanswered, can you guess the answer?
2 Why do you think the information sometimes differs in the two interviews?
3 Compare the private sector of education in England with your country.
4 What are the arguments for and against having a separate system of education for those who can afford to pay for it?

2 Work in groups and add to the following chart. Remember that public schools are in fact private!

What I know about English Public Schools.	What I would like to know about English Public Schools.
Parents have to pay.	Is it only the children of the rich who go to them?

Reading

In the following text, A. S. Neill describes his famous school, Summerhill, which he founded in 1921.
Before you read, look at the pictures. In what ways do you think life at Summerhill is different from life at a more traditional school?

Now read the first part of the text.

THE IDEA OF SUMMERHILL

This is a story of a modern school – Summerhill. Summerhill began as an experimental school. It is no longer such; it is now a demonstration school, for it demonstrates that freedom works.

5   When my first wife and I began the school, we had one main idea: *to make the school fit the child* – instead of making the child fit the school.

Obviously, a school that makes active children sit at desks studying mostly useless subjects is a bad school.
10 It is a good school only for those who believe in *such* a school, for those uncreative citizens who want docile, uncreative children who will fit into a civilization whose standard of success is money.

I had taught in ordinary schools for many years. I
15 knew the other way well. I knew it was all wrong. It was wrong because it was based on an adult conception of what a child should be and of how a child should learn.

Well, we set out to make a school in which we
20 should allow children freedom to be themselves. In order to do this, we had to renounce all discipline, all direction, all suggestion, all moral training, all religious instruction. We have been called brave, but it did not require courage. All it required was what we had – a
25 complete belief in the child as a good, not an evil, being.

My view is that a child is innately wise and realistic. If left to himself without adult suggestion of any kind, he will develop as far as he is capable of developing.
30 Logically, Summerhill is a place in which people who have the innate ability and wish to be scholars will be scholars; while those who are only fit to sweep the streets will sweep the streets. But we have not produced a street cleaner so far. Nor do I write this snobbishly,
35 for I would rather see a school produce a happy street cleaner than a neurotic scholar.

What is Summerhill like? . . .

Questions for prediction

The text goes on to describe Summerhill. Before you read, discuss what you think the answers are to these questions.

1 Can the children choose whether to go to lessons or not?
2 Is there a timetable for lessons?
3 Do children have classes according to their ages or according to their interests?

4 Does Summerhill have special teaching methods?
5 Are the children happy?
6 Is every single decision about everything made democratically by both teachers and children?
7 Does Neill find it easy to influence the children at Summerhill?

Now read the second part of the text.

. . . Well, for one thing, lessons are optional. Children can go to them or stay away from them – for years
40 if they want to. There is a timetable – but only for the teachers.

The children have classes usually according to their age, but sometimes according to their interests. We have no new methods of teaching, because we do not
45 consider that teaching in itself matters very much. Whether a school has or has not a special method for teaching long division is of no significance, for long division is of no importance except to those who *want* to learn it. And the child who *wants* to learn long division
50 *will* learn it no matter how it is taught.

Summerhill is possibly the happiest school in the world. We have no truants and seldom a case of homesickness. We very rarely have fights – quarrels, of course, but seldom have I seen a stand-up fight like the
55 ones we used to have as boys. I seldom hear a child cry,

because children when free have much less hate to express than children who are downtrodden. Hate breeds hate, and love breeds love. Love means approving of children, and that is essential in any school. You
60 can't be on the side of children if you punish them and storm at them. Summerhill is a school in which the child knows that he is approved of.

The function of the child is to live his own life – not the life that his anxious parents think he should live,
65 nor a life according to the purpose of the educator who thinks he knows what is best. All this interference and guidance on the part of adults only produces a generation of robots.

In Summerhill, everyone has equal rights. No one is
70 allowed to walk on my grand piano, and I am not allowed to borrow a boy's cycle without his permission. At a General School Meeting, the vote of a child of six counts for as much as my vote does.

But, says the knowing one, in practice of course the
75 voices of the grownups count. Doesn't the child of six wait to see how you vote before he raises his hand? I wish he sometimes would, for too many of my proposals are beaten. Free children are not easily influenced; the absence of fear accounts for this phenomenon. Indeed,
80 the absence of fear is the finest thing that can happen to a child.

Questions for discussion

1 Were your answers to the 'Questions for prediction' right?
   Were you surprised by any of the answers?
2 In what ways does a child usually have to *fit a school*? To what extent do you think Summerhill *fits a child*?
3 What are the freedoms that children at Summerhill enjoy?
4 Neill holds quite strong views on education, the innate qualities of children, and the way adults interfere with learning. Which of these views do you agree with?
5 What do you understand by the last sentence of the extract?
   What were you afraid of when you were young?
6 Here are some more of A. S. Neill's ideas. What is your reaction to them?

'I hold that the aim of life is to find happiness, which means to find interest. Education should be a preparation for life.'

'Most of the school work that adolescents do is simply a waste of time, of energy, of patience. It robs youth of its right to play and play and play; it puts old heads on young shoulders.'

'[Traditional education produces children] for a society that needs obedient sitters at dreary desks, standers in shops, mechanical catchers of the 8.30 suburban train . . .'

▶ Language focus

Read the Language study on *avoiding repetition* (page 21) and do the practice exercise.

Writing

Write about one of the following subjects:
– a teacher who had a lot of influence on me
– my memories of school days
– my school compared to Summerhill.

Discussion

Groupwork

Work in groups of four.
Look at the list below of the possible aims of education.

In column A, put a number 0–5 according to the importance attached to these aims at Summerhill school.
0 = not important at all
5 = vital

	A	B	C
Helping you to develop your personality and character	☐	☐	☐
Helping you to do as well as possible in exams	☐	☐	☐
Teaching you about right and wrong	☐	☐	☐
Showing you how to get on with other people	☐	☐	☐
Teaching you about what is going on in the world today	☐	☐	☐
Keeping you occupied	☐	☐	☐
Teaching you how to read and write well	☐	☐	☐
Helping you to get as good a job as possible	☐	☐	☐
Helping with things you will need to know when you leave school (for example about running a home and managing money)	☐	☐	☐
Making school a pleasant place to be in	☐	☐	☐

Work alone

In column B, put a number 0–5 according to the importance attached to these aims at the school *you* went to.

Pairwork

In column C, put a number 0–5 according to what you think the ideal school's priorities should be.
When you have finished, compare your conclusions as a class.

Vocabulary 2

1 Spelling and pronunciation

Here is a list of twenty-five words. Put them into the correct column according to their vowel sounds. Use the left-hand side of the column. The first one has been done for you.

weight	caught	heard	crews	sees
course	sauce	bread	waste	praise
pause	bruise	isle	rain	paste
fur	peal	sight	floor	suite
bury	key	sword	raise	hall

/eɪ/	/ɔ:/
weight	

/ɜ:/	/u:/

/e/	/aɪ/

/i:/	

2 Homophones

All the words in Exercise 1 are also homophones, that is, there is another word with the same pronunciation but a different spelling (and, of course, a different meaning).

Example
weight – wait

Try to think of the other spelling, and write it in the correct column above. Use the right-hand side of the column.

3 Rhymes

As you know, English spelling is not phonetic, so words can rhyme when their spelling is very different.
Choose some of the words in Exercise 1 and think of other words that rhyme with them.

Examples
weight – late, hate, eight
course – horse, force

LANGUAGE STUDY

1 Noun phrases

Information about a noun can be added before and after it, and in several different ways. Here are four of them.

Plural expressions become singular when used in compound adjectives.
a ten-mile walk
a fifteen-year-old girl
a three-ton lorry

Compound nouns (two nouns together) are very common.
traffic lights
pain-killer
toothpaste

After the noun, prepositional phrases and participle clauses occur.
a story about ghosts
Prepositional phrases: *a man with an axe in his hand*
a cheque for £20
a tool for cutting glass
Participle clauses: *a girl wearing green trousers*
a book written by a friend of mine

Look again at the text about Churchill's first day at school and find examples of compound nouns, prepositional phrases, and participle clauses.

▶ **Grammar reference: page 134.**

Practice

Make one sentence by combining the information in brackets into the base sentence. Use the patterns above.

a. He bought a house. (farm; eighty thousand pounds; three acres of land)
b. A girl came into the room. (twelve years old; she was wearing a clown's outfit)
c. I need some nails. (six inches long; steel)
d. Concorde is a plane. (passengers; fastest in the world)
e. Have you seen those knives? (Swiss; army; gadgets for everything)
f. She is a lecturer. (economics; Bristol University; much-respected)
g. She has just started a job. (fifteen thousand pounds a year; a firm of accountants; New York)
h. He bought a picture. (three hundred years old; two men; working in a field)
i. We had a meal. (four courses; two bottles of wine; splendid; less than fifteen pounds)
j. It was a long flight. (twelve hours; stop-overs in Delhi and Moscow)
k. The pile-up has finally been cleared by police. (on the M1; forty cars; it was caused by yesterday's freak weather conditions)
l. Passengers can expect delays. (three hours; Pan Am Airways; those who are flying to New York)

2 Avoiding repetition

Look at the following extracts from the text about Summerhill.

. . . the vote of a child of six counts for as much as my vote **does**. (lines 72–3)
Doesn't the child of six wait to see how you vote before he raises his hand? I wish he sometimes **would** . . . (lines 75–7)

In the first sentence, the writer has avoided repeating **counts** by using **does** instead. In the second sentence, he has left out part of the sentence which is understood.
I wish he sometimes would (wait to see how I vote).

▶ **Grammar reference: page 134.**

Practice

Fill each gap in the following sentences with an auxiliary verb or a modal verb. Sometimes you will need to add **not**.

a. I tried to repair the car at the weekend, but I _____. I didn't have the right tools.
b. A Come on, John! It's time you were getting up!
   B I _____! I'll be down in a second.
c. A You look awful. Why don't you see a doctor?
   B I _____. He just gave me some pills and told me to take things easy.
d. A It's a long journey. Take care on the motorway.
   B Don't worry. I _____.
e. I met your sister last night. She thought we'd met before, but we _____.

f. A Have you read those reports?
   B No, I _____, but I _____, I promise.
g. The weather forecast said that it could rain this afternoon. If it _____, we'll have to call off the tennis.
h. My car isn't working at the moment. If it _____, I could give you a lift. Sorry.
i. The baby very nearly fell into the fire last night. If I hadn't managed to catch her just in time, she _____. (*two words*)
j. I learned this morning that I got the job I applied for. I was delighted. I really didn't think I _____.
k. A I think I'll give Robert a ring.
   B You _____. You haven't been in touch for ages, and he'd be pleased to hear from you.
l. A Andrew easily beat me in our match yesterday.
   B I knew he _____. He's been playing very well recently.
m. I went to a party last night, but I wish I _____. It was awful.
n. My husband insists on doing the cooking, but I wish he _____. What he cooks is uneatable.
o. A Are you still going to America for your holidays?
   B We _____. We haven't made up our minds yet.
p. A The party was wonderful until Andy got drunk and started insulting everyone.
   B He _____. It's terrible the way he's always doing that.

REVISION

1 'A' or 'an'?

Why do we say **an** *umbrella*
　　　　　　　an unusual event
　　　　　　　an hour
　　　　　　　an MA
but　　　　　*a uniform*
　　　　　　　a unique event
　　　　　　　a hill
　　　　　　　a Master of Arts?

Think about the pronunciation, not the spelling!

▶ **Grammar reference: page 134.**

Put **a** or **an** before the following:

_____	university	_____	MP
_____	used car	_____	UFO
_____	honest man	_____	uncle
_____	human being	_____	unfair result
_____	X-ray	_____	urgent message
_____	umpire	_____	unilateral declaration
_____	European	_____	united country
_____	useful tool		

2 'The' – /ðə/ or /ðɪ/?

Remember that **the** is pronounced /ðɪ/ before a vowel-sound.

Put 1 or 2 next to the following according to whether *the* is pronunced /ðə/ (1), or /ðɪ/ (2).

	Union Jack ( )		Atlantic Ocean ( )
	office ( )		EEC ( )
the	air we breathe ( )	the	UK ( )
	heir to the throne ( )		MP for Leicester ( )
	USA ( )		USSR ( )
	universe ( )		English Channel ( )

Put **the** before the words in Exercise 1, and practise pronouncing it.

▶ **Grammar reference: page 134.**

UNIT 2

Literature

Discussion

The people in the pictures are all characters from English literature.
Who are they?
Which books are they from?
What are they famous for?
Their names are upside-down at the bottom of the page.

Romeo and Juliet; Lemuel Gulliver; Sherlock Holmes; Alice in Wonderland; Oliver Twist

23

Reading

Matching stories

Here are the opening and closing paragraphs of five different books. There is an autobiography, a detective story, a romance, a spy story, and a fairy story.
Read them carefully and match them up.

1 I was born on 16 April 1889, at eight o'clock at night, in East Lane, Walworth. Soon after, we moved to West Square, St George's Road, Lambeth. According to Mother my world was a happy one. Our circumstances were moderately comfortable; we lived in three tastefully furnished rooms. One of my early recollections was that each night before Mother went to the Theatre, Sydney and I were lovingly tucked up in a comfortable bed and left in the care of the housemaid.

2 'I wouldn't marry you if you were the last man left on earth!'
　　Netta faced him defiantly, a tiny figure shaking with outrage, her spirit as fiery as the colour of her copper curls.
　　'The feeling's mutual,' he snapped back through tight lips. 'Don't imagine I enjoy the prospect of being saddled with you for a wife, for however short a time it may be.'
　　'Then let's forget the whole crazy idea.'

3 At the palace, the King was glad to welcome his son's bride. He arranged a magnificent wedding for the Prince and his chosen wife. The kings and queens, and the princes and princesses from many lands came to the wedding. The wedding feast lasted a whole week. And they all lived happily ever after.

4 With such happiness, I sometimes sit out on our terrace at sunset and look over a vast green lawn to the lake in the distance, and beyond the lake to the reassuring mountains, and in this mood think of nothing, but enjoy their magnificent serenity.

5 Once upon a time there was a little girl called Cinderella. Her mother was dead, and she lived with her father and two elder sisters.
　　Cinderella's sisters were beautiful and fair of face, but because they were bad-tempered and unkind, their faces grew to look ugly. They were jealous of Cinderella because she was a lovely child, and so they were often unkind to her.

6 When I have finished writing, I shall enclose this whole manuscript in an envelope and address it to Poirot. And then – what shall it be? Veronal? There would be a kind of poetic justice. Not that I take any responsibility for Mrs Ferrars' death. It was the direct consequence of her own actions. I feel no pity for her.
　　I have no pity for myself either.
　　So let it be veronal.
　　But I wish Hercule Poirot had never retired from work and come here to grow vegetable marrows.

7 Castle, ever since he had joined the firm as a young recruit more than thirty years ago, had taken his lunch in a public house behind St James's Street, not far from the office. If he had been asked why he lunched there, he would have referred to the excellent quality of the sausages; he might have preferred a different bitter from Watney's, but the quality of the sausages outweighed that. He was always prepared to account for his actions, even the most innocent, and he was always strictly on time.

8 'You didn't let me tell you how lovely you look,' he murmured afer a long, sweet time had passed between them. 'I tried to tell you, when you joined me in the ballroom tonight, but you thought I was going to say you were late coming down.'
　　He laughed softly at the memory, and she joined in gaily. She had been wonderfully, blissfully on time. She started to tell him so, but his lips claimed her own, masterfully silencing the words that no longer needed to be spoken.

9 Mrs Ferrars died on the night of the 16th-17th September – a Thursday. I was sent for at eight o'clock on the morning of Friday the 17th. There was nothing to be done. She had been dead some hours.
　　It was just a few minutes after nine when I reached home once more. I opened the front door with my latchkey, and purposely delayed a few moments in the hall, hanging up my hat and the light overcoat that I had deemed a wise precaution against the chill of an early autumn morning. To tell the truth, I was considerably upset and worried.

10 She asked, 'Have you friends?'
　　'Oh yes, I'm not alone, don't worry, Sarah. There's an Englishman who used to be in the British Council. He's invited me to his *dacha* in the country when the spring comes. When the spring comes,' he repeated in a voice which she hardly recognized – it was the voice of an old man who couldn't count with certainty on any spring to come.
　　She said, 'Maurice, Maurice, please go on hoping,' but in the long unbroken silence which followed she realized that the line to Moscow was dead.

What helped you to match the extracts? Was it content (names, details), language, or style?

Titles and authors

Here are the titles and authors, again mixed up.
Match each book with its correct title and author.

The Human Factor   Sue Peters
The Murder of Roger Ackroyd   Charlie Chaplin
Cinderella   Graham Greene
Marriage in Haste   Agatha Christie
My Autobiography   (traditional fairy story)

Kinds of books

Of course, stories are not entirely predictable, but we expect certain things to happen in different kinds of book.

Work in groups of three.

1 Choose one of the following kinds of book:
   – detective story
   – fairy story
   – romance
   – spy story
   – science fiction

2 Talk about the typical characters, setting, and plot for the kind of book you chose.

3 Your teacher will give you an imaginary title for your choice of book.
   Write either the opening or the closing paragraph for it. When you have finished, read it out to the rest of the class.

▶ Language focus

Do the practice exercise on *narrative tenses (1)* in the Language study (page 31).

Reading

You will read extracts from Oscar Wilde's book *The Picture of Dorian Gray*.
Before you read, work in groups of four.
Prepare questions to ask your teacher about the writer Oscar Wilde and the book *The Picture of Dorian Gray*.

About the writer	About the book
When did he live?	What sort of story is it?

At the beginning of the story, Basil Hallward, an artist, has just finished the portrait of Dorian Gray, a remarkably beautiful young man. Dorian thinks the portrait is very good, but is then struck by the realization that in time his good looks will vanish.

Read extract 1.

Extract 1

Yes, there would be a day when his face was wrinkled and wizen, his eyes dim and colourless, the grace of his figure broken and deformed. The scarlet would pass away from his lips, and the gold steal from his hair. The
5 life that was to make his soul would mar his body. He would become dreadful, hideous, and uncouth.
    As he thought of it, a sharp pang of pain struck through him like a knife, and made each delicate fibre of his nature quiver. His eyes deepened into amethyst,
10 and across them came a mist of tears. He felt as if a hand of ice had been laid upon his heart.
    'How sad it is!' murmured Dorian Gray, with his eyes still fixed upon his own portrait. 'How sad it is! I shall grow old, and horrible, and dreadful. But this
15 picture will remain always young. It will never be older than this particular day of June . . . If it were only the other way! If it were I who was to be always young, and the picture that was to grow old! For that – for that – I would give everything! Yes there is nothing in the
20 whole world I would not give! I would give my soul for that!'

(2) *wizen*   having a dried-up appearance
(5) *mar*   spoil
(6) *uncouth*   (here) horrible
(9) *amethyst*   a precious stone, purple or violet in colour

Comprehension check

1 What is Dorian's fear?
2 What is his wish?
3 What impression do you have of Dorian?

A little later, Dorian falls passionately in love with an actress and promises to marry her, but then he suddenly deserts her in a very cruel manner. She is heart-broken and commits suicide.
The next day, Dorian is at home.

Now read extract 2.

Extract 2

As he was turning the handle of the door, his eye fell upon the portrait Basil Hallward had painted of him. He started back as if in surprise. Then he went on into
25 his own room, looking somewhat puzzled. After he had taken the buttonhole out of his coat, he seemed to hesitate. Finally he came back, went over to the picture, and examined it. In the dim arrested light that struggled through the cream-coloured silk blinds, the
30 face appeared to him to be a little changed. The expression looked different. One would have said that there was a touch of cruelty in the mouth. It was certainly strange.

He turned round, and, walking to the window, drew
35 up the blind. The bright dawn flooded the room, and swept the fantastic shadows into dusky corners, where they lay shuddering. But the strange expression that he had noticed in the face of the portrait seemed to linger there, to be more intensified even. The quivering,
40 ardent sunlight showed him the lines of cruelty round the mouth as clearly as if he had been looking into a mirror after he had done some dreadful thing.

He rubbed his eyes; and came close to the picture, and examined it again. There were no signs of any
45 change when he looked into the actual painting, and yet there was no doubt that the whole expression had altered. It was not a mere fancy of his own. The thing was horribly apparent.

He threw himself into a chair, and began to think.
50 Suddenly there flashed across his mind what he had said in Basil Hallward's studio the day the picture had been finished. Yes, he remembered it perfectly. He had uttered a mad wish that he himself might remain young, and the portrait grow old; that his own beauty
55 might be untarnished, and the face on the canvas bear the burden of his passions and his sins; that the painted image might be seared with the lines of suffering and thought, and that he might keep all the delicate bloom and loveliness of his then just conscious boyhood.
60 Surely his wish had not been fulfilled? Such things were impossible. It seemed monstrous even to think of them. And, yet, there was the picture before him, with the touch of cruelty in the mouth.

(24) *started* jumped
(26) *buttonhole* a flower worn in the buttonhole
(29) *blinds* a shade for a window
(36) *dusky* dark
(47) *a mere fancy* just his imagination
(55) *untarnished* unspoilt
(56) *bear the burden* take the responsibility
(57) *seared* burnt, marked

Comprehension check

4 What is beginning to happen to the portrait?
5 Is this change real, or is Dorian imagining it?

Dorian is tormented by the thought that his 'mad wish' might have come true. Is he really prepared to give his soul away so that he can stay beautiful?

Now read extract 3.

Extract 3

He felt that the time had really come for making his
65 choice. Or had his choice already been made? Yes, his life had decided that for him – life, and his own infinite curiosity about life. Eternal youth, infinite passion, pleasures subtle and secret, wild joys and wilder sins – he was to have all these things. The portrait was to bear
70 the burden of his shame: that was all.

For there would be a real pleasure in watching it. He would be able to follow his mind into its secret places. This portrait would be to him the most magical of mirrors. As it had revealed to him his own body, so it
75 would reveal to him his own soul. And when winter came upon it, he would still be standing where spring trembles on the verge of summer.

Comprehension check

6 What is the choice that Dorian has to make?
7 In fact 'life' has made the choice for him. What sort of life is he going to lead in the future?
   How does Dorian feel about the prospect of such a life?
8 What role will the portrait play in Dorian's future?

Dorian decides to hide the portrait in an old upstairs room, so that no-one can see how 'hour by hour, and week by week, the thing upon the canvas was growing old'. Dorian, meanwhile, stays forever beautiful. Over the years, he lives a life of indulgence and sensual pleasure. There is much scandal surrounding his life, and people who befriend him are disgraced, or die in mysterious circumstances. Dorian takes to disappearing for days on end to sordid opium houses.

Now read extract 4.

Extract 4

Often, on returning home from one of those mysterious and prolonged absences that gave rise to such strange
80 conjecture among those who were his friends, or thought that they were so, he himself would creep upstairs to the locked room, open the door with the key that never left him now, and stand, with a mirror, in front of the portrait that Basil Hallward had painted of
85 him, looking now at the evil and ageing face on the canvas, and now at the fair young face that laughed back at him from the polished glass. The very sharpness of the contrast used to quicken his sense of pleasure. He grew more and more enamoured of his
90 own beauty, more and more interested in the corruption of his own soul. He would examine with minute care, and sometimes with a monstrous and terrible delight, the hideous lines that seared the wrinkling forehead, or crawled around the heavy sensual mouth,
95 wondering sometimes which were the most horrible, the signs of sin or the signs of age. He would place his white hands beside the coarse bloated hands of the picture, and smile. He mocked the misshapen body and the failing limbs.

(80) *conjecture*   guessing
(89) *enamoured of*   in love with
(91) *minute* /maɪˈnjuːt/   detailed
(97) *bloated*   swollen
(98) *mocked*   ridiculed

Comprehension check

9 Why does Dorian go to look at the portrait particularly after he has 'sinned'?
10 What thoughts go through his head as he looks at the portrait?
11 What do you think is happening to Dorian's mental stability?

His old friend Basil tries to warn him about what people in London society are saying about him. Dorian decides to show him the portrait, then stabs him to death as Basil is looking at it. He blackmails another old friend to dispose of the body. The years go by, and Dorian becomes more tortured by the sins of his past. One night, he is back in the room where his portrait is hidden.

Now read extract 5.

Extract 5

100 But this murder – was it to dog him all his life? Was he always to be burdened by his past? Was he really to confess? Never. There was only one bit of evidence left against him. The picture itself – that was evidence. He would destroy it. Why had he kept it so long? Once it
105 had given him pleasure to watch it changing and growing old. Of late he had felt no such pleasure. It had

kept him awake at night. When he had been away, he had been filled with terror lest other eyes should look upon it. It had brought melancholy across his passions.
110 Its mere memory had marred many moments of joy. It had been like conscience to him. Yes, it had been conscience. He would destroy it.

He looked round, and saw the knife that had stabbed Basil Hallward. He had cleaned it many times, till there
115 was no stain left upon it. It was bright, and glistened. As it had killed the painter, so it would kill the painter's work, and all that that meant. It would kill the past, and when that was dead he would be free. It would kill this monstrous soul-life, and, without its hideous
120 warnings, he would be at peace. He seized the thing, and stabbed the picture with it.

There was a cry heard, and a crash. The cry was so horrible in its agony that the frightened servants woke, and crept out of their rooms. Two gentlemen who were
125 passing in the Square below, stopped, and looked up at the great house. They walked on till they met a policeman, and brought him back. The man rang the bell several times, but there was no answer. Except for a light in one of the top windows, the house was all
130 dark. After a time, he went away and stood in an adjoining portico and watched.

'Whose house is that, constable?' asked the elder of the two gentlemen.

'Mr Dorian Gray's sir,' answered the policeman.
135 They looked at each other, as they walked away, and sneered.

Inside, in the servants' part of the house, the half-clad domestics were talking in low whispers to each other. Old Mrs Leaf was crying and wringing her
140 hands. Francis was as pale as death.

After about a quarter of an hour, he got the coachman and one of the footmen and crept upstairs. They knocked, but there was no reply. They called out. Everything was still. Finally, after vainly trying to force
145 the door, they got on the roof, and dropped down on to the balcony. The windows yielded easily; their bolts were old.

When they entered they found, hanging upon the wall, a splendid portrait of their master as they had last
150 seen him, in all the wonder of his exquisite youth and beauty. Lying on the floor was a dead man, in evening dress, with a knife in his heart. He was withered, wrinkled and loathsome of visage. It was not till they had examined the rings that they recognized who it
155 was.

(100) *dog*   pursue, torment
(136) *sneered*   smiled contemptuously
(137) *half-clad*   half-clothed
(152) *withered*   dried up
(153) *loathsome of visage*   with a horrible face

Comprehension check

12 How had the portrait 'been like conscience to him'?
   In what ways had Dorian's attitude to his portrait
   changed?
13 What did he hope to achieve by destroying the portrait?
14 Why did the two gentlemen sneer?
15 What had happened to the portrait?
   What had happened to Dorian?

Questions for discussion

1 How did Dorian die?
2 The final extract is, in fact, the end of the novel. Do you
   think it is a good ending? Why/why not?
3 'As it had revealed to him his own body, so it would
   reveal to him his own soul' (lines 74–5). Explain this
   sentence.
4 How does Dorian's character change as the story
   unfolds?
5 Paraphrase the sentence (lines 4–5) 'The life that was to
   make his soul would mar his body.'
   In life, what do we gain as we grow old, and what do we
   lose?
   Is youth fanciful or immature?
   Is old age realistic or wise?
6 There is a Zen saying 'By the age of thirty we are all
   responsible for our face'.
   To what extent do you think our appearance reflects the
   life that we have led?

Oscar Wilde's epigrams

Oscar Wilde was famous for his epigrams (short, witty
sayings). Here are a few.

To love oneself is the beginning of a lifelong romance.

I have nothing to declare except my genius.

There is only one thing worse than being talked about, and that is not being talked about.

I can resist everything except temptation

When one is in love, one always begins by deceiving oneself, and one always ends by deceiving others. This is what the world calls a romance.

I never travel without my diary. One should always have something sensational to read in the train.

▶ Language focus

Read the Language study on *narrative tenses (2)* and
reflexive pronouns (page 31) and do the practice exercises.

Vocabulary 1
1 Positive and negative meaning

In the extracts from *The Picture of Dorian Gray* there are
many words (especially adjectives) that describe beauty or
ugliness. For example, in lines 1–5, **wrinkled**, **dim**,
colourless, **broken**, and **deformed** contrast with **grace**,
scarlet, and **gold**.
Find more examples of such words with positive and
negative meanings in lines 4–15, 78–99, and 148–55.

2 Dramatic style

Oscar Wilde writes in a dramatic, somewhat exaggerated
style, and so chooses words to express extremes.
Match a word from the extracts in column **A** with a more
neutral word in column **B**.

A		B
(6)	hideous	pain
(9)	quiver	came suddenly
(37)	shuddering	tremble
(38)	to linger	sadness
(50)	flashed	endless
(66)	infinite	loaded down
(77)	the verge	ugly
(101)	burdened	beautiful, excellent
(109)	melancholy	the edge
(115)	glistened	shone
(120)	seized	shaking
(123)	agony	to remain
(150)	exquisite	picked up

Speaking and writing

Devising a horror story

Work in groups of four.
You are going to outline the plot of a horror story. Select from the list of 'ingredients' below and, if you want to, add your own ideas.
Appoint a spokesperson to take notes.
When you have finished, compare your stories.

Location	Period	Characters	Events
a cemetery	1860	a honeymoon couple	people disappear
an old castle on a hill	the Middle Ages	a mad scientist	a monster is created
a church	when there's a new moon	a witch	man-eating plants invade
a remote country mansion	present time	a psychiatrist	Earth
a house with secret passages	some time in the future	a poltergeist	someone collects people for a
an aeroplane		a young girl who, if angered,	human zoo
a dark wood		has the power to make	the dead return to life
		strange things happen	an operation that goes wrong
		an army of androids	a successful operation!
		someone who has a grudge	inexplicable accidents
		against society	
		rats, spiders, giant bees, bats	

Write the story for homework.

Listening

T.2 You will hear an interview with Graham Greene, one of the most well-known twentieth-century English novelists. His books include *The Third Man*, *Brighton Rock*, *The Heart of the Matter*, *The End of the Affair*, *The Quiet American*, *Our Man in Havana*, and *The Human Factor*.

Many of his books have been made into films.

He has been called a romantic anarchist. His novels are set in exotic locations and are peopled with fugitive heroes, with whom he tries to persuade the reader to sympathize. He had a very lonely childhood. As well as writing, he has worked as a journalist, editor, film critic, and, in the Second World War, for the Foreign Office.

In the interview, he talks about how he goes about his writing.

As you listen, take notes under the following headings:
- Graham Greene, the man – his character, appearance, and life
- What he says the qualities of a writer are
- The example he gives of how a writer should have 'a splinter of ice in his heart'
- Where he draws his characters from, and their effect on a novel
- The 'need to escape' that he feels in his life.

What do you think?

1 What impression do you have of Graham Greene from the interview?
2 Think of a writer whose work you like. Do you know anything about his/her background that explains the kind of things that appear in his/her books?

Vocabulary 2

Words with the same spelling but different pronunciation

1 Some words have two pronunciations, each with one or more different meanings.

Example
minute /'mɪnɪt/ sixty seconds
         /maɪ'njuːt/ very, very small

Work in two groups. Look at the words in your column, write the two pronunciations in phonemic script, and either a definition or a sample sentence to show each meaning. Finally, explain the words to the other group.

Group A		
bow	/	/
	/	/
tear	/	/
	/	/
row	/	/
	/	/
lead	/	/
	/	/
polish	/	/
	/	/

Group B		
used	/	/
	/	/
live	/	/
	/	/
wind	/	/
	/	/
wound	/	/
	/	/
close	/	/
	/	/

2 The following words have different meanings (and, of course, different pronunciations) depending on whether the stress is on the first or the second syllable. For each word, write two sentences that illustrate these contrasting meanings.

console	contract
entrance	object
refuse	incense
content	defect
extract	project
desert	frequent

LANGUAGE STUDY

1 Narrative tenses (1)

T.3 The recording is of an extract from a spy story. It is reproduced below with gaps.
Put the verbs in brackets in the correct tense, then listen to the tape to check your answers.
The tenses used are Past Simple and Continuous, Past Perfect Simple and Continuous, or a form of the 'future in the past' (*He was meeting*/*would meet her later*).

► **Grammar reference: page 135.**

Angus Pym (a) _____ (wake) up on the dot of six o'clock, as he always (b) _____ (do), no matter where he (c) _____ (be) or what he (d) _____ (do) the previous day. His first thought was the realization that he (e) _____ still (wear) shirt and trousers, and when his eyes (f) _____ (fall) on the reports piled up around him on the bed, the events of the previous evening (g) _____ (come) back to him. He (h) _____ (go) to his club for supper, (i) _____ just (finish) his steak tartare and (j) _____ (look) forward to a splendid zabaglione when his meal (k) _____ rudely (interrupt – *passive*) by a call from M, his controller.

After an ice-cold shower, Pym (l) _____ (think) carefully about which suit to put on. He (m) _____ (see) M at nine o'clock that morning, and he (n) _____ (want) to make a good impression. Glancing at himself in the mirror, he (o) _____ (notice) that he (p) _____ (put) on weight recently. He (q) _____ (have) to pay more attention to his diet in the future.

An hour later, as he (r) _____ (drive) through the rush-hour traffic on his way to meet M, Pym (s) _____ carefully (consider) the contents of the files. So Zircon, the organization which sought to control the free western world, was back in business? Its founder, Leon Biarrowitz, was dead. Pym (t) _____ (know) this, because he (u) _____ personally (arrange) his death. But who (v) _____ (control) Zircon now? Doubtless M (w) _____ (tell) him.

2 Narrative tenses (2)

Look again at lines 100–121 of the extract from *The Picture of Dorian Gray*, and examine the use of tenses in a narrative.
'Real time' in the narrative is expressed by the Past Simple.

Examples
There was only one bit of evidence left against him. (lines 102–3)
He looked round, and saw the knife . . . (line 113)

Events *before* this are expressed by the Past Perfect.

Examples
Why had he kept it so long? (line 104)
Once it had given him pleasure . . . (lines 104–5)

Events *after* this (the future in the past) are expressed by **was to** (+ infinitive) . . . and **would** (+ infinitive).

Examples
But this murder – was it to dog him all his life? (line 100)
He would destroy it. (lines 103–4)

Practice

Work in pairs.
1 Look at lines 1–11 and lines 64–77 and comment on the use of tenses.
2 In lines 78–99, does **would** refer to past habit or to the future in the past?

3 Reflexive pronouns

Look at the following examples from *The Picture of Dorian Gray*:

He threw himself into a chair . . . (line 49)
He had uttered a mad wish that he himself might remain young . . . (lines 52–4)
The picture itself – that was evidence. (line 103)
They looked at each other . . . (line 135)

In the first sentence, the same person is both the subject and the object. In the next two sentences, reflexive pronouns are used to give emphasis. In the last sentence, **each other** means that the action was reciprocal.

Practice

1 Compare the use or absence of pronouns in the following sentences.
   a. He got dressed and went to work.
      She's growing up fast. She can get dressed herself now.
   b. I burned/hurt/cut myself quite badly.
      I burned/hurt/cut my arm quite badly.
   c. I live by myself because I like being on my own.
      Do you like my jumper? I made it myself.
   d. My wife was talking to her.
      My wife was talking to herself.
   e. I spoke to the director.
      I spoke to the director himself.
      I spoke to the director myself.
   f. I trust my children. They look after themselves, and don't do anything dangerous.
      They look after each other very well.

2 In what situations would you say the following?

   a. Make yourself at home!
   b. Help yourself!
   c. I'm busy. Do it yourself!
   d. Pull yourself together!
   e. It was difficult, but I made myself do it.
   f. I could kick myself!
   g. Get yourself a drink!
   h. I bought myself a pair of shoes.
   i. Please yourself!
   j. Is there a D-I-Y (do-it-yourself) shop near here?

REVISION

Irregular verbs

An entry in a good learner's dictionary gives detailed information about irregular verbs.

Example

---

be·gin /bɪ'gɪn/ *v* (-**nn**-, *pt* **began** /bɪ'gæn/, *pp* **begun** /bɪ'gʌn/)

---

buy /baɪ/ *v* (*pt*, *pp* **bought** /bɔːt/)

---

let[1] /let/ *v* (-**tt**-, *pt*, *pp* **let**)

---

1 What are the forms of the following verbs?
Most of them are irregular, but not all. There are some regular verbs which are often confused, too.

beat	fall	raise
bend	feel	rise
bet	fly	shrink
bite	grind	sink
bleed	hang (× 2)	stick
blow	hurt	swear
burst	lay	swell
creep	lead	tread
deal	lend	weep
draw	lie (× 2) (*careful!*)	

2 What is special about the following verbs?

burn dream lean learn smell spell spill spoil

3 Ask each other questions, in either the Past Simple or the Present Perfect, to test the forms of the verbs in **1** and **2**.

Examples

A *Did* the wind *blow* hard last night?
B *Yes, it **blew** very hard.*

A ***Have*** *you ever **flown** in a helicopter?*
B *No, but I've **flown** in a plane.*

UNIT 3

What is normal?

Discussion

What kind of club do you think these men belong to?
What is normal behaviour in such a group?

"Look here, Hugget, the Committee would like to know why you're not wearing a club moustache"

Discuss what is normal and abnormal behaviour for the following people.

– a church congregation
– film stars
– a group of men in a pub
– the audience at a pop concert
– politicians

What groups do you belong to? Consider your working life, your home life, your leisure time.
What is normal behaviour in these groups?

Vocabulary 1

1 Idioms

Each of the following sentences contains an idiom. A key word in each idiom is missing.
If necessary, use your dictionaries to find the key word and check the meaning.

a. They were all so clever, discussing the latest scientific theory. I said nothing. I felt like a _____ out of water.

b. I always talk about the weather when I'm in England – you know, when in Rome do as the _____ do.

c. That group of lads are always hanging about together getting into trouble. I suppose birds of a _____ flock together.

d. He takes advice from nobody, he obeys no-one, he's a law unto _____ .

e. In my patched jeans and torn shirt I stuck out like a _____ thumb at that elegant cocktail party.

Which of the above refer to being the same as everyone else?
Which refer to being different?
Do you have similar idioms in your language?

2 Words with similar meaning

1 Look at the dictionary extracts. What idea do all the words express?

de·vi·ant /'diːvɪənt/ *n, adj* (*often derog*) (person who is) different in moral or social standards from what is considered normal: *a sexual deviant who assaults children* ○ *deviant behaviour*.

ec·cent·ric /ɪk'sentrɪk/ *adj* **1** (of people, behaviour) unusual; peculiar; not conventional or normal: *his eccentric habits* ○ *an eccentric old lady*. **2** (**a**) (of circles) not having the same centre. Cf CONCENTRIC. (**b**) (of orbits) not circular. (**c**) (of planets, etc) moving in an eccentric orbit.

eerie (also **eery**) /'ɪərɪ/ *adj* (**-ier, -iest**) causing a feeling of mystery and fear: *an eerie scream* ○ *an eerie silence*. ▷ **eer·ily** /'ɪərəlɪ/ *adv*. **eeri·ness** /'ɪərɪnɪs/ *n* [U].

fant·astic /fæn'tæstɪk/ *adj* **1** (**a**) wild and strange: *fantastic dreams, stories*. (**b**) impossible to carry out; not practical: *fantastic schemes, proposals, etc*. **2** (*infml*) marvellous; excellent: *She's a fantastic swimmer*. ○ *You passed your test? Fantastic!* **3** (*infml*) very large; extraordinary: *Their wedding cost a fantastic amount of money*. ▷ **fant·ast·ic·ally** /-klɪ/ *adv*: *You did fantastically well in the exam*.

freak¹ /friːk/ *n* **1** (*infml derog*) person considered abnormal because of his behaviour, appearance, ideas, etc: *People think she's a freak just because she's religious*. **2** (*infml*) person with a specified interest or obsession; fan: *health/health-food freaks* ○ *a jazz freak* ○ *an acid freak*, ie sb addicted to the drug LSD. **3** very unusual event or action: *By some freak (of chance) I was overpaid this month*. ○ [attrib] *a freak accident, storm, etc*. **4** (also **freak of 'nature**) person, animal or plant that is abnormal in form.

idio·syn·crasy /ˌɪdɪə'sɪŋkrəsɪ/ *n* person's particular way of thinking, behaving, etc that is clearly different from that of others: *One of her little idiosyncrasies is always washing in cold water*. ▷ **idio·syn·cratic** /ˌɪdɪəsɪŋ'krætɪk/ *adj*.

mon·strous /'mɒnstrəs/ *adj* **1** shocking, unjust or absurd; outrageous: *a monstrous lie* ○ *monstrous crimes* ○ *It's absolutely monstrous to pay men more than women for the same job*. **2** like a monster in appearance; ugly and frightening: *the monstrous form of a fire-breathing dragon*. **3** extremely large; gigantic.

un·canny /ʌn'kænɪ/ *adj* (**-ier, -iest**) (**a**) unnatural: *The silence was uncanny*. ○ *I had an uncanny feeling of being watched*. (**b**) beyond what is normal or expected; extraordinary: *an uncanny coincidence, resemblance, etc*. ▷ **un·can·nily** /-ɪlɪ/ *adv*: *an uncannily accurate prediction*.

weird /wɪəd/ *adj* (**-er, -est**) **1** (frightening because it is) unnatural, uncanny or strange: *Weird shrieks were heard in the darkness*. **2** (*infml often derog*) unconventional, unusual or bizarre: *weird clothes, hairstyles, taste* ○ *I found some of her poems a bit weird*.

2 Although the words are similar in meaning, they are not exact synonyms. In the following sentences, the words are used incorrectly. Correct them, referring to the dictionary extracts. Sometimes more than one of the words is possible.

a. Did you hear the wind and rain last night? Surely it was a deviant storm for the time of year.

b. We sat round a table and held hands. She closed her eyes and then a really idiosyncratic voice came out of her mouth. I'm sure it was Uncle Harry!

c. Listen to that owl hooting! It sounds really monstrous on such a dark, moonless night!

d. His hair is green and spiky and he wears an ear-ring in his nose. You can imagine how uncanny his grandmother thinks he is.

e. What a freakish design for a building, so big and so beautiful!

f. My aunt can read people's minds. It's eccentric how she knows exactly what you are thinking.

g. He's a millionaire but he wears shabby old clothes; he owns three Rolls Royces but he never goes out; he keeps a leopard and a tiger as pets. He's altogether very eerie.

3 Collocation

Which of the adjectives in box **A** can combine with a noun in box **B**? Sometimes several combinations are possible.

A	B	
weird	dream	fashion
eerie	behaviour	effect
deviant	accident	sound
fantastic	experience	appearance
eccentric	style of painting	clothes
freak	feeling	place
idiosyncratic	person	

Reading

Pre-reading task

You will read an article from the *Independent* newspaper about a young man who lives in New York.
Work in groups of four.

1 What do you know about New York, its people, and their life-styles?
2 Look at the title and the last paragraph of the article. What can you infer about the writer's opinion of Americans generally, and about his opinion of Mr Redman, the young man?
3 Mr Redman would be considered by many as an eccentric. What clues are given in the title as to how he might be eccentric?

Reading for information

Read the article (on page 36) and find out whose ideas were closest to the facts.
What is the dream that became a reality?
What aspects of the story do you think the writer finds comforting?

A happy landing for the Tarzan of Central Park

It all proves, I suppose, that America is still the land of opportunity in which dreams – even such seemingly impossible dreams – can become reality. And in the tirelessly competitive atmosphere of the United States, it is comforting every now and then just to remember that Mr Redman exists.

A happy landing for the Tarzan of Central Park

ANYBODY visiting New York for the first time should take a room high up in one of those over-priced, slightly tacky hotels at the southern end of Central Park merely for the extraordinary view it will afford. The park extends northwards until it is lost to sight, a sea of treetops flanked on each side by enormous, impenetrable cliffs of stone and cement.

During recent years legends have grown up among people who frequent or live near the park, legends of life among the treetops. One story went that the park contained whole tribes of mysterious tree-dwellers playing tom-toms by night. Another was of a young and handsome man who had been spotted from time to time lurking among the branches.

That such rumours should arise is not altogether surprising. Central Park covers a huge area — some 850 acres — and accommodates a multitude of strange and sinister happenings. In this case one of the rumours turned out to be true. There *was* a young and handsome man and he *had* been living among the treetops for eight years until he was brought to book not long ago by the city authorities.

It is a touching tale. Bob Redman, now 22, had always been addicted to trees, which might normally be regarded as a misfortune for a boy brought up by his mother in a tiny apartment on Manhattan's Upper West Side. But when he was 14, Redman went into the park and built himself a tree house.

It was the first of 13 such houses he was eventually to build, each more elaborate and lavish then the last. "I like to be in trees," he explained to a reporter from the *New York Times*. "I like to be up, away from everything. I like the solitude. I love most of all to go up in the tree houses and look at the stars. The view at night, of the city lights and the stars, is beyond description."

Mr Redman built his tree houses as birds build nests, with pieces of scrap-wood that he managed to scrounge. He carried the pieces of wood little by little into the park and then hoisted them up secretly into the tree tops. A lean and muscular young man, he can scale tall, branchless tree trunks with remarkable agility. Entry to his houses is often 40ft above the ground, with several levels above that.

His final house was the grandest of them all. Constructed at the top of a towering beech tree from 1,000lb of timber, it was what an estate agent would describe as a five-room split-level home commanding spectacular views of the city skyline and of all of Central Park. It included ladders and rope bridges — one leading to an adjacent tree — as well as wooden benches and tables he had made. Who can imagine what the rent would be?

> 'A young man
> who had been spotted
> lurking among
> the branches.'

Mr Redman would go to great pains to conceal his tree houses, building them in neglected corners of the park and camouflaging them with branches and green paint. He would call them after his favourite stars, his last house bearing the name Epsilon Eridani. Friends would come to visit him in them, sometimes as many as 12 people at a time, bringing sandwiches and radios and books and torches. They were given a set of rules, which, among other things, prohibited branch-breaking, fires, litter and loud noise. His brother Bill sometimes brought a set of conga drums to the tree houses and played them very late at night, giving rise to the rumours of a tree-dwelling tribe.

Although the park authorities quickly became aware of his activities, the houses would often go undetected for long periods of time. Some lasted as long as a year before the sleuths of the Parks Department would find them and tear them down, often with Mr Redman watching mournfully from a distance. His final and most magnificent structure went unnoticed for four months. Then they got him.

He was awoken one morning by the voice of Frank Serpe, Director of Horticulture for Central Park. "Come down! The party's over!" he yelled from the foot of the tree. And Mr Redman climbed down to meet not only Mr Serpe but 10 officers of the Parks Enforcement Patrol. It was victory for Mr Serpe, who had been hunting Mr Redman for years. But, after his triumph, he paid a generous tribute. "We marvelled at the spectacular workmanship," he said. "The last house had floors strong enough to hold a truck, and not one nail was driven into the tree."

You will be glad to hear at this stage that the story has a happy ending. As the officers formed a huddle to decide his fate, Mr Redman offered to go up and help the workmen dismantle the tree house. "I told him I supposed that was all right," said one of the officers later. "Well, he *walked* up the tree. It was amazing."

Mr Serpe concluded that, rather than lock him up, perhaps they should offer him a job. And now, having made a solemn promise to build no more tree houses, Mr Redman is a professional pruner and tree-climber for the Central Park Conservancy. He says he still cannot believe that a job so perfect for him could possibly exist. His mother is happy, too. He finally has work and is back living at home.

It all proves, I suppose, that America is still the land of opportuntity in which dreams — even such seemingly impossible dreams — can become reality. And in the tirelessly competitive atmosphere of the United States, it is comforting every now and then just to remember that Mr Redman exists.

(*Independent* 8 October 1986)

Comprehension check/language work

Work in pairs.
Here are the answers to some questions about the article.
What are the questions?

1 High up in a hotel overlooking Central Park.
2 Tribes of mysterious tree-dwellers.
3 Since he was fourteen.
4 Thirteen.
5 He likes to look at the stars.
6 With pieces of scrapwood.
7 He used branches and green paint.
8 Four months.
9 The fact that he hadn't banged a single nail into the tree.
10 He (the writer) thinks he (Mr Redman) is a lovable eccentric.

Roleplay

Work in pairs.
One of you is Mr Redman.
The other is a journalist. Conduct an interview about Mr Redman's past and present life.

Vocabulary guessing

Try to work out the meaning of the following words from the context.

(16) tom-toms	(56) hoisted (them) up
(19) lurking	(58) scale
(32) touching	(97) sleuths
(43) elaborate and lavish	(100) mournfully
(54) to scrounge	(124) dismantle

▶ Language focus

Read the Language study on *as* (page 40) and do the practice exercises.

● Vocabulary 2

Introduction

You are going to listen to and read a song by a very famous English song-writer called Noël Coward.
First read the biographical extract.

COWARD, Sir Noël (b. Dec. 16, 1899, Teddington, near London – d. March 30, 1973, St Mary, Jamaica). Playwright, actor, and composer whose highly polished comedies of manners continued the same English stage tradition developed by William Congreve and Oscar Wilde. He caught in his work the clipped speech and brittle life-style of the generation that emerged from World War I. His songs struck the world-weary note of his times. He sings in a quavering but superbly timed and articulate baritone. Coward was knighted in 1970 and late in life, for health and tax reasons, lived outside England, chiefly in the Caribbean and Switzerland.

The song is called 'Mad dogs and Englishmen'. It was written in the 1930s, a time when the British Empire was starting to decline.
In it Coward pokes fun at the Englishman's refusal to adapt his life-style to local customs and conditions when living abroad.

Questions to discuss before you listen

1 How do the British behave as visitors to your country? Is there a difference between those who come as tourists and those who perhaps come to live and work there?

2 How do you feel other countries view your compatriots when they visit?
3 Can you name any countries that were once part of the British Empire?
4 In the left-hand column are the names of some countries as they are known today.
In the right-hand column are their names under colonial rule (not just British). Try to match them.

a. Zimbabwe	**1** The Belgian Congo
b. Sri Lanka	**2** Tanganyika
c. Tanzania	**3** Abyssinia
d. Zaire	**4** The Gold Coast
e. Belize	**5** Ceylon
f. Ghana	**6** British Honduras
g. Ethiopia	**7** Rhodesia

37

| T.4 | Look at the first verse before you listen.

Try to fill the gaps with the best word from the column at the side.
Consider the rhyme and the poetic flow of the lines to help you choose
which is most appropriate. Saying the lines aloud might help you do this.
Work in pairs, and use your dictionary if necessary.

Now listen to the first verse and check your words.

Repeat this procedure for the following verses.

Mad Dogs and Englishmen

In tropical _____ there are certain times of day
When all the _____ retire
To take their clothes off and _____.
It's one of those rules that the greatest fools

5 _____
Because the sun is far too _____
And one must avoid its ultry violet ray.
The natives grieve when the whitemen leave their

10 Because they're obviously, definitely _____ !

sultry/hot
citizens/people
houses/huts
nuts/crazy
follow/obey
perspire/sweat
climes/countries

Mad dogs and Englishmen go out in the midday sun.
The Japanese don't care to,
The Chinese wouldn't dare to.
Hindus and Argentines sleep _____ from twelve
15   to one.
But Englishmen _____ a siesta.
In the Philippines they have lovely _____
To protect you from the _____.
In the Malay States there are _____ like plates
20 Which the Britishers won't wear.
At twelve noon the natives _____
And no further work is done.
But mad dogs and Englishmen go out in the midday
       sun.

detest/hate
shoes/hats
screens/parasols
swoon/faint
firmly/soundly
glare/sun

25 It's such a surprise for the Eastern eyes to see,
That though the English are _____ ,
They're quite _____ to heat.
When the whiteman rides every native hides in

30 Because the simple creatures hope he
Will _____ his solar topee on a tree.
It seems such a _____ when the English claim
    the _____
That they give rise to such _____ and mirth.

happiness/glee
impale/stick
shame/pity
weak/effete
laughter/hilarity
world/earth
closed/impervious

35 Mad dogs and Englishmen go out in the midday
    sun.
  The toughest Burmese _____
  Can never understand it.
  In Rangoon the heat of noon is just what the natives
40 _____
  They put their _____ or Rye down and lie
    down.
  In a _____ town where the sun _____ down
  To the rage of man and beast,
45 The English _____ of the English *sahib*
  Merely gets a bit more _____ .
  In Bangkok at twelve o'clock
  They _____ at the mouth and run
  But mad dogs and Englishmen go out in the midday
50   sun.

  Mad dogs and Englishmen go out in the midday sun.
  The smallest Malay _____
  Deplores this foolish habit.
55 In Hong Kong they _____ a gong
  And fire off a noonday _____
  To reprimand each _____ who's in late.
  In the mangrove _____ where the python

60 There is peace from twelve to two.
  Even caribous lie around and _____ ,
  For there's nothing else to do.

  In Bengal to move at all is _____ if ever done.
  But mad dogs and Englishmen go out in the midday
    sun.

whisky/Scotch
jungle/desert
clothes/garb
crumpled/creased
foam/salivate
avoid/shun
shines/beats
robber/bandit

inhabitant/inmate
bang/strike
sleep/snooze
plays/romps
gun/cannon
infrequently/seldom
chicken/rabbit
swamps/marshes

Glossary

solar topee – pith helmet, a type of sun-hat worn in the tropics, typical of colonial times
mangrove – tropical tree or shrub
caribou – a large deer
sahib /saːb/ – (Indian) form of address for a man

Discussion

Culture shock!

Discuss these questions in small groups.
1 Have you visited any country or countries that you felt were very different from your own?
2 What did you find that was very strange to you?
3 Which aspects of life in your country do you think might seem strange or unusual to a first-time foreign visitor?
4 Which nationalities do you think would find your country most different? Which would find it similar?
  You can consider the following areas if you wish.

  – food   – natural features
  – clothes   – public holidays
  – ceremonies   – daily routine
  – celebrations   – leisure activities
  – religion   – modes of transport
  – attitudes to work – climate

Writing

Write about a time in your life when you found your surroundings and the customs going on around you strange or different. This could be the first time you went abroad on your own, or a holiday that you took away from your parents; perhaps your first day at school, or going to stay with someone in your own country who organized their life in a way you found strange.

Do the exercise on linking cause and result in the 'Writing' section of Unit 3 of the Workbook before you write your essay.

Listening

T.5 You will hear an interview with Quentin Crisp, an English writer and raconteur. He talks about why he has always felt different from other people.

He has a droll, self-deprecatory sense of humour, which is sometimes funny and sometimes sad. 'I am not a drop-out', he says at the beginning of his autobiography, 'I was never in.'

Listen to the interview and answer the questions.

Comprehension check

1 'I was never going to be able to join the human race.' What does he mean by this?
2 What is his attitude towards his family?
3 A *hooligan* nowadays means someone who behaves in a violent and noisy way. What does Quentin Crisp use the word to mean?
4 What do you think his family thinks of him?
5 What is his ideal home?
6 How do you think he views himself?

▶ Language focus

Do the practice exercise on *verb patterns* in the Language study (page 41).

LANGUAGE STUDY

1 'As'

As has many uses in English.

There are seven examples of **as** or **as . . . as** in the text about Bob Redman. Find them and try to identify the different uses.

'As' versus 'like'
Look at the following sentences.

*He works **as** a professional tree climber.*
*He climbs trees **like** a monkey.*
*He built his tree houses **as** birds build nests.*
*He used his shoe **as** a hammer.*

Both **as** and **like** are used for comparison.
Which two of the above sentences are comparisons?
How do these two sentences differ? What is the rule?
What do the other two sentences have in common?

▶ Grammar reference: page 136.

Practice

Complete the following sentences with either **as** or **like**.
a. The skyscrapers of New York are _____ impenetrable cliffs of stone and cement.
b. She appeared on the screen _____ Florence Nightingale but no-one could be less _____ a nurse in reality.
c. Since he got that job _____ a traffic warden, he regards every motorist _____ a potential criminal!
d. The estate agent described it _____ 'cosy' and 'well-fitted'. It was _____ a prison cell!
e. John is easy-going _____ his mother but Jeff gets worked up about the slightest little thing, just _____ his father always does.

'As . . . as' for comparison

1 Transform the following sentences, using **as . . . as** or **not as/so . . . as**.
a. She enjoys her work more than Alan does.
b. This is the happiest day of my life!
c. He's a lot less interesting to talk to than he used to be.
d. His later books don't have the same appeal as his earlier ones.
e. I speak better German than Alice.
f. She's less arrogant than I thought.

2 Put one suitable word into each gap.
a. There were as _____ as one thousand guests at the wedding.
b. He said I could have as _____ money as I wanted.
c. As _____ as working during the day in an office, she also works in the evening in a restaurant.

d. You can borrow it as _____ as you promise to look after it.
e. As _____ as I heard the news, I told all my friends.
f. You can do what you like as _____ as I'm concerned.

2 Verb Patterns

Which of the four verbs or verb phrases in each of the following sentences belongs there grammatically?

Change each sentence in as many ways as are necessary to use each of the other three verbs in the grammatical construction.

a. He | enjoys / used / is used / would rather | to live in the trees.

b. I | have decided / am thinking / had better / made him | to look for a job.

c. I | was made / expect you / am trying / don't mind | cleaning the house.

d. I | stopped / want / hoped / let | him to go.

e. I | remember him / succeeded / am looking forward / reminded him | to come home early.

f. I | avoided / managed / happened / helped her | meeting him.

g. I | can't help / stopped / don't feel like / saw him | to do it.

REVISION

Future forms

There are more forms to express future time in English than in many other languages.

▶ **Grammar reference: page 136.**

1 Match a future form in box **A** with its definition in box **B**.

A
a. You'll have a long and happy life, my dear.
b. I'll give you my phone number in case you need to contact me.
c. I'm going to study medicine at university.
d. I feel dizzy. I think I'm going to faint.
e. We're meeting Emma for a drink after work.
f. My plane leaves at midday next Thursday.
g. Don't phone around 8.00 – they'll be putting the children to bed.
h. This is your captain speaking. Welcome aboard this flight. We'll be flying at 35,000 feet.
i. We'll have completed the survey by the twentieth of the month.

B
1 An activity which will be in progress at a certain time
2 An arrangement between people
3 A planned intention
4 A spontaneous intention
5 A future fact based on a calendar or timetable
6 A simple prediction
7 A prediction about the future based on present evidence
8 An action that will be finished *before* a definite time
9 An action that will happen in the natural course of events

a. ____ b. ____ c. ____ d. ____ e. ____

f. ____ g. ____ h. ____ i. ____

2 Here are the names of the future forms.
Write the letter from box **A** that corresponds to each.
Sometimes a form will have two letters as it has two uses.
The Present Continuous ____
The Future Continuous ____
Will + infinitive ____
The Present Simple ____
Going to + infinitive ____
The Future Perfect ____

41

3 Put the verb in brackets in a suitable future form. Sometimes more than one form is possible.

A What (a) _____ you _____ for Christmas this year? Have you made any plans?

B Yes, we (b) _____ (go) to my wife's family on Christmas Eve. We (c) _____ (stay) at her sister's because there (d) _____ (not be) enough room at her parents' house. We (e) _____ probably (come) back home on Boxing Day, but we haven't decided yet. What about you?

A We have decided we (f) _____ (do) something different this year.
We (g) _____ (visit) some friends in Australia, so on Christmas Day we (h) _____ (lie) on the beach, I hope.

B How long (i) _____ you _____ (be) away for?

A Two weeks. The new term (j) _____ (start) on January 6th, and we (k) _____ (be) back in time for that, of course.

A How long (l) _____ you _____ (stay) at this school, Maria?

B Till the end of the month.

A And what (m) _____ you _____ (do) then?

B I (n) _____ (go) back to Spain. I hope that by the end of the month my English (o) _____ (improve) enough for me to pass my exams.

A And if you pass them, what (p) _____ you _____ (do)?

B I don't know. I (q) _____ (have to) see how good my grades are. If they are good enough, I (r) _____ (go) to the same university as my sister.

A Well, good luck.

A I'm going to Germany tomorrow on business.

B What (s) _____ you _____ (do) there?

A I (t) _____ (meet) some new clients. I hope to sell them a new million-pound computer.

B How (u) _____ you _____ (do) that?

A I don't know yet. But if I do, then I (v) _____ (sell) ten new computer systems this year.

B It sounds as if you (w) _____ (make) a lot of money soon, if you aren't already. What (x) _____ you _____ (do) with it all?

A I (y) _____ (let) you know!

4 Divide into four groups.
Your teacher will give you a role card.
Groups **A** and **B** should prepare the questions.
Groups **C** and **D** should prepare the answers.
When you are ready, conduct the interview.
When you have finished, ask each other similar questions about your future plans.

UNIT 4

From the cradle to the grave

Discussion

1 It is said that children learn more in the first two years of life than at any other stage. What kinds of things have most children learnt by the age of two? What do they learn themselves, and what are they taught?

2 Say what you think are the three most important qualities of an ideal parent. Are there any other qualities that you would like to add to your list?

3 How would you rate the way that your parents brought you up? If you are a parent, how do you rate yourself? If you are not a parent, do you think you would make a good one?

'May I borrow him? We need to get rid of some visitors.'

'Congratulations ! He seems very bright.'

'That's all I needed – a baldheaded sister.'

CHILDREN LEARN WHAT THEY LIVE

A	B
If a child lives with criticism, *She learns to condemn.*	she learns to be patient.
If a child lives with hostility,	he learns justice.
If a child lives with ridicule,	she learns to be shy.
If a child lives with shame,	he learns confidence.
If a child lives with tolerance,	she learns to have faith.
If a child lives with encouragement,	he learns to like himself.
If a child lives with praise,	she learns to condemn.
If a child lives with fairness,	she learns to appreciate.
If a child lives with security,	he learns to fight.
If a child lives with approval,	he learns to feel guilt.
If a child lives with acceptance and friendship,	he or she learns to find love in the world.

4 The sentences above appear on a chart that is often found in baby clinics and child centres, but the second halves of the sentences have been mixed up.
Match the first half of a sentence in column **A** with an appropriate second half in column **B**. The first one has been done for you.

5 Devise a 'Good parents' charter' based on the points in the chart. One way of starting might be:

Good parents shouldn't be too critical, because if they are, their child will . . .

44

Listening

T.6 You will hear six people commenting on their childhood and their parents. Stop the tape after each one and discuss the following:

1 Relate their comments to the points on the chart. Some comments may relate to more than one point.
2 Each person on the tape could continue by assessing the effects of their upbringing on their lives today. Do this for them.
   For example, the first person might start:

Maybe that's why I'm never nervous about exams and interviews. When I got this job . . .

● Vocabulary 1

1 Word building

Complete the following sentences with an appropriate word formed from the root of one of the words in the children's chart on page 44.

Example
*It was only after he'd been **unfaithful** for the third time that she asked for a divorce.*

In some cases you will need to use the following prefixes and suffixes:

dis- un- in- -able -ant -ed -ingly -ive

a. The priest visited the _____ man in his cell.
b. As an actor, he has never recovered from the _____ reception the critics gave his last performance.
c. I don't believe that theft is ever _____, even if you are starving.
d. Why should you get a hundred pounds when I only get fifty? That's hardly a _____ deal.
e. My neighbours had always been noisy, but when they bought an organ and started playing it at two in the morning, the level of noise became _____ and I had to move.
f. She's a good teacher with the bright kids, but she's too _____ of those who are less able.
g. 'Tut, tut! Smoking at your age!' he said _____.
h. Management offered employees a two per cent pay rise, but the union found this offer _____.
i. The teacher helped the student with private lessons and extra homework. When the student passed her exam, she was most _____ and bought her teacher a present.
j. 'I know you feel fed up, but don't let one failure _____ you. It was your first interview, after all. There'll be more.'

2 Prepositions

Nouns, verbs, and adjectives often have dependent prepositions which simply have to be learnt.
Put an appropriate preposition in the following gaps.

a. She felt so guilty _____ not telling the truth. She knew that because of this he had been found guilty _____ murder.
b. How could she have been so unfaithful _____ him when he had such faith _____ her?
c. She criticizes everything _____ him. She criticizes him _____ not being ambitious enough, and she's even critical _____ the way he eats his breakfast cereal!
d. He may be patient _____ his own children, but he shows absolutely no tolerance _____ anybody else's.
e. I'm always so shy _____ strangers. I know I should have more confidence _____ myself but I can't help it.
f. They just take her for granted. They show no appreciation _____ all she does for them. They should be ashamed _____ themselves.
g. Those children were hostile _____ her as their stepmother right from the start. Mind you, in fairness _____ them, she is not very easy to get on with.
h. I feel secure _____ the knowledge that I have done nothing wrong, although I know you don't approve _____ the way I acted.

Reading

You are going to read an article from an American magazine called *Harper's*. It is about creating better and brighter babies.

Background information

1 Divide into two groups of equal size.

Group A

T.7 You will hear a short extract from a talk given in 1973 by Dr Benjamin Spock, a world famous pediatrician and author of books on child care.
Listen and take notes under the following headings:

– relationships between parents and children up until the middle of the twentieth century
– the influence of Freud
– the influence of Dewey
– Dr Spock's interpretation of Freud and Dewey
– the effect of these influences on children.

Group B
Read the letter written to a newspaper, and answer the questions.

a. According to the writer, what have children lost these days, and what have they gained?
b. What is wrong with school?
c. How does he characterize the 1960s and the 1980s?
d. What are youth's problems?
e. In what ways does the writer criticize youth? Is it for the things parents are traditionally critical about (for example being untidy, irresponsible, or lazy), or is it something different?

Discuss your answers in your own groups.

Pennington Street, The Highway, London E1 9XW

Our Children's Future

As a parent and an observer of mankind, I grow increasingly concerned about the life that our children inherit, the values that they hold dear, and their expectations for the future. Childhood seems to last but a few years until children become a market force to be bombarded with advertisements on the television. They demand to have all that they see, and regard it as their right to be entertained every waking moment.

At school, most children are bored by the lessons, which they see as irrelevant to life as they perceive it. Life is about having fun, and having fun *now*. Or, at the other extreme, school is fiercely competitive, and pupils are pushed by parents to achieve at all costs.

The 1960s were a time of great liberalization, when youth thought it could right all wrongs. Its ideals of love and peace are now much scorned as hollow, hippy phrases. If the world veered to the left in '68, then it has lurched to the right in the past fifteen years. The 1980s are undoubtedly a more selfish, inward-looking era, with the individual out to look after himself, regardless of the effect this might be having on others. The new gods are money and materialism, and teenagers want *now* what it took their parents half a generation to achieve.

If youth has learnt to question the wisdom of its elders, it has so far found nothing to replace it with. No wonder there is drug abuse on a scale never seen before. No wonder so many children seek the help of psychiatrists. What are they to fill the emptiness of their souls with?

JAMES STUART,
Gloucester.

2 Work in pairs.
Find a partner from the other group.
Summarize for each other the content of your texts.
Dr Spock was speaking in 1973. Which war was he referring to?
What would the writer of the letter have to say to Dr Spock, if the two ever met?

Pre-reading task

1 Look at the cartoon in the article 'Bringing up a better baby'. Who are the people? What are they doing?
2 Read the first paragraph of the article.
Why do present-day Americans disagree with Dr Spock?

Reading for information

Now read the article.
As you read, underline anything that surprises you in Glenn Doman's thinking. Can you find any flaws in his arguments?

Comprehension check

Are the following statements true or false? Put **T** or **F** in the box by each one.

T/F

1 Dr Spock reassured generations of parents that their babies were instinctively sociable. ☐

2 The main ambition of many American professional parents these days is for their children to become integrated members of society. ☐

3 The Better Baby Institute runs courses for especially gifted children. ☐

4 Doman believes that any individual could be a genius as great as Shakespeare as long as training is started early enough. ☐

5 Doman believes that a baby would prefer to learn Greek to its mother tongue because Greek is more challenging. ☐

6 Doman maintains that babies can learn to read hundreds of new words and phrases every day. ☐

7 Scientists have proof that Glenn Doman's theory is correct. ☐

8 It is a full-time job for parents if they embark on the training programme. ☐

9 Josh Pereira has difficulty getting on with other children. ☐

10 Dr Spock believes it is desirable that parents make every effort to increase their baby's cognitive abilities. ☐

Bringing up a better baby
(and goodbye Dr Spock)

Dr Benjamin Spock, the famous American pediatrician, reassured several generations of anxious parents in his best selling *Baby and Child Care*. He wrote 'Your baby is born to be a reasonable friendly human being'. Today's parents are not sure this is enough. There is a growing number of American professional parents with obsessive ambitions for their children. They are dedicating their lives to creating brilliant children. The Age of Spock is over! Why have a merely 'normal' baby when you can have an improved model, a Better Baby? In the world of baby care, common sense has given way to competition and connoisseurship.

The Better Baby Institute

This was founded by an American called Glenn Doman. Four to six times a year the Institute opens its doors to a group of about eighty parents who have paid $490 each for a seven-day seminar entitled 'How to multiply your baby's intelligence'. After studying children for over forty years, Doman has developed an apparently brilliant, internally consistent, and completely idiosyncratic brand of science that commingles developmental psychology, neurology and anthropology. He introduces the parents to his '89 Cardinal Facts for Making Any Baby into a Superb Human Being'.

Cardinal Fact No. 6: 'Our individual genetic potential is that of Leonardo da Vinci, Mozart, Michelangelo, Edison and Einstein.'

Doman claims that up until the age of six, when brain growth slows, a child's intellectual and physical abilities will increase in direct proportion to stimulation. Thus any child, given the proper stimuli, can become the next Leonardo.

Cardinal Fact No. 26: 'Tiny kids would rather learn than eat.'

Doman claims that they'd rather learn Greek than baby talk, since higher orders of complexity offer more stimulation. He makes the average adult seem like a tree sloth in comparison with a two-year-old. 'Every kid,' he asserts, 'learns better than every adult'. Parents at the Better Baby Institute learn to regard their mewling puking infants not so much with respect as awe.

So the question is now one of technique. How can parents create the kind of brain growth that leads to expertise in reading, math, gymnastics, and the like? Say you want to teach your six-month-old how to read. Write down a series of short, familiar words in large, clear letters on flashcards.

Show the cards to your infant five or six times a day, simultaneously reciting the word written on each one. With his extraordinary retentive powers he'll soon be learning hundreds of words, then phrases. The idea is to try to treat the baby's mind as a sponge. By the age of three, Doman guarantees, your child will be entertaining himself and amazing your friends by reading 'everything in sight'. In like manner he can learn to perform staggering mathematical stunts, or to distinguish and thoughtfully analyze the works of the Great Masters or the classical composers.

Doman declines to prove his claims to the scientific community; he's happy, he says, as long as parents are convinced. These Professional Mothers (it is usually the mother) turn out to be paragons. Attractive young Mrs DiBattista printed up 9,000 flashcards for five-year-old Michael. Stout, solemn Mrs Pereira patiently explained that she 'took time off' from her all-day routine of teaching eleven-year-old Josh to devote several weeks exclusively to making Josh's French and Spanish flashcards for the coming year. Wasn't Josh lonely? 'No', his proud mother replied. He was 'socially excellent'.

What does Dr Benjamin Spock think of the better baby phenomenon? Like most octogenarians he thinks the world has gone to hell; he argues that competitive pressures are taking a psychic toll on most Americans, especially young people, and blames 'excessive competitiveness' for the extraordinary rise in teenage suicide over the last twenty years. Efforts to improve infants' cognitive abilities only prove to him that the scramble for success has finally invaded the cradle.

(adapted from an article in *Harper's and Queen* March 1986)

Points for discussion

1 How do you feel you would have responded as a baby or child if you had been trained in the manner described in the article?

2 Would you want your children to be trained like this? Why? Why not?

3 What is the difference between 'learning' and 'playing' for a baby?

4 Do you think that an institute like Glenn Doman's would be popular in your country? Why? Why not? What kind of people do you think it might be popular with?

5 Can you envisage any problems that might result for both parents and children who embark on such a programme of training?

▶ Language focus

Read the Language study on *modal auxiliary verbs* (page 50) and do the practice exercises.

Speaking

Roleplay

Imagine that you are a group of parents and you have just listened to a talk given by Glenn Doman in which he has described the Better Baby Institute.
It is now question time.

In pairs prepare at least six questions that you would like Doman to answer about his ideas.
Either your teacher or another member of the class will try to respond to your questions as they feel Doman might do.

Writing

Write an essay on one of the following topics. Present both sides of the argument, and then give your own views with reasons.

– Should parents try to teach their children before they go to school?

– Who is mainly responsible for a child's academic success, the parents or the teachers?

– A competitive society brings out the best in every individual.

– 'Most of the school work that adolescents do is simply a waste of time, of energy, of patience. It robs youth of its right to play and play . . .' A. S. Neill (see page 19)

Do the exercises on linking words and phrases to show similarity and comparison in the 'Writing' section of Unit 4 of the Workbook before you write your essay.

Listening

T.8

How to Live to a Hundred or More

Introduction

You are going to listen to some advice given by American comedian George Burns, who is now in his nineties. George Burns won enduring popularity in Britain with the 'Burns and Allen Show', a television series featuring himself and his wife Gracie Allen. Gracie died in the 1960s, but George continues doing shows and acting in films.

Note-taking

George discusses the following in his recipe for a long life:
– exercise   – work
– stress and tension   – the past
– hobbies   – the future
– attitude

Listen, and make notes under these headings.
In pairs, discuss your notes.

Listening for specific points

George is famous for his witticisms. Listen again and note all the ways in which he tries to be funny.
How would you describe the manner in which he tries to be humorous?

Vocabulary 2

Euphemisms

A euphemism is a polite way of expressing something thought to be unpleasant.

Here is a newspaper article, in which the writer complains about the use of euphemistic language.

The euphemisms have been blanked out, and appear on the right. Match them to the correct place in the article.

STOP BEING COY
I will die—not "pass away"

I AM an old cripple, drawing an old-age pension, working hard to raise vast quantities of vegetables on an allotment and well aware that, one of these days, I shall die. All this is fact.

If, however, I listen to the voice of officialdom, it turns out that I am a **1** _____ , registered as **2** _____ , drawing a **3** _____ , renting a **4** _____ , and, presumably, immortal because I shall never die – I shall merely **5** _____ .

According to *Encyclopaedia Britannica*, 'Euphemisms are considered overly squeamish and affected by contemporary writers, unless used for humorous effect.' This may be so among the cognoscenti but there is little evidence to show that the masses, especially the administrators, have read their encyclopaedia. The clichés which pour from the lips of trade union leaders are endless. **6** '_____ ' or **7** '_____ ' equals 'going on strike' and **8** '_____ ' equals 'being bloody minded'.

Again quoting the encyclopaedia: a euphemism is a 'figure of speech in which something of an unpleasant, distressing, or indelicate nature is described in less offensive terms'. For example, to describe Uncle George as a sex maniac might not endear you to Auntie Mabel but she would be proud to hear him referred to as a **9** _____ .

Examples of gross understatement may also appeal to some of us. A native of the Lake District who describes himself as being 'nobbut middlin', is approaching a state of collapse and coma; if he says he's 'proper poorly', there will be a funeral in the near future.

These more robust euphemisms may, for all I care, stay. But let us, please, do away with the following: **10** '_____ ' *(poor)*, **11** '_____ ' *(ill)*, **12** '_____ ' *(stupid)*, **13** '_____ ' *(dole)*, **14** '_____ ' *(Ministry of War)*, **15** '_____ ' *(talk)*, and **16** '_____ ' *(pet)*.

All this effort to avoid unpleasantness is certain to fail, because the euphemism quickly acquires the stigma of the word it replaced. I, and probably others, do not feel younger because I am called a 'senior citizen'.

BRYAN HEATH
(Retired vet)

(The Sunday Times 29 June 1980)

a. withdrawing our services
b. leisure garden
c. pass away
d. low IQ
e. Ministry of Defence
f. companion animal
g. disadvantaged senior citizen
h. working to rule
i. unemployment benefit
j. disabled
k. manly man
l. under the weather
m. retirement pension
n. lower income brackets
o. taking industrial action
p. have a dialogue

What do you think the following euphemisms refer to?

– The rebel fighters were neutralized.
– The Prime Minister was economical with the truth.
– With all due respect, I think your figures are misleading.
– Could you please regularize your bank account?
– We had a frank, open exchange of views.
– This is not a non-risk policy.
– The company is in a non-profit situation.

LANGUAGE STUDY

1 Modal auxiliary verbs, present and future

One of the main uses of modal verbs is to express varying degrees of likelihood or probability.

Examples
A *It'll rain tomorrow, you'll see.*
B *It might not. It could stay fine.*

A *Give Anne a ring. She should be home by now.*
B *She can't be. The traffic's too bad. She'll be stuck in a traffic jam.*

▶ **Grammar reference: page 137.**

Practice

1 Look at the following sentences and identify those which express degrees of likelihood. The modal verbs are in italics.

a. You *can* borrow the car, I don't need it.
b. He *can't* still be at the office, it's after 9 o'clock.
c. I *can't* hear you very well, the line's bad.
d. That *won't* be the postman at the door, he's been already.
e. *Will* you give me a hand with this? It's so heavy.
f. John's awful. He simply *won't* admit that he's made a mistake!
g. A What's that scratching noise?
   B Don't worry. It*'ll* be the cat trying to get in.
h. He*'ll* be at the airport by now.
i. No, you *may* not leave before the end.
j. We *may* be in for a rough crossing, there's a storm coming.
k. He *might* change his mind, if we keep on at him.
l. You *mustn't* give up yet, try just once more.
m. He always looks so exhausted, he *must* have a very demanding job.
n. If you hurry up, we *could* be there by 6 o'clock.
o. You *should* drive more slowly round there, it's a dangerous corner.
p. You *should* have no trouble passing, it's your best subject.

2 When you have identified those sentences that express likelihood, try to group them according to whether they express certainty, probability, or possibility.

3 Other uses of modals are to express *obligation* (mild or strong), *permission*, *ability*, and *willingness*.
Categorize the remaining sentences under these headings.

2 Modal auxiliary verbs in the past

Modal auxiliary verbs often have different forms to refer to past time depending on the meaning.

Example
must
I had to go the dentist. (obligation)
It must have been an awful shock. (deduction)

▶ **Grammar reference: page 138.**

Practice

Fill the gap in (ii) by putting the concept expressed by the verb form in (i) into the past. Notice that in some cases a different form of the modal verb is needed, and in others a totally different verb.

a. (i) She *can ski* really well.
   (ii) She _____ really well when she was five.
b. (i) I *can finish* it by Friday, but it won't be easy.
   (ii) I _____ by Friday, but it wasn't easy.
c. (i) John *can't live* here. This is the wrong street.
   (ii) Shakespeare _____ in that house. It wasn't built until 1840.
d. (i) *May I leave* the room? I don't feel well.
   (ii) I _____ the room because I didn't feel well.
e. (i) I *must check* the oil before we leave.
   (ii) I _____ the oil before we left.
f. (i) It *must be raining*. Everyone has their umbrella up.
   (ii) It _____. The ground is wet.
g. (i) Thank you very much. You *needn't give* me a lift, but it's very kind.
   (ii) You _____ me a lift, but it was very kind.
h. (i) He *needn't collect* me from the station. I'll walk.
   (ii) He _____ me from the station. I walked.
i. (i) Why don't you take the exam? You *might pass*.
   (ii) Why didn't you take the exam? You _____.
j. (i) He *should stop* smoking before it's too late.
   (ii) He _____ smoking before it was too late.
k. (i) I *could visit* you next Sunday.
   (ii) I _____ you last Sunday. Why didn't you ask me?
l. (i) There's the phone. It*'ll be* Paul.
   (ii) Did he have a deep voice? It _____ Paul.
m. (i) He*'ll sit* in the armchair for hours, staring into space.
   (ii) He _____ in the armchair for hours, staring into space.
n. (i) Let's take the map. We *may get lost*.
   (ii) I wonder where they are. They _____.

3 Modal auxiliary verbs: past, present, and future

Look at this very unnatural sounding monologue.
Replace the words in italics with appropriate modal verbs to make it sound more natural.

'Wonderful, it's Sunday and (a) *not necessary for me* to get up at 7 o'clock. (b) *I'll possibly* stay in bed a bit longer although (c) *I think* the children *are probably* awake now and I'll (d) *be obliged* to get their breakfast soon. They (e) *refuse to* make it for themselves. (f) *It would be a good idea for me to* get up immediately because (g) *perhaps* they *will* wreck the house. However, it is still very early and they (h) *are probably not* very hungry yet. (i) *It would have been a good idea if I had* put out the cornflakes and milk yesterday evening. But all this thinking and not acting is really silly! (j) *It is* really *necessary for me to* get up this minute. Now where are my bedroom slippers? – That damn dog (k) *has probably* hidden them again! (l) *It would be a good idea for us to train* it better, but I suppose we (m) *weren't obliged* to buy it in the first place, and after all, it's only a puppy.

Oh, I'd forgotten! (n) *It's just possible that* Alan *will* be back from his business trip today – marvellous! One adult isn't enough to look after four children, a puppy, and three goldfish! Why (o) *did he refuse to* take me with him? (p) *It was possible for us to get* his mother to come and look after the children. Never again!'

REVISION

Reply questions

1 **T.9**   Listen to this short conversation between a man and a woman.
Listen particularly to how the man replies.
How does he show interest in what the woman is saying?
Work in pairs and try to remember the exact words of the conversation. Practise saying it together.

2 We often reply to statements by making short questions, containing just an auxiliary verb and a pronoun.
These *reply questions* are not real questions asking for information.
They are used to express interest, concern, surprise, or just to show that we are listening.
The intonation always rises.

3 You need to be careful to use the right auxiliary verb.
Work in pairs.
Underline the correct auxiliary verb in the reply questions below, and say why it is correct.

   a. **A** I have an English lesson every Monday.
      B Have/do you?

   b. **A** I have never tasted such a delicious wine!
      B Haven't/don't you?

   c. **A** She has the most amazing green eyes!
      B Has/does she?

   d. **A** I had a row with the boss yesterday.
      B Had/did you?

   e. **A** I have to go now.
      B Have/do you?

   f. **A** He'd gone before I arrived.
      B Would/had/did he?

   g. **A** Ask Peter. He'd help you.
      B Had/would/did he?

4 Look at the following statements.
Work in pairs and try to respond to each one with a reply question.
See if you can continue the response a little.

   Example
   A We're having lobster for dinner.
   B *Are we? How delicious!*

   a. Jeremy's won first prize in a raffle!
   b. I've got a terrible pain down at the bottom of my spine.
   c. I often have pains in my back.
   d. I had a nightmare last night.
   e. I never used to have a birthday party when I was a kid.
   f. I'd crawl under the bedclothes and cry about it for hours.
   g. I went to a party last Saturday but I was so late they'd finished the food when I arrived.
   h. Did you know that Paul never does any work?
   i. Yet he still earns over £30,000 a year.
   j. The thing that amazes me is that he never has to pay any tax, either.

5 Work in pairs.
   Student A You are reading the newspaper, and only half listening to **B**. Answer **B** using reply questions.
   Student B You are trying to tell **A** about what you did last night, and what you intend doing today.

UNIT 5

War and peace

Discussion

Work in groups of three.
Look at the list of quotations on the subject of war and decide if they come from ancient or modern history.
Match the quotation with one of the sources listed opposite.

1 'I came, I saw, I conquered.'

2 'People say, well, I could never kill a man. That's bullshit. They can. Anybody can kill. It takes more to make one man kill than it does the next. The training helps a lot. But combat – you know, once they start shooting at you, if you don't shoot back, you're a damned fool.'

3 'What did you do in the Great War, daddy?'

4 '. . . we shall fight on the beaches, we shall fight on the landing grounds, we shall fight in the fields and in the streets, we shall fight in the hills; we shall never surrender.'

5 'You shall show no mercy: life for life, eye for eye, tooth for tooth.'

6 'Happiness lies in conquering one's enemies, in driving them in front of oneself, in taking their property, in savouring their despair, in outraging their wives and daughters.'

7 'We knew the world would not be the same. A few people laughed. A few people cried. Most people were silent. I remembered the line from Hindu scripture, "Now I am become Death, the destroyer of worlds." I suppose we all felt that, one way or another.'

8 'You know, I turn back to your ancient prophets in the Old Testament and the signs foretelling Armageddon, and I find myself wondering if – if we're the generation that's going to see that come about . . . There have been times in the past when we thought the world was coming to an end, but never anything like this.'

9 'Resist not evil: but whosoever shall smite thee on thy right cheek, turn to him the other also.'

Sources

a. the Old Testament
b. the New Testament
c. Julius Caesar
d. Genghis Khan
e. a recruiting poster for World War I, 1914–1918
f. Winston Churchill
g. Robert Oppenheimer, inventor of the atomic bomb
h. Ronald Reagan
i. US veteran of Vietnam

What were the clues that helped you match a quotation and its source?

Vocabulary 1

Here are a number of words connected with defence.

1 Use your dictionary to check those you are not sure of, and put them (where possible) into chronological order.

fortress shield minefield moat helmet
air-raid shelter bullet-proof vest barbed wire
gas mask drawbridge
armour parapet
sandbag trench fall-out shelter

2 Give an example of a context in which each of the words could be used. Who might be defended, and against what?

Example

Noun	Defending who?	Against what?
bullet-proof vest	the president of a country	an assassination attempt

53

Reading

You will read an extract from a book called *War* by
Gwynne Dyer.
Dyer used to be Senior Lecturer in War Studies at the
Royal Military Academy, Sandhurst.
The extract is from Chapter 1, 'The roots of war'.

Pre-reading task

Work in pairs to discuss the following questions.

1 When do you think the first war in history took place, and
   why?
2 In what ways has war changed through the ages?
3 In what ways hasn't it changed?

When you have finished, compare your ideas as a group.

Reading for information

Now read the text and find the answers to these questions.
1 What are the differences between primitive warfare and
   the battles described in the text?
2 What is the importance of military drill?
3 What happened on the battlefield as a result of drilling
   and formations?
4 What reasons are given in the text to explain why
   ordinary men can take part in such battles?

What do you think?

1 Can you think of any *other* reasons why ordinary,
   civilized men are able to act so uncharacteristically
   violently in battle?
2 What do you think are the most common causes of war?
   Give specific examples from wars past or present.
3 Make a personal list of causes for which you feel you
   would fight in a war. Compare your answers with others
   in the group.
4 Do you believe that aggression is innate in man, that it is
   in his genes?

THE ROOTS OF WAR

It can never be proved, but it is a safe assumption that the first time five thousand male human beings were ever gathered together in one place, they belonged to an army. That event probably
5 occurred around 7000 BC – give or take a thousand years – and it is an equally safe bet that the first truly large-scale slaughter of people in human history happened very soon afterward.

The first army almost certainly carried weapons
10 no different from those that hunters had been using on animals and on each other for thousands of years previously – spears, knives, axes, perhaps bows and arrows. Its strength did not lie in mere numbers; what made it an army was discipline and
15 organization. This multitude of men obeyed a single commander and killed his enemies to achieve his goals. It was the most awesome concentration of power the human world had ever seen, and nothing except another army could hope
20 to resist it.

The battle that occurred when two such armies fought has little in common with the clashes of primitive warfare. Thousands of men were crowded together in tight formations that moved
25 on command and marched in step. Drill, practised over many days and months until it became automatic, is what transformed these men from a mob of individual fighters into an army. (The basic forms of military drill are among the most
30 pervasive and unchanging elements of human civilization. The Twelfth Dynasty Egyptian armies of 1900 BC stepped off 'by the left', and so has every army down to the present day.)

And when the packed formations of well-drilled
35 men collided on the forgotten battlefields of the earliest kingdoms, what happened was quite impersonal, though every man died his own death. It was not the traditional combat between individual warriors. The soldiers were pressed
40 forward by the ranks behind them against the anonymous strangers in that part of the enemy line facing them, and though in the end it was pairs of individuals who thrust at each other with spears for a few moments before one went down, there was
45 nothing personal in the exchange. 'Their shields locked, they pushed, fought, killed and died. There was no shouting, and yet not silence either, but rather such a noise as might be made by the angry clash of armed men.'
50 The result of such a merciless struggle in a confined space is killing on an unprecedented scale. Hundreds or thousands of men would die in half an hour, in an area no bigger than a couple of football fields. 'The battle over, one could see on the site of

55 the struggle the ground covered with blood, friend and foe lying dead on one another, shields broken, spears shattered and unsheathed swords, some on the ground, some fixed in corpses, some still held in the hands of the dead. It was now getting late, so
60 they dragged the enemy corpses inside their lines, had a meal and went to rest.'*

And the question we rarely ask, because our history is replete with such scenes, is, How could men do this? After all, in the tribal cultures from
65 which we all come originally, they could not have done it. Being a warrior and taking part in a ritual 'battle' with a small but invigorating element of risk is one thing; the mechanistic and anonymous mass slaughter of civilized warfare is quite another, and
70 any traditional warrior would do the sensible thing and leave instantly. Yet civilized men, from 5000 BC or from today, will stay at such scenes of horror even in the knowledge that they will probably die within the next few minutes. The invention of
75 armies required more than just working out ways of drilling large numbers of people to act together, although that was certainly part of the formula. A formation of drilled men has a different psychology – a controlled form of mob psychology – that tends
80 to overpower the personal identity and fears of the individuals who make it up.

We assume that people will kill if they find themselves in a situation where their own survival is threatened, and nobody needs lessons to learn
85 how to die. What is less obvious is that practically anybody can be persuaded and manipulated in such a way that he will more or less voluntarily enter a situation wherein he must kill and perhaps die. Yet if that were not true, battles would be impossible,
90 and civilization would have taken a very different course (if indeed it arose at all).

* Written by Xenophon, the Greek general and historian, about the Battle of Coronea in 394 BC.

Summary writing

There are seven paragraphs in the text.
Look at each and try to summarize the main point, or points, in one, or possibly two, sentences.
Now try to join these sentences with appropriate linking words or phrases to produce a more coherent, flowing summary.

▶ Language focus

Read the Language study on *ways of adding emphasis* (page 58) and do the practice exercises.

Vocabulary 2

Here is a poem by an English poet called Siegfried Sassoon.

'They'

The Bishop tells us: 'When the (1) _____ come back
They will not be the same; for they'll have fought
In a (2) _____ (3)_____; they lead the last attack
On Anti-Christ; their (4) _____ blood has bought
New right to breed a(n) (5) _____ race.
They have (6) _____ Death and dared him face to face.'

'We're none of us the same!' the (7) _____ reply.
'For George lost both his (8) _____; and Bill's
(9) _____ blind;
Poor Jim's shot through the (10) _____ and like to die;
And Bert's gone (11) _____: you'll not find
A chap who's (12) _____ that hasn't found *some*
change.'
And the Bishop said: 'The ways of God are strange!'

Which war do you think this poem refers to? Why?

Gap filling

Now work in pairs and choose the best words from these lists to fill each gap.
Be prepared to explain why you chose the words.

1 chaps/boys/men/lads
2 just/fair/bloody/good
3 battle/war/cause/struggle
4 comrades'/pals'/companions'/chums'
5 glorious/honourable/distinguished/great
6 courted/overcome/seen/challenged
7 friends/fellows/men/boys
8 eyes/pals/legs/guns
9 gone/stone/completely/all
10 lungs/head/foot/heart
11 mad/syphilitic/neurotic/away
12 served/fought/been/enlisted

Checking and discussion

1 Compare your version with those of other members of the class.

2 [T.10] Now listen to the actual poem.
How close were you to Sassoon's original?
Would you argue that any of your choices were better than his? If so, why?

3 What is the basic message of this poem?

4 Both the Bishop and the boys agree that the war will change men. How do their views of the change differ?

5 How would you describe the Bishop's attitude to the war and the soldiers who fought in it?

6 The first verse expresses the Bishop's views.
The second verse expresses the views of the soldiers.
How does the style and choice of individual words emphasize the difference in their views?
Are there any words you would not expect to find in a poem?

7 Ordinary soldiers are sometimes described as 'cannon fodder'.
What is the implication of this?
How do governments get the support of the people for wars?

8 What do you think is Siegfried Sassoon's attitude to
– religion?
– the establishment?
– the ordinary soldier?
– war?
(Bear in mind that he fought in the 1914–1918 war.)

Listening

A Christmas story

[T.11]

Part 1
You will hear a short extract from a musical play (later made into a film) called '*Oh What a Lovely War!*'
Listen and answer the questions.

1 Which war is it?
2 What happens?
3 What nicknames do the Germans and the British have for each other?
4 The scene portrays the beginning of the so-called Christmas Truce. Do you know what this was, or can you guess what it might have been?

Now listen to an interview about the truce.

Part 2
1 How similar is Graham Williams's account of the first contact with the Germans to the scene from the play?
2 What is 'no-man's land'?
3 Which nicknames are mentioned in this part?
4 Why does the interviewer think that they might have felt frightened and suspicious?
5 List the surprising things that happened.
6 How is it possible that Harold Startin can say: 'We were the best of pals, although we were to kill one another, there were no two ways about that at all'?

Part 3
1 How long did the truce last?
2 What was the significance of the three rifle shots?
3 Who is Otto from Stuttgart?

Part 4
1 Why does Malcolm Brown, the writer of a book about the Christmas Truce, think it is an event which should not be forgotten?
2 In what ways was the truce a 'first'?

What do you think?

– Such events as these do not normally appear in the history books. Why do you think this could be? What kind of event *does* appear in history books?

– How old will the men who were interviewed be now? In what ways might the memory of this event have been important to them during the rest of their lives?

– Could such a wartime incident happen nowadays? If so, where? How? If not, why not?

▶ Language focus

Do the practice exercise on *tenses* in the Language study (page 59).

Writing

Describe an event, major or minor, ancient or modern, in the history of your country. Choose something that really interests you, and include in your description the reason for your interest. You could choose something which, like the Christmas Truce, does not normally appear in history books.

Postscript

A modern war poem

What is the main message of this poem?
Compare it with the message in 'They'.
Identify each of the 'men'.

THE RESPONSIBILITY

I am the man who gives the word,
If it should come, to use the Bomb.

I am the man who spreads the word
From him to them if it should come.

I am the man who gets the word
From him who spreads the word from him.

I am the man who drops the Bomb
If ordered by the one who's heard.
From him who merely spreads the word
The first one gives if it should come.

I am the man who loads the Bomb
That he must drop should orders come
From him who gets the word passed on
By one who waits to hear from him.

I am the man who makes the Bomb
That he must load for him to drop
If told by one who gets the word
From one who passes it from him.

I am the man who fills the till,
Who pays the tax, who foots the bill
That guarantees the Bomb he makes
For him to load for him to drop
If orders come from one who gets
The word passed on to him by one
Who waits to hear it from the man
Who gives the word to use the Bomb.

I am the man behind it all,
I am the one responsible.

LANGUAGE STUDY

1 Ways of adding emphasis

The following sentences are similar to lines found in the text on war.
Compare them with these lines and work out the ways in which the writer gives emphasis to the points she is making.

Discipline and organization made it an army.
(lines 14–15)
These men were transformed . . . into an army by drill.
(lines 25–8)
. . . pairs of individuals thrust at each other with spears.
(lines 42–3)

There are many ways of emphasizing a part of a sentence. Here are some further sentences based on the three patterns from the text.

1a

What	made it an army I like about John annoys me most	was is	discipline and organization. his honesty. people who are always late.

or

1b

What	made it an army I like about John annoys me most	was is	the way it was organized. the fact that he is so honest. the way some people are always late.

2

Drill Money John	is what is who	transformed these men into an army. makes the world go round. you should talk to.

3

It	was is	pairs of individuals John money	who that	thrust at each other. broke the vase. makes the world go round.

what = the thing which/that
who = the person who/that
where = the place which/that

Practice

1 | T.12 | It is important to make such sentences *sound* emphatic when you are speaking. You will hear the first two sentences only from each of the four boxes above. Listen and mark the main stresses, then decide where the stresses are in the third sentence.

Example

What made it an army was discipline and organization.

Practise saying the sentences in pairs.

2 Restructure the following statements to make them more emphatic. Try to use patterns **1a**, **2**, and **3**.
  a. We doubt his sincerity.
  b. I admire the efficiency of the Swiss.
  c. She hates having to get up at 6 o'clock every morning.
  d. His approval of the scheme is important.
  e. Their self-righteousness is annoying.
  f. You should go to Spain for your holidays.
  g. I like London because it has beautiful parks.
  h. Nobody likes losing.

3 Join each of the following sentence-pairs using **the way** or **the fact**, and beginning with *What . . .*
  a. He never makes a fuss. I admire this.
  b. She's always on time. I appreciate this.
  c. This government has treated the Health Service so badly. This irritates everybody.
  d. The Health Service wastes less money than it used to. This is of no consequence.

4 Look at this sentence, based on lines 66–9 of the text on war. What device has the writer used to make the point more emphatically than it is made here?

  The . . . anonymous mass slaughter of civilized warfare is worse than . . . taking part in a ritual 'battle' with a small . . . element of risk.

  Restructure the following statements using the same device.
  a. Working until midnight occasionally is fine, but working until midnight every night isn't.
  b. Being woken by a pneumatic drill is worse than being woken by birdsong.
  c. I like living in a caravan when I'm on holiday, but I wouldn't like to live in one permanently.

5 Work in pairs.
  Prepare to talk for one minute on one of the topics below, or any other topic that you feel particularly strongly about. Try to use some of these patterns for emphasis:

  What really annoys me about . . .
  What is most surprising . . .
  It is the way some people . . . that . . .
  What most people don't realize is the fact that . . .

litter	badly-behaved children
smoking	the weather
bad drivers	learning English
politics	people who wear fur coats
football	teachers who set too
exams	much homework

2 Review of tenses

In this summary of the story of the Christmas Truce the verbs are omitted. Choose the appropriate verb from beneath and put it in the correct tense, and in active or passive, positive or negative form.

The war (a) _____ for only a few months when on Christmas Eve 1914, an extraordinary event (b) _____ . At midnight, lights (c) _____ and carols (d) _____ from the German trenches. Soon the British (e) _____ with English carols and in the end both sides (f) _____ together.

At first they (g) _____ in no-man's land, and within a short space of time many friendships (h) _____ . Not only did they (i) _____ to bury each other's dead, but often German and British (j) _____ together in the same grave. Tools (k) _____ and defences (l) _____ . If they (m) _____ frightened or suspicious of each other, such a truce (n) _____ never _____ .

It (o) _____ now _____ that the truce (p) _____ much longer than historians previously (q) _____ , probably as long as six weeks. Incredibly, some of the friendships (r) _____ a lifetime. Harold Startin (s) _____ many times by his German friend, Otto, from Stuttgart. They (t) _____ in touch regularly over the years.

Now everybody (u) _____ that, almost certainly, no future war (v) _____ in the same way.

Use each verb *once* only.

see	sing	fight	take place
hear	borrow	keep	form
strengthen	know	last	go on
continue	join in	happen	feel
believe	think	bury	meet
visit	help		

REVISION

The perfect aspect

The Present Perfect, Past Perfect, and Future Perfect are formed with the auxiliary verb **have** (in the appropriate tense) + the past participle.

The perfect aspect expresses the following ideas:

1. An action that happened before now, when is not important.

   Have you ever been to Greece?
   I think I've seen her somewhere before.

2. An action that is completed before a certain time.

   Present Perfect
   She has written her books. (some time before now)
   When I arrived, he had already left. (some time before I arrived)
   I will have finished the letter by two o'clock. (some time before two o'clock)

Practice

1 Complete the following sentences using your own ideas, and with a perfect tense of the verb in brackets.

Example
I can't phone anyone. My telephone _____ (cut off) . . .
I can't phone anyone. My telephone has been cut off because I forgot to pay the bill.

a. Our house is looking very smart at the moment. We _____ (decorate) . . . and _____ (buy) . . .
b. What do snails taste like? I _____ (never try) . . .
c. I finally got to bed at four in the morning. I _____ (spend) the whole night . . .
d. When Queen Victoria died in 1901, she _____ (reign) . . .
e. Come and collect your shoes on Thursday. I _____ (repair) . . . by Wednesday night . . .
f. The shop assistant was sacked because he _____ (steal) . . .
g. You look different! What _____ you _____ (do) . . . ?
h. Henry Froggat retired at the age of 65. He _____ (be) with the same company since . . .
i. It is our wedding anniversary next month. We _____ (be) married for . . .
j. A Where has my car gone?
   B It _____ (tow) away because you were parking . . .
k. When we went outside, we saw the old apple tree lying on the grass. It _____ (blow) down in the storm . . .
l. The drug Altercone, which was prescribed for arthritis, _____ (withdraw) from the market because research (show) . . . serious side effects.

2 In the following dialogues there are some mistakes in the use of tenses. Find them and correct them.
   a. A Have you heard? The Prime Minister has resigned!
      B Has it said on the news why she has done that?
   b. A Of course, I'm an excellent skier.
      B When have you ever been skiing?
      A Before I'd met you, dear. I did a lot of things in my life that you don't know about.
      B This is the first time since we've been married that you ever mentioned going skiing. Have you enjoyed it?
      A It's been very exciting.
   c. A Who's broken my knife?
      B I have. Sorry. I've broken it by accident.
   d. A Darling? Did you ever meet my friend Andy?
      B No. Hello, Andy.
      C Hi! I heard a lot about you.
   e. I'm doing a pottery course at night school. I've learned a lot in the few weeks I'm going.

3 Groucho Marx (of the Marx Brothers) said to his hosts on leaving a party, 'I've had a lovely evening, but this wasn't it'.
   The joke rests on two different uses of the Present Perfect. What are they?

UNIT 6

A sense of taste

Discussion

Objective descriptions

Divide into four groups.
Each group should choose a different picture and produce a detailed, objective description of it in note form.

Give your description to the other groups and introduce them to any items of vocabulary they may not know.

Subjective descriptions

Still in your groups, discuss whether you like or don't like your picture. Give specific reasons.
Would you feel happy to be in that room?
Is it decorated in a style that appeals to you?
Look at all the rooms and decide which you like best and which you like least. Why?
Take a class vote to see to what extent you all have the same taste.

Vocabulary 1

Your taste in clothes

1 Look at the pictures. Which of the clothes and fashions
   appeal to you, and which don't? Why?

62

2 Which of the following items of clothing can you see in the pictures on these two pages? Which of them do you consider to be
- fashionable now?
- old-fashioned?
- always fashionable?

denim jeans
trousers with turn-ups
faded denim jacket
pin-striped suit
waistcoat
bomber jacket
sheepskin coat
tracksuit
jumpsuit
tailored suit
wide-brimmed hat
beret
flared trousers
leggings
silk stockings
polo-neck sweater
T-shirt
straight skirt

stiletto heels
canvas shoes
baggy shirt
baggy jumper
ankle socks
pleated skirt
blazer
dungarees
frayed jeans
pill-box hat
full-length evening gown
duffle-coat
frilly dress
leg warmers
woolly tights
sweatshirt
mini skirt
trainers

Is there anything omitted that you feel is definitely fashionable at the moment?

3 How fashion-conscious are you?
Do you give time and thought to what you wear each day?
Do you think that having good taste in clothes is linked with being fashionable?
Do you think clothes reveal character? If so, what can you tell about the characters of the people on page 62?

Reading

Pre-reading task

Discuss the following questions in small groups.

1 What kind of pictures do you have decorating your house or room?
Who are your favourite artists?
Why do you like their work?

2 Are there any members of the class who are artistically talented?
Is there a great diversity of taste and talent within the class?

3 You are going to read a newspaper article on 'Artspeak'. What do you think this is?

4 Three paintings illustrate the article, which is on the next page.
Exchange opinions on the paintings and try to give a title to each work.
Now compare your opinions and titles with the captions printed upside-down at the bottom of the page.

Reading for the main ideas

Read the text quickly and answer the questions.

1 What is the aim of the course given by William Quinn?
2 What is your opinion of the course?
3 What is your opinion of William Quinn?
4 What is the purpose of the text? Choose from the alternatives below, as many as you think appropriate.

- to criticize
- to amuse
- to make fun of
- to inform
- to surprise
- to mock
- to warn
- to educate
- to shock
- to cause discussion

Text organization

The following four sentences have all been removed from the text. Read it again more carefully and decide where each sentence should go.
Work in pairs.

a. 'You needn't waste a minute listening to tunes you don't instantly recognize,' it says.
b. If so, what do you say when you visit an art gallery?
c. In other words, places where the public can hear you.
d. 'One should speak of the boldness of the interpretation.'

Exposed! The fine art of Artspeak

Or the instant way to be a classic bluffer

ARE you one of those unfortunates who knows little about art and, worse still, hasn't the foggiest idea *what* you like or *why* you like it?

It's obvious. You look at the pictures and declare sagely:
That's very nice or
Yes, I like that, or
Hmm . . . interesting.

10 Well, sorry, that just isn't good enough. In New York, discussions about art are the currency of social life. Just like in the Woody Allen films, your worth is measured by your Artspeak.

15 Which is why William Quinn, a young Irishman from County Mayo, is the new hero of the smart set.

He is running a £33 course on how to say intelligent things about works of art in 20 public places. And people are queuing to join his remedial class in art bluffery.

Quinn – an increasingly well-known artist who paints giant versions of the computer bar codes on supermarket pro- 25 ducts – aims to teach the 'basic but critical vocabulary' of art.

'People like to feel sophisticated,' he says. 'But they can't unless they know at least something about art.'

30 'If they're at a dinner party and start talking about the Modigliani heads being inspired by the example of Brancusi, other people pay attention.'

As one student says: 'This course 35 teaches you how to sound halfway intelligent about art when you're not.'

Indeed, after a few evenings on Quinn's course, you can be an 'expert' without even seeing works you discuss. And *everyone* 40 defers to an 'expert'.

Just like Liberace – who once revealed that his gift was to play Tchaikovsky by leaving out the boring bits – Quinn's proteges go into New York's social whirl 45 armed with just the interesting snippets they need.

For this is the age of art for survival, where people would rather die than have nothing to say about something.

50 A huge TV advertising campaign is running in America for a series of records of the most tuneful pieces of 100 classical music favourites.

Quinn gets very shirty at his students' 55 go-for-it attitude to art consumption. Yet he agrees that his course title – called Meeting People at the Great Museums – does not sound, well enormously deep.

Warmth

Meanwhile, over in the Metropolitan 60 Museum of Art, one student gazes lamely at Pierre Bonnard's The Terrace at Vernon and says: 'I like this one.'

'Insufficient', says Quinn. 'And if you're with a sophisticate, you should add: 'The 65 daily intimacies of family life add warmth to Bonnard's art.'

See, it's easy when you get the hang of it!

(*Daily Mail* 22 February 1987)

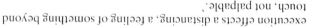

Joan Miro
WORK: *Harlequin's Carnival*
● Unintelligent comment: 'Is it the right way up?'
● Intelligent comment: 'Miro's work of this period is characterized by humour, a naive awkwardness and violent colours.'

Constant
WORK: *Uit de Oorlog*
● Unintelligent comment: 'Interesting.'
● Intelligent comment: 'One cannot really know Constant without taking into account the profound nostalgia in his soul.'

Bernice Howard
WORK: *Forever*
● Unintelligent comment: 'That's a white wiggly line.'
● Intelligent comment: 'Its meticulous presentation and execution effects a distancing, a feeling of something beyond touch, not palpable.'

Comprehension check

Which of the following statements are true or false, or don't you know?
Tick the appropriate box.

	True	False	Don't know
1 It is important to be able to speak sensibly about art in New York.	☐	☐	☐
2 William Quinn is one of New York's smart set.	☐	☐	☐
3 William Quinn gives courses on art appreciation.	☐	☐	☐
4 The courses are extremely popular.	☐	☐	☐
5 They produce experts on art who everyone listens to.	☐	☐	☐
6 After doing Quinn's course you can speak with seeming authority about paintings you have never seen.	☐	☐	☐
7 There is a series of records of 100 complete classical music favourites.	☐	☐	☐
8 Quinn gets annoyed by the course participants' superficial attitude to art.	☐	☐	☐

Pairwork

Look at the paintings on this page.
Decide on a title.
As in the captions that accompany the article, describe each painting:
– with an 'unintelligent' comment.
– with an 'intelligent' comment.
Compare your ideas with the rest of the class.

▶ Language focus

Read the Language study on *adjective order* and *adverbs with two forms* (page 71) and do the practice exercises.

Reading and listening

You are going to read and hear several extracts from a play by George Bernard Shaw (1856–1950), which has the title *Pygmalion*. (In Greek mythology, Pygmalion was a king who fell in love with a statue he had sculpted, and which his prayers had brought to life.) Shaw was very concerned with the state of the English language, particularly its spelling, punctuation, and pronunciation. He campaigned for the simplification of the written language, for example writing short forms, like **haven't** and **can't**, as 'havnt' and cant'. In the Preface to the play, he writes the following:

The English have no respect for their language, and will not teach their children to speak it. They cannot spell it because they have nothing to spell it with but an old foreign alphabet of which only the consonants – and not all of them – have any agreed speech value. Consequently no man can teach himself what it should sound like from reading it; and it is impossible for an Englishman to open his mouth without making some other Englishman despise him.

The reformer we need most today is an energetic phonetic enthusiast: that is why I have made such a one the hero of a popular play.

Questions for discussion

1 Do you personally have a regional accent in *your* language?
   If so, how strong is it?
2 What are the main regional accents in your language?
   Which is considered to be the 'standard'?
   What is the reputation of the other accents?
3 In your country, is it true that people draw conclusions about others from the way they speak?

Background to the play

Pygmalion was written in 1913, and is set in London. The main characters are as follows:

Henry Higgins: a Professor of Phonology and a bachelor
Colonel Pickering: his friend and colleague, also a language expert and also a bachelor
Eliza Doolittle: a Cockney flower-seller

In Act One, we are introduced to Eliza (Liza) selling flowers in Covent Garden. As various people speak, Professor Higgins is in the background making notes and phonetic transcriptions of the way they talk. He can identify where people come from, 'sometimes within two streets', according to their accent. He correctly notes that Liza comes from Lisson Grove, an area in London. He boasts to the crowd that he is a teacher of phonetics, and, as such, 'in three months (he) could pass that girl (Liza) off as a duchess at an ambassador's garden party.' Out of sympathy, he gives her a large tip.

Extract 1

Read extract 1, which is the stage-set instructions for Act Two. What impression do you have of Professor Higgins?

ACT II

Next day at 11 a.m. Higgins's laboratory in Wimpole Street. It is a room on the first floor, looking on the street, and was meant for the drawing room. The double doors are in the middle of the back wall; and persons entering find in
5 *the corner to their right two tall file cabinets at right angles to one another against the walls. In this corner stands a flat writing-table, on which are a phonograph, a life-size image of half a human head, shewing in section the vocal organs, and a box containing a supply of wax cylinders for the*
10 *phonograph.*

Further down the room, on the same side, is a fireplace, with a comfortable leather-covered easy-chair at the side of the hearth nearest the door, and a coal-scuttle. There is a clock on the mantelpiece. Most of the side wall is occupied by
15 *a grand piano, with the keyboard at the end furthest from the door, and a bench for the player extending the full length of the keyboard.*

Pickering is seated at the table, putting down some cards and a tuning-fork which he has been using. Higgins is
20 *standing up near him, closing two or three file drawers which are hanging out. He appears in the morning light as a robust, vital, appetizing sort of man of forty or thereabouts, dressed in a professional-looking black frock-coat with a white linen collar and black silk tie. He is of the energetic, scientific type,*
25 *heartily, even violently, interested in everything that can be studied as a scientific subject, and careless about himself and other people, including their feelings. He is, in fact, but for his years and size, rather like a very impetuous baby 'taking notice' eagerly and loudly, and requiring almost as much*
30 *watching to keep him out of unintended mischief. His manner varies from genial bullying when he is in a good humour to stormy petulance when anything goes wrong; but he is so entirely frank and void of malice that he remains likeable even in his least reasonable moments.*

Extract 2

Extract 2 is the opening scene of Act Two.

T.13a Listen and read at the same time.

35 HIGGINS [*as he shuts the last drawer*] Well, I think thats the whole show.

PICKERING It's really amazing. I havnt taken half of it in, you know.

HIGGINS Would you like to go over any of it again?

40 PICKERING [*rising and coming over to the fireplace, where he plants himself with his back to the fire*] No, thank you; not now. I'm quite done up for this morning.

HIGGINS [*following him, and standing beside him on his left*] Tired of listening to sounds?

45 PICKERING Yes. It's a fearful strain. I rather fancied myself because I can pronounce twenty-four distinct vowel sounds; but your hundred and thirty beat me. I cant hear a bit of difference between most of them.

HIGGINS [*chuckling, and going over to the piano to eat*
50 *sweets*] Oh, that comes with practice. You hear no difference at first; but you keep on listening, and presently you find theyre all as different as A from B. [*Mrs Pearce looks in: she is Higgins's housekeeper*]. Whats the matter?

55 MRS PEARCE [*hesitating, evidently perplexed*] A young woman wants to see you, sir.

HIGGINS A young woman! What does she want?

MRS PEARCE Well, sir, she says youll be glad to see her when you know what she's come about. She's
60 quite a common girl, sir. Very common indeed. I should have sent her away, only I thought perhaps you wanted her to talk into your machines. I hope Ive not done wrong: but really you see such queer people sometimes – youll excuse me. I'm sure, sir –

65 HIGGINS Oh, thats all right, Mrs Pearce. Has she an interesting accent?

MRS PEARCE Oh, something dreadful, sir, really. I dont know how you can take an interest in it.

HIGGINS [*to Pickering*] Lets have her up. Shew her
70 up, Mrs Pearce [*he rushes across to his working table and picks out a cylinder to use on the phonograph*].

MRS PEARCE [*only half resigned to it*] Very well, sir. It's for you to say. [*She goes downstairs*].

HIGGINS This is rather a bit of luck. I'll shew you
75 how I make records. We'll set her talking; and I'll take it down first in Bell's visible Speech; then in broad Romic; and then we'll get her on the phonograph so that you can turn her on as often as you like with the written transcript before you.

80 MRS PEARCE [*returning*] This is the young woman, sir.

Comprehension check

1 Which ability of Professor Higgins greatly impresses Pickering?
2 Why is Higgins so anxious to meet the *common girl*?
3 What does he want to do?

Extract 3

T.13b Now listen only to the next scene.
While you listen, note down ways in which Higgins teases the girl in the course of the conversation.

Comprehension check

1 Describe the attitude of Higgins, Pickering, and Mrs Pearce to Liza.
2 At first, Higgins is disappointed when he realizes who the girl is. Why?
  How, and why, does his interest in her revive?
3 What does Liza want?
4 How does she work out the price for the lessons?
5 How does Higgins calculate that this is 'the biggest offer (he) ever had'?
6 What is Liza's reaction to this calculation?
7 Why does Higgins point out the difference between her handkerchief and her sleeve?
8 Why does Pickering laugh when Liza snatches the silk handkerchief from Mrs Pearce?
9 What is the precise nature of the bet?

Now listen again and read the tapescript on page 150 at the same time. Underline anything said by Liza that you think is an example of Cockney English.

Reading aloud and pronunciation

You will now read a scene from Act Three.
Higgins has been giving Liza lessons in how to speak 'properly'. He is pleased with her progress and feels the time has come to 'try her out in public', although she has only been groomed to talk about the weather and health! He takes her, beautifully dressed, to a tea party at his mother's house.

He has been able to help her a lot with her pronunciation, but unfortunately she has little idea about what constitutes polite conversation!

Work in groups and allocate parts for the scene.
Practise it together, checking any unknown vocabulary.

Extract 4

Characters

Mrs Higgins: Professor Higgins's mother, a kind and wise lady
Mrs Eynsford-Hill: Mrs Higgins's high-society friend
Freddy Eynsford-Hill: her son, in his early twenties
Clara Eynsford-Hill: sister to Freddy
Professor Higgins
Colonel Pickering
Eliza Doolittle

LIZA [*speaking with pedantic correctness of pronunciation and great beauty of tone*] How do you do, Mrs Higgins? [*She gasps slightly in making sure of the H in Higgins, but is quite successful*]. Mr Higgins told me I might come.

85 MRS HIGGINS [*cordially*] Quite right: I'm very glad indeed to see you.

PICKERING How do you do, Miss Doolittle?

LIZA [*shaking hands with him*] Colonel Pickering, is it not?

90 MRS EYNSFORD-HILL I feel sure we have met before, Miss Doolittle. I remember your eyes.

LIZA How do you do? [*She sits down on the ottoman gracefully in the place just left vacant by Higgins*].

MRS EYNSFORD-HILL [*introducing*] My daughter Clara.

95 LIZA How do you do?

CLARA [*impulsively*] How do you do? [*She sits down on the ottoman beside Liza, devouring her with her eyes*].

FREDDY [*coming to their side of the ottoman*] Ive certainly had the pleasure.

100 MRS EYNSFORD-HILL [*introducing*] My son Freddy.

LIZA How do you do?

A long and painful pause ensues.

MRS HIGGINS [*at last, conversationally*] Will it rain, do you think?

105 LIZA The shallow depression in the west of these islands is likely to move slowly in an easterly direction. There are no indications of any great change in the barometrical situation.

FREDDY Ha! ha! how awfully funny!

110 LIZA What is wrong with that, young man? I bet I got it right.

FREDDY Killing!

MRS EYNSFORD-HILL I'm sure I hope it wont turn cold. Theres so much influenza about. It runs right

115 through our whole family regularly every spring.

LIZA [*darkly*] My aunt died of influenza: so they said.

MRS EYNSFORD-HILL [*clicks her tongue sympathetically*]!!!

LIZA [*in the same tragic tone*] But it's my belief they

120 done the old woman in.

MRS HIGGINS [*puzzled*] Done her in?

LIZA Y-e-e-es, Lord love you! Why should she die of influenza? She come through diphtheria right enough the year before. I saw her with my own eyes.

125 Fairly blue with it, she was. They all thought she was dead; but my father he kept ladling gin down her throat til she came to so sudden that she bit the bowl off the spoon.

MRS EYNSFORD-HILL [*startled*] Dear me!

130 LIZA [*piling up the indictment*] What call would a woman with that strength in her have to die of influenza? What become of her new straw hat that should have come to me? Somebody pinched it; and what I say is, them as pinched it done her in.

135 MRS EYNSFORD-HILL What does doing her in mean?

HIGGINS [*hastily*] Oh, thats the new small talk. To do a person in means to kill them.

MRS EYNSFORD-HILL [*to Eliza, horrified*] You surely dont believe that your aunt was killed.

140 LIZA Do I not! Them she lived with would have killed her for a hat-pin, let alone a hat.

MRS EYNSFORD-HILL But it cant have been right for your father to pour spirits down her throat like that. It might have killed her.

145 LIZA Not her. Gin was mother's milk to her. Besides, he'd poured so much down his own throat that he knew the good of it.

MRS EYNSFORD-HILL Do you mean that he drank?

LIZA Drank! My word! Something chronic.

150 MRS EYNSFORD-HILL How dreadful for you!

LIZA Not a bit. It never did him no harm what I could see. But then he did not keep it up regular. [*To Freddy, who is in convulsions of suppressed laughter*] Here! what are you sniggering at?

155 FREDDY The new small talk. You do it so awfully well.

LIZA If I was doing it proper, what was you laughing at? [*To Higgins*] Have I said anything I oughtnt?

160 MRS HIGGINS [*interposing*] Not at all, Miss Doolittle.

LIZA Well, thats a mercy, anyhow. [*Expansively*] What I always say is –

HIGGINS [*rising and looking at his watch*] Ahem!

LIZA [*looking round at him; taking the hint; and rising*]

165 Well: I must go. [*They all rise. Freddy goes to the door*]. So pleased to have met you. Goodbye. [*She shakes hands with Mrs Higgins*]

MRS HIGGINS Goodbye.

LIZA Goodbye, Colonel Pickering.

170 PICKERING Goodbye, Miss Doolittle. [*They shake hands*].

LIZA [*nodding to the others*] Goodbye, all.

FREDDY [*opening the door for her*] Are you walking across the Park, Miss Doolittle? If so –

175 LIZA Walk! Not bloody likely. [*Sensation*]. I am going in a taxi. [*She goes out*].

Pickering gasps and sits down. Freddy goes out on the balcony to catch another glimpse of Eliza.

Pronunciation check

| T.13c | Listen to the scene.

Compare your version with the actors' and actresses'. Practise some parts again to improve your performance.

How does it end?

Liza makes great progress, and Higgins wins his bet! She goes to a high society gathering where she is taken for a princess. Higgins continues to treat Liza with contempt, but too late realizes that he is in fact very fond of her. She leaves him to marry Freddy. In the film version (*My Fair Lady*) the ending is different! In what way, do you think?

▶ Language focus

Read the Language study on *adverbs and expressions of opinion* (page 72) and do the practice exercises.

Speaking

Work in groups of three or four.
Look at these pictures.

Each one is someone's treasured possession.
Describe the objects using both factual and opinion
adjectives, and taking care with the adjective order.
Now try to imagine why it could be important to the owner.
Finally, describe something that is of personal importance
to you.
Tell the other students why this is so. If possible bring it to
class.

Writing

Either:
Write a description of a treasured possession.
Give its history, saying why it is important to you.
Or:
Describe your favourite room, saying why you like it.

70

Vocabulary 2

Adverb and verb collocations

Many adverbs of manner go with a particular verb.

Examples
The sun shone brightly.
They were waiting patiently.
He ate his food greedily.

1 Match a verb in column **A** with an adverb, or group of adverbs, in column **B**. Sometimes there is more than one possibility.

A	B
a. rain	**1** peacefully
b. breathe	**2** violently, impetuously
c. fight	**3** forcefully, convincingly
d. explain	**4** heavily
e. die	**5** longingly, enviously
f. look	**6** clearly, concisely
g. argue	**7** courageously
h. react	**8** deeply

A	B
i. behave	**9** thoroughly
j. sleep	**10** gently
k. whisper	**11** deeply, soundly, fitfully
l. stroke	**12** badly, correctly, erratically
m. investigate	**13** softly
n. listen	**14** steadily
o. consider	**15** carefully
p. progress	**16** attentively

2 Write six sentences to practise some of the above collocations, adding any necessary words.

Examples
She explained the case against the death penalty very convincingly.
He whispered softly in her ear, 'I adore you.'

LANGUAGE STUDY

▶ **Grammar reference: page 138.**

Practice

Put the adjectives in brackets into an order that sounds natural to you.

a. He gave us some bread. (brown; delicious; home-made)
b. A lady suddenly arrived. (little; old; funny)
c. I bought a shirt. (silk; striped; blue and white)
d. He was smoking a cigar. (fat; revolting; Havana)
e. I've got a racket. (new; tennis; great; metal)
f. She was wearing a dress (summer; plain; cotton)
g. Thieves stole a painting. (French; priceless; Impressionist)
h. He showed me into his room. (airy; living; high-ceilinged)
i. He introduced me to his daughter. (ten-year-old; little; pretty)
j. I've just met a student. (young; chemistry; very interesting)

Practice

In the following sentences, put the correct form of the adverb into each gap.

clean/ly
a. The thief got _____ away and was never seen again.
b. He pulled the cork out of the bottle _____ .

clear/ly
c. Steer _____ of that man. He'll do you no good.
d. If you look at the situation _____ , you'll see that I'm right.

71

easy/easily

e. He beat me _____ . He was much too good.

f. Take it _____ ! You push yourself too much.

free/ly

g. He _____ admits that he has never done a day's work in his life.

h. A lot of teenagers spend their time trying to break _____ from their parents.

high/ly

i. I can throw a ball _____ into the sky.

j. I've heard a lot about you from Paul. He speaks very _____ of you.

most/ly

k. I've spent a lot of time abroad, _____ in the States.

l. Which part of the States do you like _____ ?

right/ly

m. Don't move. Stay _____ here.

n. He was sacked for incompetence, and _____ so.

tight/ly

o. The houses were _____ packed together, with hardly a space between them.

p. Hold _____ ! We're going to move soon.

wide/ly

q. She left the door _____ open.

r. My views on this subject are already _____ known.

wrong/ly

s. He was _____ accused of treason. He was in fact a most loyal citizen.

t. Oh dear! Did I do something _____ ?

3 Adverbs and expressions of opinion

There are many adverbs and expressions which give the speaker's attitude to what he or she is saying.

Examples

Quite honestly, I think you should leave the job. (This is my honest opinion.)

Admittedly, it's well-paid. (I know this contradicts the opinion I've just expressed.)

Surely you want promotion? (I am sure you do.)

Anyway, I want your job. (What I said before doesn't matter. This is the main point.)

Practice

1 **T.14** You will hear a woman speaking, but you will have to listen very carefully to realize what she is talking about.

There are two or three key words.

Work in pairs to answer the questions.

a. Apart from the speaker, how many people are mentioned?

b. Who is *he*?

c. What is the speaker's attitude towards him?

d. What are the key words? Find them in a dictionary if necessary.

e. So what is she talking about?

2 The woman uses many adverbs and expressions which indicate her attitude to what she is saying.

Listen again and try to write down as many as you can. Then read the tapescript on page 151 and discuss the meaning of them.

3 Work in pairs.

Here are some unfinished dialogues. Finish them in a way that seems appropriate.

Example

A *There's some crab in the fridge if you're hungry, but I don't suppose you like seafood, do you?*

B *As a matter of fact, **I adore seafood**.*

1 A Have you heard that Jane is thinking of getting married to that chap Paul?
   B Quite honestly, . . .

2 B I don't know where she met him.
   A If I remember rightly, . . .

3 A I wonder if they'll have a church wedding or go to a registry office?
   B Presumably, . . .

4 B He's been married three times before. Did you know that?
   A Actually, . . .

5 A I think she's too young, too immature, for marriage.
   B I really don't think so. After all, . . .

6 B I wonder why they want to get married?
   A Obviously, . . .

7 A I'm sure they'll both be very happy.
   B So am I. Incidentally, . . .

8 B I'd like to congratulate them, but I don't know when I'll see them again.
   A As a matter of fact, . . .

9 A Ah, well. Good old Jane and Paul.
   B Mmm. Best of luck to them. Anyway, . . .

4 **T.15** You will hear the unfinished dialogues in exercise 3. Listen carefully to both **A** and **B**'s intonation, then practise the dialogues, inserting the line(s) that you added for **A** and **B**.

Compare your answers as a class.

There are further exercises on adverbs and expressions of opinion in Unit 6 of the Workbook.

REVISION

The position of an adverb can change the meaning of a sentence.

Example
Naturally, she played with the children. (Of course she did.)
She played with the children naturally. (in a natural way)

Practice

Place the adverb in brackets in at least two positions in the following sentences and explain the difference in meaning.

a. I'm sure he's clever. (quite)
b. I knew you had a lot of money. (never)
c. I can't answer that question. (frankly)
d. He realized that she wasn't well. (obviously)
e. They knew he was able to play chess. (well)
f. I don't think she can answer your questions. (honestly)
g. I saw him yesterday at the theatre. (only)
h. He told her what he thought of her. (actually)
i. I love you more than Peter. (still)
j. George likes French cooking. (even)
k. He discussed the design with her. (very sensibly)
l. I can see what he's doing. (just)

Conscience doth make cowards of us all

Reading and discussion

Read the accounts of the seven court cases on this and the next page.

In each one, the sentence imposed by the judge has been blanked out. Working in groups of four, say what you think the sentence should have been. There is no need to try and replace the exact words. Just say what sentence should have been imposed.

Former judge sentenced over driving offences

A 61-YEAR-OLD former High Court judge, who gave a false name when stopped for speeding while disqualified, pleaded guilty yesterday to attempting to pervert the course of justice.

The disgrace of former judge Vivian Price, of Redwall Farmhouse, Linton, Kent, was chronicled in Maidstone Crown Court as he ▬▬▬▬▬▬▬.

His counsel Mr George Carman, QC, said that for a former deputy High Court judge to "plead guilty to a charge of trying to pervert the course of justice is a unique situation as far as I know in the courts of this country."

He added that "the law has often reserved its most severe punishment for those in positions of public eminence. Great privilege carries with it great responsibility."

Miss Heather Hallett, prosecuting, said Price gave his correct date of birth when stopped for speeding but the name of a member of his family. He continued the deceit by pressurising a member of his family to take the blame. He had been disqualified for drink-driving the same year.

The first offence took place on the Canterbury by-pass where he was stopped after driving at 98 mph. He was later stopped again doing 50 mph at Coxheath, near Maidstone, in a 30 mph limit.

For attempting to pervert the course of justice he was sentenced to ▬▬▬▬▬▬▬ for driving while disqualified the first time. For the second driving offence, he was sentenced to ▬▬▬▬▬▬▬. He was also banned from driving for ▬▬▬.

for Mob leader

TERRY LAST, the ringleader of the Chelsea Mob who planned violence at Britain's football grounds was ▬▬▬▬▬ today.

His Honour Judge Shindler described 24-year-old solicitor's clerk Last as a man who "glorified and revelled in violence" and who had a "perverted lust for violence."

The judge, who lists watching soccer as a hobby in his Who's Who entry, said Last and his gang of four other Chelsea fans had brought terror to the terraces forcing ordinary fans to stay away.

Attack

Judge Shindler, who follows Crystal Palace, sentenced Last, of Bow, East London to ▬▬▬▬▬ for conspiring to fight at Britain's soccer grounds and ▬▬▬▬▬ for taking part in an attack on Everton fans in Liverpool in December, 1985.

Driver

▬▬▬▬▬

A drink-driver who killed a man while fleeing from police was ▬▬▬▬▬ at Birmingham Crown Court. It was the second conviction involving drinking and driving in five months for Shabir Sabar, 30, who ran down Stanley Crofts, 51.

████████ for boy who killed a school bully

SIMON LUNDIE, 17, suffered years of hell at the hands of a school bully. Finally he snapped —and stabbed his tormentor to death.

"This was a wicked and terrible thing you did," Mr Justice Alliott told Simon today at the Old Bailey.

He accepted that Lundie had been provoked but had decided that such outrageous behaviour demanded stern punishment. Lundie's mother wept as he was sentenced to ████████.

The boy he stabbed was 17-year-old Robert Tucker, whose parents silently watched as Lundie was taken to the cells.

Mr Timothy Langdale, prosecuting, said Tucker bullied and threatened Lundie. "Every day for 18 months he forced him to hand over his dinner money of 75p."

Tucker constantly telephoned Lundie at home—sometimes five times in a day.

"He carried on threatening him and making even greater demands for money" said counsel. "Lundie was very nervous and frightened of the other boy."

Two weeks before his death Tucker ordered Lundie to have a fight with one of his cronies. Lundie was reluctant, but there was a minor scuffle involving Tucker as well.

When arrested Lundie told detectives: "It is a long story. This has been going on for years. I could not take any more."

Lundie, of Rochford Avenue, Waltham Abbey, pleaded not guilty to murder but admitted manslaughter.

His plea was accepted.

Night intruder
████████

A JILTED lover smashed his way into his ex-girlfriend's home and said, after grabbing her throat: "I could kill you. No-one knows I am here," a court heard on Monday.

Jobless David Jones, formerly of Bedwyn Walk, Aylesbury, appeared at Aylesbury Magistrates Court only three days before his 22nd birthday and admitted assault occasioning actual bodily harm, and criminal damage.

The court ████ Jones ████████ , and ordered him to pay £32 compensation for the window and £30 towards costs.

Double rapist
████████

A MAN who raped a 25-year-old bank clerk less than a month after being bailed for a similar offence was ████ at Birmingham Crown Court yesterday ████.

Steven Wilson, aged 25, of Coventry, met the woman in a night club in Coventry last New Year's Eve. Four weeks earlier he had committed a similar rape on a girl aged 20, whom he also met in a night club.

How Erica put drug dealer behind bars

DRUG dealer Anthony Dorrington has been ████████ after he was trapped by a police operation code-named 'Erica'.

Throughout the summer weeks of last year crack drug squad officers from Herts mounted a secret surveillance operation on Dorrington's flat.

They logged down all the visitors before mounting a raid on the premises in Abbey View, Garston.

Dorrington, 35, and flatmate Neil Hornsby, 27, were both arrested after officers found unknown substances, syringes and needles.

It turned out the pair had been dealing in heroin.

Discussion

1 The sentences imposed were as follows:
   – five years' youth custody
   – ten years' imprisonment
   – eighteen months' imprisonment
   – a fine of £110
   – four years' imprisonment
   – ten years' imprisonment
   – a nine-month suspended jail sentence.

In your opinion, which sentence goes with which court case?

2 After you have decided, your teacher will tell you the answers.
Do you think the decisions were fair?
Was anyone treated unduly harshly or leniently?
Did the sentences reflect a proper order of priorities; that is, was the most serious crime punished most severely?

▶ Language focus

Read the Language study on *verb patterns* (page 81) and do the practice exercises.

Reading

Pre-reading task

Discuss the following questions in groups of four.

1 'Crime doesn't pay' is a well-known English saying. Can you think of any recent news stories that either prove or disprove this saying?

2 Can you think of any recent court cases where you feel the law has been unjust – for example, an excessively lenient or harsh decision?

3 You will read an interview with a burglar, published in the *Guardian* newspaper. Read the text just beneath the heading.
Can you guess the meaning of the following?

a ten-year stretch   living it up   a pro

4 The article deals with the following topics:
The time the writer himself was burgled
Recent research into burglary
The sentences burglars can expect
Danny (the burglar interviewed)
– his background
– his introduction to crime
– how he carries out a burglary
– his attitude to the people he steals from.

Write questions that you would like answered from the article.

Reading and matching

Now read the article.
The ten key sentences below have been removed. Decide where they should go.

a. Research by Maguire and Bennett suggests that burglary has a considerable effect on people's lives, leaving them uneasy, insecure, even feeling violated.

b. It was dead easy.

c. But the lad I did the house with got caught on another job.

d. Nobody was ever suspicious.

e. Research in Sheffield suggests that nearly three-quarters of burglars travel less than two miles from their homes to commit the crime.

f. If I got a job, I'd have to change my whole lifestyle.

g. In ten years' time I'll either be doing a ten-year stretch or living it up.

h. Research by Mike Maguire and Trevor Bennett (*Burglary in a Dwelling*, Heinemann 1982) into several hundred victims of burglary revealed that wilful damage was caused in less than one in a hundred cases.

i. Burglary is more popular today than ever before.

j. Within six months Danny had graduated to houses.

GRASSROOTS

Meet the burglar

'If I got a job I'd have to change my whole lifestyle . . . Burglary is the only real skill I've got. In ten years' time I'll either be doing a ten–year stretch or living it up.' Danny is still only 20, reports Geoffrey Beattie, but already he's a pro.

I HAVE only been burgled once, and the burglar wasn't even that successful; he ended up leaving me some of his goods rather than leaving with mine. I could hear him pottering about. I shouted, he ran, leaving a typewriter behind, doubtless removed from a neighbour's house. I considered myself lucky because of the stories about the mess burglars make when they're on the job — the ransacked rooms, the broken furniture, the meals they cook themselves, the urine.

Crime prevention advertisements exploit such images to persuade people to lock their windows. But my burglar wasn't like that — he was careful, meticulous, and tidy (even if a bit noisy), he didn't try to cook himself a meal or use my house as a toilet. Apparently he's like many other burglars. **1** . . .

. . . .
But what kind of person could go into the home of a total stranger and have the skill to find something of value (certainly difficult in my house) — and have no twinge of conscience about removing whatever he could lay his sticky little fingers on? And what's the probability of it happening again?

According to Maguire and Bennett's research it is very likely to happen again. They reckon that the "average British citizen" can expect to be burgled two or three times during his or her lifetime. **2** . . . .

. . . . Sentences for house burglary can be quite stiff — the maximum is 14 years — but many burglars today end up in magistrates'

courts facing fines. As another burglar put it to me, "I'd enough in my piggy bank for the first fine."

But what are burglars really like? How could I meet some personally?

A chain of association eventually led me to Danny (name changed). Still only 20 but already a pro: he's served his time at his chosen profession in more ways than one. Several hundred burglaries in five years, and two stretches in Borstal and one in prison. In official terms he's a recidivist. He puts it bluntly: "Money, clothes, and having a good time is my life. **3** . . . .

. . . . What would I do with £80 a week? I can spend that in one night. Burglary is the only real skill I've got."

Danny's profession runs in the family (his father is currently on the run for an armed robbery offence) but he says his family had nothing to do with it. It was his mates. He was 15, they were 16, he was their eager pupil. He started with a warehouse. "We were careful to choose one without a burglar alarm. We got in through a ground floor window. **4** . . . . We all had a look about and I found a cashbox in a drawer with a hundred quid in it. I couldn't believe it. It was money for old rope. We blew the money in two days on Indian meals, taxis, and drinks. Then we went out again about three days later. We just get the bus a couple of miles down the road to the Moor or Bramall Lane and have a wander about." **5** . . . .

. . . .
Danny enjoyed his new pas-

time. "Some nights we'd do three places in the one spot. Sometimes of course you'd find nothing but occasionally you'd hit the jackpot." **6** . . . .

. . . . We'd usually get the bus to Gleadless, which was a good spot because it borders on a wood. Dead easy to get away. We'd go up in the afternoon and just pick a house that looked empty.

"My two mates would stay in the next street and I'd just go up and knock on the door. If anyone answered I'd say 'Is Paul in please?' **7** . . . .

. . . . They'd just say 'Sorry, you must be at the wrong house.' If nobody answered I'd just go and get my mates and we'd go round the back and steam in. If the windows were locked we'd put a coat up to the window and knock it in. When I was in, I'd head straight for the bedroom to look for the jewellery case. I'd also look under the mattress straight away. Then it was down to the kitchen. You'd be amazed how many people keep money in the oven, but I've even found money stashed in cornflakes boxes.

"We never made a mess, at least deliberately — some houses would look a bit untidy afterwards but that's because you're looking for things in a hurry. You haven't got all day. The most I ever got from a house when I was a kid was eight and a half grand in goods — at least that's what the local paper said. Me and another kid only got a grand and a half for the jewellery and stuff. **8** . . . .

. . . . He grassed on me. I got a £554 fine plus probation. Of course, the fine wasn't that bad. I'd made quite a lot by then. My mum had to pay the fine, though. I'd spent what I'd made."

Danny leans back in his chair. "It might seem to you that I haven't been that successful, but I've done hundreds of jobs and I've never actually been caught on the job. It's usually people wanting to do themselves a favour with the coppers. I know I've got the bottle and the skill. **9** . . . .

. . . . I'm not going to change my life style."

As he got up to go, sun tan, streaked blond hair, expensive leather jacket, all the trimmings of the pop star, I asked him the key question. Do you ever think about your victims? **10** . . . . .

. . . .

Danny doesn't think about this. "Why should I? The people I burgle can afford it and jewellers are all bent and bump up the insurance claims. Another thing, I never burgle poor people or old people."

Danny was beginning to sound like Robin Hood. "But just a minute, you've burgled council houses, isn't that right?"

"Yes," Danny says, "but loads of ordinary people have stacks of dough stashed away."

"But do you really mean that if you went to all the trouble of breaking into a house and then discovered that it belonged to an old person, you wouldn't take anything?"

"Well, not nothing," says Danny, "but I wouldn't leave them broke." And Robin Hood had, before my very eyes, started to metamorphose into the Sheriff of Nottingham. Just enough left in the kitty to survive, when Danny's high demands were met.

(*Guardian* 20 October 1984)

Comprehension check and inferring

1 Which of the questions that you wrote are answered in the article?
Did you find any of the information surprising?

2 What do the following extracts tell us about Danny's attitude to a life of crime, and life in general?
'If I got a job I'd have to change my whole lifestyle.' (line 72)
'You'd be amazed how many people keep money in the oven . . .' (line 136)
'Of course, the fine wasn't that bad.' (line 156)
'My mum had to pay the fine, though.' (line 158)
'It might seem to you that I haven't been that successful . . .' (line 162)
'The people I burgle can afford it . . .' (line 181)

3 '. . . he's served his time . . . in more ways than one.' (line 63)
What does the writer mean by this?

4 What do you know about Robin Hood?
If necessary, ask your teacher questions to find out who he was!
Can you now explain the reference to Robin Hood and the Sheriff of Nottingham?

5 The writer has presented most of the article dispassionately, letting the information and Danny speak for themselves. However, there are times when the writer's attitude to burglary and Danny are apparent. Find them, and comment on his attitude. At the beginning, the writer seems curious about burglars. How does he appear to feel by the end?

Vocabulary 1
Informal language

1 There are several examples of slang and informal English in the text about the burglar.
Match an example from column **A** with a neutral equivalent in column **B**.

A	B
mates (118)	informed the police
quid (93)	dishonest, corrupt
money for old rope (94)	friends
blew the money (95)	the courage
hit the jackpot (109)	with no money
stashed (139)	pound
a grand (149)	a thousand pounds
grassed on me (155)	money easily obtained
the coppers (168)	spent the money
the bottle (169)	recklessly
bent (183)	have great success
stacks of dough (193)	lots of money
broke (202)	hidden
	the police

2 What do the following examples of slang or informal English mean?

the loo   She's very uptight.   booze   He's thick.
What a rip-off!   Stop hassling me!
Who's pinched my book?   What a drag!
It was a very heavy situation.
He's got a lot of hang-ups.

3 'It was dead easy.' (line 89)
Dead here is an informal way of intensifying **easy**, meaning **very easy**. Put one of the following words into each gap to intensify the meaning of the adjective. One of them is used twice.

fast   wide   solid   bone   stiff   boiling   brand
sick   stone

a. My son won't get out of bed. He's _____ idle.
b. Careful with the soup. It's _____ hot.
c. I can't eat the ice-cream. It's frozen _____ .
d. The first thing I do every morning is have a cold shower. Then I feel _____ awake.
e. Thank goodness you phoned! I've been worried _____ about you!
f. I didn't hear the phone. I must have been _____ asleep.
g. The film was awful. I was bored _____ from beginning to end.
h. Ugh! This tea is _____ cold.
i. Look after my bike, won't you. It's _____ new.
j. I'm scared _____ at the sight of dogs. I don't know why. They just frighten me.

Language focus

Read the Language study on *conditional sentences* (page 82) and do the practice exercises.

Listening
Pre-listening task

Discuss the following questions:

1 What are the most popular television programmes in your country?
2 Which of the following possible aims of television do you think is the most important?
   – to instruct
   – to inform
   – to entertain
   – to distract
3 If you controlled a television channel, what sort of programmes would you put on it?
Would you limit the amount of sex and violence portrayed, or influence the political nature of the programmes?
4 What controls exist on TV output in your country?

Jigsaw listening

Divide into two groups.

T.16a   **Group A** You will hear an interview with Joanna Bogle, a member of the National Viewers' and Listeners' Association, a group which aims to monitor the output of television and radio in Britain.

T.16b   **Group B** You will hear an interview with Kate Adie, a news reporter for the BBC and a documentary maker.

They talk about similar topics, but not in the same order. Listen to the interview and answer the questions.

1 What sort of programmes does she find offensive? Why? What examples does she give?

2 Does she feel people can tell the difference between fantasy and reality?
Does she think it matters whether they can?
What examples does she quote to support her view?
What sort of programmes do you think these are?

3 Does she think television reflects society, or influences society?
Does she feel that television has positive as well as negative influences?

When you have answered your questions, find a partner from the other group.
Compare your answers and swap information.

Writing

In groups, discuss the information contained in these statistics about television. Then write a report on one of the following subjects, using the statistical information to illustrate your own opinions where appropriate.
- television output in your country compared to other countries
- the place of television in our lives
- 'Television is chewing-gum for the eyes.'
- Does television realize its potential?

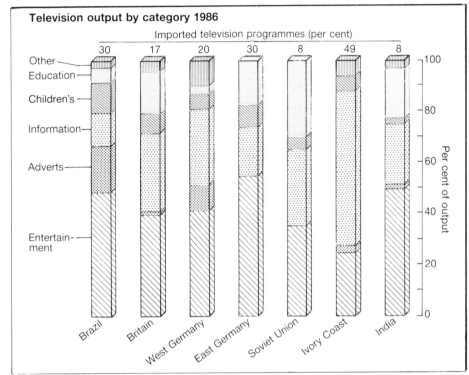

Sources: UNESCO, Screen Digest

	Number of TV homes (millions) 1985	Number of domestic national channels 1985	Average adult TV viewing per day (hours/minutes)‡ 1984	Annual TV advertising expenditure per head, 1983§	TV advertising expenditure as a % of total advertising expenditure 1985	Number of households connected to cable mid-1985** (millions)
West Germany	24.6	3	2.13	$8.40	10.7%	1.47
Britain	20.0	4	3.10	$26.10	31.0%	1.95
France	19.6	3	2.9	$8.30	17.7%	0.75
Italy	17.6	7	2.4	$11.20	49.6%	n/a
Spain	9.8	2	3	$8.30	31.8%	n/a
Holland	4.6	2	1.27*	$5.60	5.0%	2.58
Sweden	3.2	2	2	none	–	0.2
Belguim	3.2	4	2.55	none	–	2.8
Portugal	2.7	2	3	$4.90	47.0%	n/a
Greece	2.6	2	3	$7.10	48.4%	n/a
Austria	2.5	2	2.18	$12.60	27.5%	0.6
Switzerland	2.0	3	1.34	$9.60	8.0%†	0.95
Denmark	2.0	1	1.54	none	–	0.32
Finland	1.8	2	2	$15.50	n/a	0.18
Norway	1.3	1	1.18	none	–	0.26

*Evenings only. § On domestic national channels.†1980 ‡Estimates. **Includes relay systems carrying only broadcast channels.
Sources: Young and Rubicam. Saatchi & Saatchi Compton Worldwide. Mackintosh International. European Institute for the Media, Screen Digest, John Tydeman and Ellen Kelm: "New Media in Europe" (McGraw-Hill. 1986). The Goodall Partnership.

THE ECONOMIST DECEMBER 20 1986

Speaking

Dilemma!

You're going to play a game where you have to predict how one of your colleagues would behave in a given situation. Your teacher will give you three cards similar to this one.

SITUATION

You are a taxi driver.
You find a bag in your cab with £5,000 in it.
The name of the owner is on the bag, but not the address.

What would you do?

Read your cards and choose one of them. Then choose someone in the room (but don't say who yet). Write down on a piece of paper how you think he or she would react in that situation. When it is your turn, ask your question to the person you chose. He or she must say how he/she would react. If your prediction is right, you score a point! If you don't agree, or think they are lying, you can challenge them! The secret is to match a person and a situation, and then it is a question of how well you know your colleagues. Be prepared for some surprises!

Vocabulary 2

Rhyming words

Work in pairs.
Find as many words as you can that rhyme with the words below. Many of them might be homophones (two words with the same pronunciation but different spelling).
Use a dictionary to check the spelling of words you are not sure of.

a. steak   *stake, bake*
b. weak
c. fear
d. wear
e. pain

A poem

English spelling, as you know, is irregular!

1 Practise the following poem in pairs.

Here is some pronunciation.
Ration never rhymes with nation,
Say prefer, but preferable,
Comfortable and vegetable.
B must not be heard in doubt,
Debt and dumb both leave it out.
In the words psychology,
Psychic and psychiatry,
You must never sound the *p*.
Psychiatrist you call the man
Who cures the complex, if he can.
In architect, *ch* is *k*,
In arch it is the other way.

Please remember to say iron
So that it'll rhyme with lion.
Advertisers advertise,
Advertisements will put you wise.
Time when work is done is leisure,
Fill it up with useful pleasure.
Accidental, accident,
Sound the *g* in ignorant.
Relative, but a relation,
Then say creature but creation.
Say the *a* in gas quite short,
Bought remember rhymes with thwart,
Drought must always rhyme with bout,
In daughter leave the *gh* out.

2 **T.17** Listen to the poem to check your pronunciation.

3 There are many words with two or more syllables in the poem. Which stress pattern do they have?

1 O o		'ration
2 o O		pre'fer
3 O o o		'preferable
4 o O o o		psy'chology
5 o O o		
6 O o o o		
7 o o O o		
8 o o o O o		

Wear a boot upon your foot,
Root can never rhyme with soot.
In muscle, *sc* is *s*,
In muscular, it's *sk*, yes!
Choir must always rhyme with wire,
That again, will rhyme with liar.
Then, remember it's address,
With an accent like possess.
G in sign must silent be,
In signature, pronounce the *g*.

Please remember, say towards
Just as if it rhymed with boards.
Weight's like wait, but not like height,
Which should always rhyme with might.
Sew is just the same as so,
Tie a ribbon in a bow.
When you meet the queen you bow,
Which again must rhyme with how.
In perfect English make a start.
Learn this little rhyme by heart.

LANGUAGE STUDY

1 Verb patterns

In Unit 3, several verb patterns were presented. This unit deals with verb patterns in reported speech. Dictionaries provide information about these. In the *Oxford Advanced Learner's Dictionary*, a code refers to a list of verb patterns.

Example

> **warn** /wɔːn/ *v* **1 (a)** [Tn, Tn·pr, Dn·f, Dn·w] ~ **sb (of sth)** give sb notice of sth, esp possible danger or unpleasant consequences; inform sb in advance of what may happen: *'Mind the step,' she warned.* ○ *I tried to warn him, but he wouldn't listen.* ○ *She has been warned of the danger of driving the car in that state.* ○ *The police are warning (motorists) of possible delays.* ○ *If you warn me in advance, I will have your order ready for you.* ○ *They warned her that if she did it again she would be sent to prison.* ○ *I had been warned what to expect.* **(b)** [Tn·pr] ~

Tn (Transitive verb + noun)
*A small boy **opened** the **door**.*

Tn·pr (Transitive verb + noun + prepositional phrase)
*The accused **convinced** the **court** of his innocence.*

Dn·f (Double-transitive verb + noun + finite 'that' clause)
*Colleagues **told Paul that** the job wouldn't be easy.*

Dn·w (Double-transitive verb + noun + wh-clause)
*The porter **reminded guests where** they should leave their luggage/**where** to leave their luggage.*

This information can be difficult to understand and absorb. It is often easier to look at the example sentences to find out
– if the verb needs an object or not. (i.e. is it transitive or intransitive, or can it be both?)
– if it takes a certain preposition
– if it is followed by an infinitive or an **-ing** form
– if it can be followed by **that** + clause.

Further information about verb patterns is sometimes given in an entry.

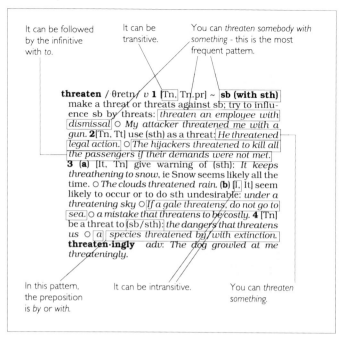

It can be followed by the infinitive with *to*.

It can be transitive.

You can *threaten somebody with something* - this is the most frequent pattern.

threaten /θretn/ *v* **1** [Tn, Tn.pr] ~ **sb (with sth)** make a threat or threats against sb; try to influence sb by threats: *threaten an employee with dismissal* ○ *My attacker threatened me with a gun.* **2** [Tn, Tt] use (sth) as a threat: *He threatened legal action.* ○ *The hijackers threatened to kill all the passengers if their demands were not met.* **3** **(a)** [It, Tn] give warning of (sth): *It keeps threatening to snow,* ie Snow seems likely all the time. ○ *The clouds threatened rain.* **(b)** [I, It] seem likely to occur or to do sth undesirable: *under a threatening sky* ○ *If a gale threatens, do not go to sea.* ○ *a mistake that threatens to be costly.* **4** [Tn] be a threat to (sb/sth): *the dangers that threatens us* ○ *a species threatened by/with extinction.* **threaten·ingly** *adv*: *The dog growled at me threateningly.*

In this pattern, the preposition is *by* or *with*.

It can be intransitive.

You can *threaten something*.

▶ **Grammar reference: page 139.**

The Grammar section gives a list of verbs that follow four common patterns:
verb + object + infinitive
verb + that + clause
verb + -ing
verb + infinitive

There is one more common pattern, which is *verb + preposition + object*.
Remember that prepositions are followed either by a noun or an -ing form.

Examples
He apologized for the inconvenience.
being late.

Practice

1 Put the correct preposition into each gap.
  a. He was accused _____ stealing from the till.
  b. I apologized _____ the mess.
  c. She blamed me _____ losing the contract.
  d. She's always boasting _____ her children's achievements.
  e. I wish you'd stop complaining _____ everything!
  f. The manager complimented her staff _____ their loyalty and devotion.
  g. He congratulated me _____ passing my exams.
  h. I managed to convince him _____ the need to invest his earnings.
  i. She never forgave me _____ losing the ring she had given me.
  j. He insisted _____ leaving immediately.

2 Report the following direct speech, using one of the verbs in Exercise 1 of the Grammar section.
Make the sentences quite short. Report the essence of the direct speech, not every word.

Example
'Listen, I really am terribly sorry about scraping your car. I'll get it repaired, honestly,' he said.
He apologized for scraping her car, and offered to get it repaired.
NOT
*He said that he really was sorry about scraping her car, and that he would honestly get it repaired.

  a. 'Peter, don't forget about the phone bill. Otherwise, we might get cut off,' she said.
  b. 'I wasn't involved in the bank robbery at all,' James Last told the police.
  c. 'You've had a boy! That's great! Well done!' he said to Sheila.
  d. 'True,' she said to Henry, 'I haven't always told you the whole truth, but I have never, absolutely never, told you a lie.'
  e. 'I really do think you should take the job in America, Joanna. I'll pay the air fare for you,' said John.
  f. 'What absolutely appalling weather!' Lisa said to her husband. 'It's your fault. You wanted to come to Scotland in winter.'
  g. 'Actually, Lisa,' said Malcolm to his wife, 'we came to Scotland because you went on and on and on about visiting your friends here.'
  h. 'Why don't you open a second shop?' said the bank manager to Alice. 'Of course, the bank would be prepared to lend you the capital.'
  i. 'But don't forget that I already have debts of over ten thousand pounds!' replied Alice. 'And anyway, the market isn't big enough for two shops.'

Listening and writing

T.18 You will hear a conversation between Alice Barron, the Director of a small company, and James Dunlop, the union representative. They are talking about the annual pay rise. Listen to the conversation, and then write a report of the meeting.

Begin like this:
Alice Barron, the Director of the company, offered to give her staff a five per cent pay rise, and explained to James Dunlop, the union representative, that . . .

2 Conditional sentences

Work in pairs.
Compare the use of tenses and verb forms in the following pairs of sentences, and discuss how the meaning changes.

  a. If I get a job, I'll be able to pay off my debts.
    If I got a job, I'd have to change my whole lifestyle.

b. **A** Give me a ring tomorrow.
   B I will if I can.

   A Give me a ring tomorrow.
   B I would if I could.

c. If you *will* play with matches, then it's your fault if you get burnt.
   If you play with matches, you might burn yourself.

d. If he doesn't come, let me know.
   If he won't come, let me know.

e. Will it be all right if I use your phone?
   Would it be all right if I used your phone?

f. If I had spoken more confidently at the interview, they would have offered me the job.
   If I spoke Spanish, they would have offered me the job.

g. If I had accepted the job, my husband would have been pleased.
   If I had accepted the job, I would be in Spain now.

h. I would come with you tomorrow if I hadn't already arranged to go to Paris.
   I would come with you tomorrow if I weren't going to Paris.

i. If I had accepted the job, I'd be Director now.
   If I had accepted the job, I'd be earning a good salary now.

▶ **Grammar reference: page 139.**
▶ Grammar reference: page 139.

1 In the following sentences, put the verbs in brackets in the most appropriate tense or verb form.

   a. Where on earth are we? If we _____ (bring) the map with us,
      we _____ (know) where we are.
      we _____ (not get) lost.
      we _____ (arrive) by now.

   b. I'd go to the party
      if someone _____ (tell) me about it earlier.
      if I _____ (know) who else _____ (go) to it.
      if I _____ (not have) an exam tomorrow.
      if I _____ (not go) out with Susan.

   c. I can't help you. I'm sorry. If I _____ (know) anything about cars,
      I _____ (can) tell you what to do.
      I _____ (repair) my own car last month.
      I _____ (not buy) this old car. It's a wreck!

   d. Just look at the weather! What a horrible day! If it _____ (not rain),
      we _____ (go) for a picnic.
      we _____ (play) tennis now.
      we _____ (not sit) here with nothing to do.

2 Put the verb in brackets in an appropriate tense or verb form. When there is no verb (_____), insert an auxiliary verb. Sometimes more than one form is possible.

I didn't go to university when I was younger, but I'm sure I (a) _____ (enjoy) it if I (b) _____.
I (c) _____ (study) medicine. I always wanted to be a doctor, but I was no good at science. Instead, I (d) _____ (study) business administration at a polytechnic. Now I (e) _____ (work) in a textile factory. I still think I (f) _____ (be) a good doctor. If I (g) _____, I (h) _____ (earn) a lot more than I (i) _____ now.

A I (j) _____ (drive) to London tomorrow to see some friends.
B Really? (k) _____ it _____ (be) possible for you to deliver a parcel for me? It's very valuable, and it (l) _____ (be) much safer if you (m) _____ (take) it than if I (n) _____ (post) it.
A Certainly. If you (o) _____ (give) it to me and (p) _____ (tell) me the address, I (q) _____ (deliver) it with pleasure.
B I've had another thought. (r) _____ you _____ (mind) if I (s) _____ (come) with you? Then I (t) _____ (can) deliver it myself.
A My car is full of books, I'm afraid, so there (u) _____ (not be) room for you. Sorry.

REVISION

Get

Get is one of the most frequent verbs in spoken English, although it is used much less often in written English.

1 Here are some examples from the text about the burglar on pages 76–7.
Rephrase the sentence without using **get**.
   a. If I got a job, I'd have to change my whole lifestyle. (line 72)
   b. Burglary is the only real skill I've got. (line 76)
   c. We got in through a ground floor window. (line 87)
   d. We just get the bus . . . (line 98)
   e. Dead easy to get away. (line 114)
   f. . . . I'd just go and get my mates . . . (line 126)
   g. . . . the lad I did the house with got caught . . . (line 153)
   h. I got a £554 fine plus probation. (line 155)

2 When **get** + adverb or preposition is used *literally*, it nearly always refers to movement.
Write sentences using each of the following to describe a movement.

get down	get up	get in	get out
get back	get off	get on	get away
get by	get under	get over	get through

Can you think of some metaphorical uses of **get** + adverb or preposition where the meaning can be guessed from the literal meaning?

Example
to get over an illness = to recover

UNIT 8

Storytime

Discussion

1 Work in pairs.
Look at the following cartoons.
Do you know which famous stories they are based on?
Which do you find funny? Why?

"After I'd got rid of the rats
they asked me to get rid of the
environmental health officers."

"What a pity, I didn't expect you to come!"

"Listen, I didn't
make the booking.
Talk to my agent."

*"Good morning,
sir. I represent the
Inland Revenue. I understand you
have a goose that lays golden eggs."*

*"For us you always stay young
and beautiful, Snow White!"*

*"It's always the same—you
think you have a job for
life and then your boss
kills himself laughing."*

*"I wonder what excuse you have
this time, Robinson?"*

2 Choose a couple of the stories with which you are fairly familiar and work together to remind yourselves of the whole story.

3 Tell some of the stories to the rest of the class. Who can remember additional parts?

4 How many of these stories are well-known in your country? Which other stories are popular? Have you got a personal favourite?

Pronunciation

T.19 You are going to read and listen to a more modern version of the story of 'Little Red Riding Hood' in the form of a poem.

Pre-listening task

1 Check round the class how much you know of the traditional tale.

2 Look at the following list of adjectives. In the traditional tale, which would apply to Red Riding Hood and which to the wolf?

innocent	cunning	cruel	cold-blooded
sly	clever	evil	quick-thinking
naïve	helpless	greedy	weak

3 What is the moral or message of the original?

Now read and listen at the same time, paying particular attention to the manner in which the poem is read.
Which adjectives in this version apply to Red Riding Hood, and which to the wolf?
What does the poem suggest about modern girls?

Reading aloud

Work in pairs.
Take it in turns to practise reading the poem or parts of the poem to each other.
Try to read it with as much feeling and humour as possible.

LITTLE RED RIDING HOOD AND THE WOLF

by Roald Dahl

As soon as Wolf began to feel
That he would like a decent meal,
He went and knocked on Grandma's door.
When Grandma opened it, she saw
5 The sharp white teeth, the horrid grin,
And Wolfie said, 'May I come in?'
Poor Grandmamma was terrified,
'He's going to eat me up!' she cried.
And she was absolutely right.
10 He ate her up in one big bite.
But Grandmamma was small and tough,
And Wolfie wailed, 'That's not enough!
'I haven't yet begun to feel
'That I have had a decent meal!'
15 He ran around the kitchen yelping,
I've got to have another helping!'
Then added with a frightful leer,
'I'm therefore going to wait right here
'Till Little Miss Red Riding Hood
20 'Comes home from walking in the wood.'
He quickly put on Grandma's clothes,
(Of course he hadn't eaten those.)
He dressed himself in coat and hat.
He put on shoes and after that
25 He even brushed and curled his hair,
Then sat himself in Grandma's chair.
In came the little girl in red.
She stopped. She started. And then she said,
'What great big ears you have, Grandma.'
30 'All the better to hear you with,' the Wolf replied.
'What great big eyes you have, Grandma,'
     said Little Red Riding Hood.
'All the better to see you with,' the Wolf replied.

He sat there watching her and smiled.
35 He thought, I'm going to eat this child.
Compared with her old Grandmamma
She's going to taste like caviare.

Then Little Red Riding Hood said, 'But Grandma,
what a lovely great big furry coat you have on.'
40 'That's wrong!' cried Wolf. 'Have you forgot
'To tell me what BIG TEETH I've got?
'Ah well, no matter what you say,
'I'm going to eat you anyway.'
The small girl smiles. One eyelid flickers.
45 She whips a pistol from her knickers.
She aims it at the creature's head
And bang bang bang, she shoots him dead.

A few weeks later, in the wood,
I came across Miss Riding Hood.
50 But what a change! No cloak of red,
No silly hood upon her head.
She said, 'Hello, and do please note
'My lovely furry WOLFSKIN COAT.'

Writing

Write a more up-to-date version of a folk tale or fairy story with which you are familiar. Try to include a similar 'sting-in-the-tail'.
It is not necessary to write in verse!
How do such stories often begin and end in English?

Vocabulary 1
Onomatopoeic words

Work in small groups.
What or *who* does the following? Use dictionaries to check the examples given.

bangs ( )   howls ( )
blares ( )   plops ( )
chimes ( )   roars ( )
clicks ( )   shrieks ( )
crackles ( )   squeaks ( )
creaks ( )   squelches ( )
crunches ( )   taps ( )
gasps ( )   thumps ( )
groans ( )

T.20 Now listen to each of these sounds (they are not in the same order as the words).
Put the correct number next to the words in the list above.
To you, do they really *sound* like what they mean?

Practice

1 The gaps in this passage can be filled by *one* or *two* (but *not all three*) of the words that follow in brackets. Decide which are possible.

She crept quietly down the stairs and along the hall. The floorboards (a) _____ (squeaked/crunched/creaked) and her heart (b) _____ (tapped/thumped/groaned) inside her chest. However, the television was (c) _____ (roaring/blaring/shrieking) in the living room, so they didn't hear her. She reached the front door. As usual, it was locked. She turned the old iron key, and the lock (d) _____ (tapped/clicked/crunched) back. As she opened the door, a sudden gust of wind blew it back against the wall with a (e) _____ (gasp/plop/bang). She (f) _____ (gasped/groaned/shrieked) with fear, and waited to hear her father's angry voice. Seconds passed, and still only the (g) _____ (howls/shrieks/blares) of laughter came from the Saturday night quiz show they were watching. She hurried out into the stormy night. The mighty wind (h) _____ (crackled/roared/howled) through the trees, causing the branches to (i) _____ (groan/creak/tap). It had only just stopped raining, and her feet (j) _____ (squelched/crunched/plopped) in the mud as she ran across the lawn and out of the gate at the back of the house. Now the heels of her shoes (k) _____ (clicked/thumped/tapped) even more quickly along the pavement. She felt her sense of freedom growing. The church clock (l) _____ (blared/tapped/chimed) eleven o'clock. In a few more minutes she would be in her lover's arms, and they would journey into the future together!

2 Work in small groups.
Write a similar story that contains some onomatopoeic words. Remember they can be both nouns and verbs. If you like, you can make some mistakes with the sounds and choose an inappropriate word to test your colleagues!

Reading
Pre-reading task

Roald Dahl is not only a best-selling children's author: he is also a master of 'sting-in-the-tail' short stories for adults. The following sentences are taken from such a short story called 'Parson's Pleasure'.

Work in pairs or small groups. Discuss the sentences. What do you learn about the *characters*, the *setting*, and the *plot* of the story?

1 Apart from the fact that he was at this moment disguised as a clergyman, there was nothing very sinister about Cyril Boggis. By trade a dealer in antique furniture, with a shop in the King's Road, Chelsea . . .

2 Boggis's little secret was a result of something that happened on a Sunday afternoon nearly nine years before, while he was driving in the country.

3 They bargained for half an hour, and in the end, of course, Boggis got the chairs for less than a twentieth of their value.

4 The scheme worked. In fact, it became a lucrative business.

5 And now it was another Sunday. Boggis parked some distance from the gates of his first house, the Queen Anne. He never liked his car to be seen until a deal was made. A dear old clergyman and a large station-wagon never seemed quite right together.

6 The farm owner was a stumpy man with small shifty eyes, whose name was Rummins.

7 And there it was! Boggis saw it at once and gasped . . . not daring to believe what he saw before him. It *couldn't* be true!

8 – Boggis walked casually past the commode – 'worth a few pounds, I dare say. A crude reproduction, I'm afraid.'

9 'Listen, Parson,' Rummins said, 'how can you be so sure it's a fake? You haven't even seen it underneath all that paint.'

10 'Make it fifty,' Rummins said.
'My dear man,' Boggis said softly, 'I only want the legs. The rest of it is firewood, that's all . . . I'll make you one final offer. Twenty pounds.'
'I'll take it,' Rummins snapped.

Compare ideas.
What do you think the 'sting-in-the-tail' might be?
Now read the story. How similar is your ending?

Parson's Pleasure

BY ROALD DAHL

Boggis gasped, not
daring to believe what
he saw before him.
It *couldn't* be true!

MR BOGGIS stopped the car just short of the summit, got out and looked around. It was perfect. He could see for miles.

5 Over on the right he spotted a medium farmhouse. Beyond it was a larger one. There was a house that might be a Queen Anne, and there were two likely farms over on the left. Five places in all. Then 10 he drove to the other side of the hill, where he saw six more possibles—five farms and one big Georgian house. He ruled out the latter. It looked prosperous, and there was no point in calling on the 15 prosperous.

Apart from the fact that he was at this moment disguised as a clergyman, there was nothing very sinister about Cyril Boggis. By trade a dealer in antique furni- 20 ture, with a shop in the King's Road, Chelsea, Boggis had achieved a considerable reputation by producing unusual items with astonishing regularity. When asked where he got them, he would wink 25 and murmur something about a little secret.

Boggis's little secret was a result of something that happened on a Sunday afternoon nearly nine years before, while 30 he was driving in the country. The car had overheated and he had walked to a farmhouse to ask for a jug of water.

While he was waiting for it, he glanced through the door and spotted a large oak 35 armchair. The back panel was decorated by an inlay of the most delicate floral design, and the head of a duck was carved on either arm. *Good God,* he thought. *This thing is late seventeenth century!*

40 He poked his head in further. There was another one on the other side of the fireplace! Two chairs like that must be worth at least a thousand pounds up in London.

45 When the woman of the house returned, Boggis asked if she would like to sell her chairs. They weren't for sale, she said, but just out of curiosity, how much would he give? They bargained for half an 50 hour, and in the end, of course, Boggis got the chairs for less than a twentieth of their value.

Returning to London in his station-wagon, Boggis had an idea. If there was 55 good stuff in one farmhouse, why not in others? On Sundays, why couldn't he comb the countryside? The isolated places, the farmhouses, the dilapidated country mansions, would be his target. 60 But country folk are a suspicious lot. Perhaps it would be best if he didn't let them know he was a dealer. He could be the telephone man, the plumber, the gas inspector. He could even be a clergy- 65 man . . .

Boggis ordered a large quantity of superior cards on which the following legend was engraved:

The Reverend
Cyril Winnington Boggis

President of the Society
for the Preservation
of Rare Furniture

In association with
The Victoria and Albert Museum

From now on, every Sunday, he was 70 going to be a nice old parson travelling around on a labour of love for the "Society," compiling an inventory of the treasures that lay hidden in country homes. The scheme worked. In fact, it 75 became a lucrative business.

And now it was another Sunday. Boggis parked some distance from the gates of his first house, the Queen Anne. He never liked his car to be seen until a deal 80 was made. A dear old clergyman and a large station-wagon never seemed quite right together. But there was nothing of value in the house.

At the next stop, no one was home. 85 The third, a farmhouse, was back in the fields. It looked rambling and dirty. He didn't hold out much hope for it.

Three men were standing in the yard.

When they caught sight of the small, pot- 90 bellied man in his black suit and parson's collar, they stopped talking and watched him suspiciously. The farm owner was a stumpy man with small shifty eyes, whose name was Rummins. The tall 95 youth beside him was his son Bert. The short man with broad shoulders was Claud, a neighbour.

"And what exactly might you be wanting?" Rummins asked.

100 Boggis explained at some length the aims and ideals of the Society for the Preservation of Rare Furniture.

"We don't have any," said Rummins. "You're wasting your time."

105 "Now just a minute, sir," Boggis said, raising a finger. "The last man who said that to me was an old farmer down in Sussex, and when he finally let me into his house, d'you know what I 110 found? A dirty-looking old chair in the kitchen that turned out to be worth four hundred pounds! I showed him how to sell it, and he bought himself a new tractor with the money."

115 Rummins shifted uneasily on his feet. "Well," he said, "there's no harm in you taking a look." He led the way into an exceedingly filthy living-room.

And there it was! Boggis saw it at 120 once and gasped. He stood staring for ten seconds at least, not daring to believe what he saw before him. It *couldn't* be true!

At that point, Boggis became aware 125 of the three men watching him intently. They had seen him gasp and stare. In a flash, Boggis staggered to the nearest chair and collapsed into it, breathing heavily.

130 "What's the matter?" Claud asked.

"It's nothing," he gasped. "I'll be all right in a minute."

"I thought maybe you were looking at something," Rummins said.

"No, no," Boggis said. "It's just my heart. It happens every now and then. I'll be all right."

He *must* have time to think, he told himself. *Take it gently, Boggis. Keep calm. These people may be ignorant but they are not stupid. And if it is really true . . .*

To a layman, what he had seen might not have appeared particularly impressive, covered as it was with dirty white paint. But it was a dealer's dream. Boggis knew that among the most coveted examples of eighteenth century English furniture are three pieces known as "The Chippendale Commodes."

A trifle unsteadily, Boggis began to move around the room examining the other furniture, one piece at a time. Apart from the commode it was a very poor lot.

"Nice oak table," he said. "Not old enough to be of any interest. This chest of drawers"—Boggis walked casually past the commode—"worth a few pounds, I dare say. A crude reproduction, I'm afraid."

"That's a strong bit of furniture," Rummins said. "Some nice carving on it too."

"Machine-carved," Boggis replied, bending down to examine the exquisite craftsmanship. He began to saunter off, frowning as though in deep thought. "You know what?" he said, looking back at the commode. "I've wanted a set of legs something like that for a long time. I've got a table in my own home, and when I moved house, the movers damaged the legs. I'm very fond of that table. I keep my Bible and sermon notes on it."

He paused, stroking his chin. "These legs on your chest of drawers could be cut off and fixed on to my table."

"What you mean to say is you'd like to buy it," Rummins said.

"Well . . . it might be a bit too much trouble. It's not worth it."

"How much were you thinking of offering?" Rummins asked.

"Not much, I'm afraid. You see, this is not a genuine antique."

"I'm not so sure," Rummins said. "It's been in here over 20 years. I bought it at the Manor House when the old Squire died. Bert, where's that old bill you once found at the back of one of the drawers?"

"You mean this?" Bert lifted out a piece of folded yellowing paper from one of the drawers and carried it over to his father.

"You can't tell me this writing ain't bloody old," Rummins said, holding the paper out to Boggis, whose arm was shaking as he took it. It was brittle and it crackled slightly between his fingers. The writing was in a long sloping copper-plate hand.

Edward Montagu, Esq
Debtor To Thos Chippendale:
A large mahogany Commode Table of exceeding fine wood, very neat carvd, set upon fluted legs, two very neat shapd long drawers in the middle part and two ditto on each side, with rich chasd Brass Handles and Ornaments, the whole completely finished in the most exquisite taste . . . £87

BOGGIS was fighting to suppress his excitement. With the invoice, the value had climbed even higher. What in heaven's name would it fetch now? Twelve thousand pounds? Fourteen? Maybe fifteen or even twenty?

He tossed the paper contemptuously on to the table and said quietly, "It's exactly what I thought, a Victorian reproduction. This is simply the invoice that the seller gave to his client."

"Listen, Parson," Rummins said, "how can you be so sure it's a fake? You haven't even seen it underneath all that paint."

"Has anyone got a knife?" asked Boggis.

Claud produced a pocket-knife. Working with apparent casualness, Boggis began chipping the paint off a small area on top of the commode. "Take a look."

It was beautiful—a warm little patch of mahogany glowing like a topaz, rich and dark with the true colour of its two hundred years.

"What's wrong with it?" Rummins asked.

"It's processed! Without the slightest doubt this wood has been processed with lime. That's what they use for mahogany, to give it that dark aged colour. Look closely. That touch of orange in among the dark red-brown is the sign of lime."

"How much would you give?" Rummins asked.

Boggis looked at the commode, frowned, and shrugged his shoulders. "I think ten pounds would be fair."

"Ten pounds!" Rummins cried. "Don't be ridiculous, Parson. Look at the bill! It tells you exactly what it cost! Eighty-seven pounds! Now it's antique, it's worth double!"

"If you'll pardon me, no, sir, it's not. It's a second-hand reproduction. But I'll tell you what, I'll go as high as fifteen pounds."

"Make it fifty," Rummins said.

"My dear man," Boggis said softly, "I only want the legs. The rest of it is firewood, that's all."

"Make it thirty-five," Rummins said.

"I *couldn't* sir, I *couldn't*! I'll make you one final offer. Twenty pounds."

"I'll take it," Rummins snapped.

"Oh, dear," Boggis said. "I shouldn't have started this."

"You can't back out now, Parson. A deal's a deal."

"Yes, yes, I know. Perhaps if I got my car, you gentlemen would be kind enough to help me load it?"

Boggis found it difficult not to break into a run. But clergymen never run; they walk slowly. *Walk slowly, Boggis. Keep calm, Boggis, There's no hurry now. The commode is yours!*

Back in the farmhouse, Rummins was saying, "Fancy him giving me twenty pound for a load of junk like this."

"You did very nicely, Mr Rummins," Claud told him. "You think he'll pay you?"

"We don't put it in the car till he do."

"And what if it won't go in the car?" Claud asked. "He'll just say to hell with it and drive off."

Rummins paused to consider this alarming prospect.

"I've got an idea," Claud went on. "He told us that it was only the legs he was wanting. So all we've got to do is cut 'em off, then it'll be sure to go in the car. All we're doing is saving him the trouble of cutting them off when he gets home."

"A bloody good idea," Rummins said, looking at the commode. Within a couple of minutes, Claud and Bert had carried the commode outside and Claud went to work with the saw. When all the legs were severed, Bert arranged them carefully in a row.

Claud stepped back to survey the results. "Just let me ask you one question, Mr Rummins," he said slowly. "Even now, could *you* put that enormous thing into a car?"

"Not unless it was a van."

"Correct!" Claud cried. "And parsons don't have vans. All they've got usually is piddling little Morris Eights or Austin Sevens."

"The legs is all he wants," Rummins said. "If the rest of it won't go in, then he can leave it. He can't complain. He's got the legs.'

"Now you know better'n that, Mr Rummins," Claud said patiently. "You know damn well he's going to start knocking the price if he don't get every single bit of this into the car. So why don't we give him his firewood now and be done with it."

"Fair enough," Rummins said. "Bert, fetch the axe."

It was hard work, and it took several minutes before Claud had the whole thing more or less smashed to pieces. "I'll tell you one thing," he said straightening up, wiping his brow. "That was a bloody good carpenter put this job together and I don't care what the parson says."

"We're just in time!" Rummins called out. "Here he comes!"

Comprehension check

Are the following statements true or false? Say why.

T/F

1 Boggis hit on the idea of how to obtain rare antique furniture purely by chance. ☐

2 The woman of the house finally agreed to sell the chairs because she hadn't realized how valuable they were. ☐

3 Boggis always parked some way from the houses he was going to visit in order to give himself time to consider the likelihood of finding valuable antiques in them. ☐

4 He never visited prosperous-looking houses and farms. ☐

5 Boggis was so excited when he saw the commode that he almost had a heart attack. ☐

6 Boggis told Rummins that he wanted the commode for himself to keep his Bible and sermon notes on. ☐

7 Rummins is easily convinced that the commode is only a Victorian reproduction. ☐

8 Boggis's big mistake was not to tell them that he had a station-wagon. ☐

What do you think?

1 What is the moral of the story?
2 Look again at the very end of the story. In pairs try to continue the conversation as Boggis joins the three men.
3 Do you think Boggis will continue his scheme and disguise after this incident?
4 How sympathetic do you feel to Boggis?

▶ Language focus

Read the Language study on *time clauses in the past and future* (page 93) and do the practice exercise.

Listening

You will hear an interview with Barbara Cartland, a highly prolific and successful writer of romantic fiction.

Pre-listening task

Here are the covers of just a few of her books.

Work in pairs or small groups.

1 Look at the titles and try to imagine what a typical story by Barbara Cartland might be like.
Consider the setting, the characters, and the plot.
2 What questions would you want to ask her if you were interviewing her for a TV or radio programme?

Listening for information

T.21 Listen to the interview and answer the questions.

1 The following numbers are mentioned in the interview. What do they refer to?

   1923   450   45 million   23   18th   5
   6,000–7,000   8,000   2   20–30

2 Why doesn't she know how many books she has sold?

3 She says '. . . it's very interesting, because as you know, I'm very pure . . . and I sell more than anybody else.' What is her implication?

4 Why does she read so many history books? Approximately how many history books does she read every year?

5 Why do Americans love her books so much?

What do you think?

1 Why do you think her stories are so universally popular?

2 What kind of people read them?

3 Which of the following adjectives would you use to describe the way Barbara Cartland presents herself?

   energetic   aristocratic   snobbish   prudish
   patronizing   romantic   naïve   enthusiastic

▶ Language focus

Do the practice exercises on *tenses* in the Language study (page 93).

Vocabulary 2

Homonyms

Homonyms are words with the same spelling and pronunciation but different meanings: for example, *a High Street **bank*** and *the **bank** of a river*.

Dictionaries usually give separate entries for homonyms which are different parts of speech, or when the difference between the meanings is large. However, this is not always the case.

lean¹ /li:n/ *adj* (**-er**, **-est**) **1** (of people and animals) without much flesh; thin and healthy: *a lean athletic body*. **2** (of meat) containing little or no fat: *lean beef*.

lean² /li:n/ *v* (*pt, pp* **leant** /lent/ or **leaned** /li:nd/) ⇨Usage at DREAM². **1** [I, Ipr, Ip] be in a sloping position; bend: *lean out of the window, back in one's chair, over to one side, etc* ○ *Just lean forward for a moment, please*.

grass² /grɑːs; *US* græs/ *v* **1** (**a**) [Tn, Tn·p] ~ **sth** (**over**) cover sth with turf. (**b**) [Tn] (*US*) feed (animals) with grass. **2** [I, Ipr] ~ (**on sb**) (*Brit sl usu derog*) (used by criminals) inform the police of sb's criminal plans or activities: *If anyone grasses on us, his life won't be worth living!*

Practice

Below are ten sentences. Each sentence contains a homonym that you probably don't know. Decide which word this is and then look it up in the dictionary, making sure you have the correct entry.

a. Where did we file the documents about Mr Barrington-Smythe? Was it under 'B' or 'S'?

b. The accused stood in the dock, and listened impassively to the evidence given against him.

c. Police investigations into the robbery were hampered by the lack of witnesses.

d. Many trees shed their leaves in autumn.

e. She had never been known to utter an unkind word about anybody.

f. John is a selfish person. His sole purpose in life is self-gratification.

g. Many second and third world countries are pawns in the games of the superpowers.

h. Come on! Perk up! What have you got to be so miserable about?

i. It isn't 12.30 already, is it? The clock must be fast.

j. I was lucky to survive the accident with just a few cuts and grazes.

In column **A** write a definition of the word in the sentence.
In column **B** write a sentence illustrating a different meaning of the word.
The first one has been done for you.

	Homonym	A	B
a.	File	to organize documents	You need a nail file to smooth your nails
b.			
c.			
d.			
e.			
f.			
g.			
h.			
i.			
j.			

LANGUAGE STUDY

1 Time clauses in the past and future

The following time conjunctions can be used to talk about past or future:

when	*while*
before	*until, till*
after	*once*
as soon as, immediately	*by the time (that)*
as	

Study the tenses used in these examples with **when**. Discuss the differences in meaning between them.

1 When we have the meeting, we'll decide on a price.
2 When we've had the meeting, we'll decide on a price.
3 When we had/were having the meeting, we decided on a price.
4 When we had the meeting, we had decided on a price.
5 When we had had the meeting, we decided on a price.

▶ **Grammar reference: page 140.**

Practice

Combine the sentence-pairs with each of the conjunctions in brackets, changing tenses as necessary.

a. 'I'll disguise myself as a clergyman.'
'I'll visit other farms,' said Mr Boggis. (before) (after)

b. He returned to London.
He worked out a plan. (as soon as) (while) (by the time)

c. He saw the priceless piece of furniture.
He gasped in amazement. (when) (immediately)

d. I'll search every antique shop.
I'll find the one I want. (until) (once)

e. I'll save the money.
I'll buy the picture. (as soon as) (before)

f. He went to collect his van.
They chopped the drawers into firewood. (while) (once)

g. They finished the job.
He arrived to load the van. (as) (before)

h. We'll get the money.
We'll buy a new tractor. (once) (not . . . until)

2 Review of tenses

1 Put the verb in brackets in an appropriate tense. When there is no verb (_____), insert an auxiliary verb.

My wife and I (a) _____ (live) in our present house in the country for five years. We (b) _____ (move) here after our second child (c) _____ (be) born. We (d) _____ (live) in town for ten years, and (e) _____ (decide) that as soon as we (f) _____ (can) afford it, we (g) _____ (move) away from the smoke and the noise of the city centre, which we finally (h) _____ in 1985. We (i) _____ never (regret) it. We (j) _____ (be) reminded of the wisdom of our decision every morning when we (k) _____ (draw) the curtains to see open fields stretching before us. When the children (l) _____ (have) breakfast, they (m) _____ (rush) outside to play, which they (n) _____ whatever the weather. Whilst they (o) _____ (play) outside, we somehow manage to start the day.

2 Instructions as above.

Actually, we (a) _____ (think) of moving. My wife (b) _____ (accept) a new job, which she (c) _____ (start) next month. As soon as she (d) _____, she (e) _____ (have) a journey of fifty miles there and back, and I (f) _____ (not think) that she (g) _____ (realize) just how tiring this (h) _____ (be). I (i) _____ (go) away on business for a few days next week, and while I (j) _____ (be) away, my sister (k) _____ (come) to stay, which she (l) _____ quite often. Once I (m) _____ (be) back, I (n) _____ (decide) that I (o) _____ (get) in touch with some estate agents. I (p) _____ (not feel) happy until we (q) _____ (find) a house closer to my wife's job. I wonder what the children (r) _____ (say) when they (s) _____ (hear) that we (t) _____ (move). This is the first time they (u) _____ (live) in the country, and they (v) _____ (hate) to move back to a town.

REVISION

Punctuation

1 Work in pairs.
In some, but not all, of the following sentences there are mistakes of punctuation. Correct them, and comment on the use or absence of punctuation.

a. She speaks English, French, Russian, and German.
b. She asked me, if I wanted any help?
c. The Prime Minister said, that the situation was improving.
d. 'That' said John 'is all I know. 'Why?,' asked Angela.
e. When everyone's here, we'll start the meeting.
f. We'll start the meeting when everyone's here.
g. My daughter who works in New York is getting married.
h. My wife who's in publishing is going to a book fair.
i. I was at university in the early 1970's. In 78 I went to America.
j. This book isn't Peters. It's yours'.
k. We've just had a fortnights' holiday in Spain. In a few week's time we're off to Greece.
l. The girls school was on one side of the road, the boys on the other.
m. She doesn't talk, normally.

2 The punctuation in the following examples is correct. Comment on its use.

Semicolon

a. People say that travel broadens the mind; it can also be a frustrating and dangerous experience.

b. Some people believe he is a paragon of virtue; others maintain that he is dishonest and corrupt.

Colon

c. A first-aid kit should contain the following items: cotton wool, sticking plasters, antiseptic cream, bandages, and a pair of scissors.

Brackets

d. Schooldays (so we are told) are the happiest days of our lives.

e. My wife (I hope she is wrong) thinks my project has little chance of success.

Hyphen

f. ex-champion; pro-Soviet; anti-abortion

g. re-elect; co-operate; pre-eminent

h. a nine-to-five job; a well-educated man; a ten-year-old girl; up-to-date news

▶ **Grammar reference: page 141.**

3 Here are some well-known anecdotes. Punctuate them as you think appropriate.

Groucho Marx

a. He once received a letter from his bank manager who had written to remind him of an overdraft the letter ended with the standard phrase if I can be of any service to you do not hesitate to call on me Marx immediately put pen to paper dear sir he wrote the best thing you can do to be of service to me is to steal some money from the account of one of your richer clients and credit it to mine

Paul Getty I

b. Getty once received a request from a magazine for a short article explaining his success a two hundred pound cheque was enclosed the multi millionaire obligingly wrote get up early work late strike oil

George Bernard Shaw

c. A certain Mrs Smythe who was notorious for courting celebrities sent Shaw an invitation reading Lady Smythe will be at home on Tuesday between four and six o'clock Shaw returned the card with the following annotation Mr Bernard Shaw likewise

Sir Winston Churchill

d. A lady MP once rebuked Churchill for being intoxicated at a dinner party sir she said you are drunk and you madam are ugly Churchill retorted but I shall be sober tomorrow

e. In conversation with Churchill Lady Astor expounded on the subject of womens rights Churchill opposed her on this and other causes that she held dear in some exasperation Lady Astor said Winston if I were married to you Id put poison in your coffee Churchill responded and if you were my wife Id drink it

UNIT 9

A sense of place

● Pronunciation

Limericks

1 Limericks are humorous poems. They begin by introducing a person and a place.

Examples

There was | a young man from Spain
| an old lady from Bath
| a young poet from Japan

They rhyme A A B B A, and have a strong rhythm.

A gentleman dining at Crewe
Found quite a large mouse in his stew.

Said the waiter, Don't shout,
Or wave it about,
Or the rest will be wanting one too!

In each box, there are three jumbled limericks. Sort the lines into the correct order. Some have been done for you.

Who dreamed he was eating his shoe.
One day, they suppose
Who used to eat onions in bed.
He woke up in the night
There was an old woman from Kent (1)
It's not very funny.
And found it was perfectly true.
His mother said 'Sonny,
And nobody knows where she went.
There was an old man from Crewe (6)
With a terrible fright
Whose nose was remarkably bent.
Why don't you eat people instead?'
She followed her nose
There was a young cannibal called Ned, (11)

There was a young lady from Gloucester (1)
One day for her tea
Who grew so exceedingly tall.
He could stretch out his leg
Who was awfully fond of small gherkins.
The trouble was how to defrost her.
From the fridge came a sound
There was a young lady called Perkins (6)
And turn off the light in the hall.
There was a young man called Paul (11)
And pickled her internal workings.
And at last she was found.
Whose parents thought they had lost her.
She devoured forty-three
When he got into bed

Practise saying the limericks. Remember to keep to the strong rhythm.

2 Make up your own limerick. Remember that you can exercise a certain poetic licence to change word order!

Example
There was a young student from France,
Last night he went to a dance, . . .

Reading

Pre-reading task

You will read three extracts from autobiographies written by Charlie Chaplin (the comedian), Muhammad Ali (the boxer), and Laurie Lee (the writer and poet).
Divide into three groups. Your teacher will allocate one of the three men to your group. Write questions about his life to ask your colleagues.

Jigsaw reading

First scan the three extracts quickly and decide which was written by who.
Then divide into three groups. Each group should read the extract written by the man they wrote questions about. Try to answer your questions from the information in the extract. If you can't answer a question, try to guess.

Questions

1 In which year did the events described take place? How old was he?
2 Do you get the impression that it was a happy childhood? How well-off was his family?
3 Was his upbringing in a town or in the country?
4 Which members of his family does he mention? What is his attitude towards them?
5 What forms of transport does he mention? What is the purpose of this reference?
6 Are there any aspects of his childhood that you feel he would like to recreate?
7 Summarize the theme of your extract in one phrase or sentence.

When you have answered your questions, find a partner from one of the other two groups. Compare your answers and swap information.

Now read the other two extracts.

1

London was sedate in those days. The tempo was sedate; even the horse-drawn tram-cars along Westminster Bridge Road went at a sedate pace and turned sedately on a revolving table at the terminal near the bridge. In
5 Mother's prosperous days we also lived in Westminster Bridge Road. Its atmosphere was gay and friendly with attractive shops, restaurants and music halls. The fruit shop on the corner facing the Bridge was a galaxy of colour, with its neatly arranged pyramids of oranges,
10 apples, pears and bananas outside, in contrast to the solemn grey Houses of Parliament directly across the river.

This was the London of my childhood, of my moods and awakenings: memories of Lambeth in the spring; of
15 trivial incidents and things; of riding with Mother on top of a horse-bus trying to touch passing lilac-trees – of the many coloured bus tickets, orange, blue, pink and green, that bestrewed the pavement where the trams and buses stopped – of rubicund flower-girls at the corner of
20 Westminster Bridge, making gay *boutonnières*, their adroit fingers manipulating tinsel and quivering fern – of the humid odour of freshly watered roses that affected me with a vague sadness – of melancholy Sundays and pale-faced parents and their children escorting toy windmills
25 and coloured balloons over Westminster Bridge; and the maternal penny steamers that softly lowered their funnels as they glided under it. From such trivia I believe my soul was born.

2

The last days of my childhood were also the last days of
30 the village. I belonged to that generation which saw, by
chance, the end of a thousand years' life. The change
came late to our Cotswold valley, didn't really show itself
till the late 1920s; I was twelve by then, but during that
handful of years I witnessed the whole thing happen.

35   Myself, my family, my generation, were born in a
world of silence; a world of hard work and necessary
patience, of backs bent to the ground, hands massaging
the crops, of waiting on weather and growth; of villages
like ships in the empty landscapes and the long walking
40 distances between them; of white narrow roads, rutted by
hooves and cart-wheels, innocent of oil or petrol, down
which people passed rarely, and almost never for pleasure, and the horse was the fastest thing moving. Man and
horse were all the power we had – abetted by levers and
45 pulleys. But the horse was king, and almost everything

grew around him: fodder, smithies, stables, paddocks,
distances, and the rhythm of our days. His eight miles an
hour was the limit of our movements, as it had been since
the days of the Romans. That eight miles an hour was life
50 and death, the size of our world, our prison.

This was what we were born to, and all we knew at
first. Then, to the scream of the horse, the change began.
The brass-lamped motor-car came coughing up the road,
followed by the clamorous charabanc; the solid-tyred bus
55 climbed the dusty hills and more people came and went.
Chickens and dogs were the early sacrifices, falling
demented beneath the wheels. The old folk, too, had
strokes and seizures, faced by speeds beyond comprehen-
sion. Then scarlet motor-bikes, the size of five-barred
60 gates, began to appear in the village, on which our youths
roared like rockets up the two-minute hills, then spent
weeks making repairs and adjustments.

3

I remember the summer of 1956. School was out, and my
brother Rudy and I were roaming the streets all day and
65 we'd come home hungry. My father was somewhere
across town painting signs and we looked down the
streets every few minutes hoping we'd see Bird come
with a bag of groceries, maybe hamburger and hot dogs.
Maybe, if she spent all her day's pay, chicken and
70 potatoes. Usually she kept only enough for bus fare to
go to work the next day for some white lady in the
Highlands I never met. She'd get up early in the
morning, walk four blocks to catch a bus, ride up where
the white folks lived, clean house, clean toilets, cook
75 food, take care of babies – all for four dollars a day.
Sometimes she came home too tired to cook.

There was seldom enough money for Rudy and me to
have bus fare for school, not both of us at the same time.
This is the real reason why I began to race the bus to
80 school. But since my ambition was to be the World
Heavyweight Champion, I could say I wasn't racing the
bus because I didn't have any money, I was running to

get in fight condition.

We never owned a car that was less than ten years
85 old, or even new tires for it. The neighbors could at least
buy new tires. Daddy's tires kept blowing out. If we had
gotten any money, it wouldn't have gone for cars or tires.
It would have been used to fix the house. The rain was
coming in through the roof and walls; for four years the
90 toilet needed a new flush unit; for eight years the front
porch had been falling apart. The construction man told
Dad it would cost two hundred dollars to have it
propped up temporarily. That was too much, so we lived
with a front porch ready to fall any day.

95   Most of the clothes we got came from Good Will,
including the secondhand shoes that cost maybe one or
two dollars. My father had become an expert at cutting
out cardboard and putting it in the bottoms. Now and
then there would be a new shirt, and once I remember
100 Daddy buying a cheap little suit for me to wear to church
and Sunday School.

Questions for discussion

1 In your opinion, which extract:
   – is most factual?
   – is most nostalgic?
   – is most poetic?
   – is about change?
   – is about memories?
   – is about poverty?

2 What is Muhammad Ali's father's job?
   Who do you think Bird is?
   Can you guess the occupations of Laurie Lee's and
   Charlie Chaplin's parents?

3 What does Laurie Lee mean by the following?
   . . . the end of a thousand years' life. (line 31)
   . . . hands massaging the crops . . . (lines 37–8)
   . . . waiting on weather and growth . . . (line 38)
   . . . and almost never for pleasure . . . (lines 42–3)
   . . . and more people came and went . . . (line 55)

4 Which words tell us Laurie Lee's attitude to life before and after the arrival of the motor car?

5 Use your imagination to say what you think were the sounds and the smells of the three men's childhood.

Vocabulary

Find words in the texts that mean the same or similar to the following.

Lines 1–28
- **a.** calm
- **b.** carefree, merry
- **c.** unimportant
- **d.** handling
- **e.** shaking
- **f.** taking, carrying
- **g.** went smoothly

Lines 29–62
- **h.** fingering, touching
- **i.** lined
- **j.** helped
- **k.** food for horses
- **l.** noisy
- **m.** mad

▶ Language focus

Read the Language study on *relative clauses* (page 102) and do the practice exercises.

Writing

Write an essay or a story about the sounds and smells (and tastes, if you like!) of your childhood.

● Vocabulary 1

1 Varieties of English

Dictionaries provide information about the style of a word (*formal*, *informal*, *slang*, *colloquial*). They also tell us if a word comes from a particular country or region.

> **bairn** /beən/ *n* (*Scot*) child.

> **side**¹ /saɪd/ *n* [. . .]
> **'sidewalk** *n* (*US*) = PAVEMENT 1.

1 Look back at the extract from Muhammad Ali's autobiography.
There are several examples (grammar, spelling, and vocabulary) of American English. Find them, and say what their equivalent is in British English.

2 Here are some more Americanisms.
Write their equivalents in British English.
- **a.** He ain't gonna help.
- **b.** I gotta go.
- **c.** Monday thru Friday.
- **d.** Did you have a good vacation?
- **e.** Boy, he was real mad!
- **f.** Wanna cookie?
- **g.** I arrived in the fall.
- **h.** Waiter! The check, please.
- **i.** I'm going downtown.
- **j.** What did you do on the weekend?

2 Specialist registers

Dictionaries also say if a word belongs to a particular profession, occupation, or field of activity.

> **dribble** /'drɪbl/ *v* **1** [I, Ipr] allow saliva to run from the mouth: *The baby's just dribbled down my tie.* **2** [I, Ipr, Ip, Tn, Tn·pr] (cause a liquid to) fall in drops or a thin stream: *water dribbling out (of a tap)* ○ *Dribble the oil into the beaten egg yolks.* **3** [I, Ipr, Tn, Tn·pr] (in football, hockey, etc) move (the ball) forward with repeated slight touches: *He dribbled (the ball) past the goalie to score.*

> **mal·prac·tice** /ˌmæl'præktɪs/ *n* (*law*) (**a**) [U] careless, illegal or unethical behaviour by sb in a professional or official position: *lawyers, doctors, etc sued for malpractice.* (**b**) [C] instance of this: *Various malpractices by police officers were brought to light by the enquiry.*

With which profession or field of activity do you associate the following?
What features of each extract led you to your decision?

a. This contract shall be deemed null and void should any of the aforesaid clauses not be met in any way whatsoever.

b. Our Father, Which art in Heaven, Hallowed be Thy name. Thy kingdom come, Thy will be done, on earth as it is in Heaven. Give us this day our daily bread, and forgive us our trespasses, as we forgive them that trespass against us.

c. Kessler serves, Jones returns with a backhand passing shot. Kessler volleys at the net, Jones tries to lob him but the German wins the point with a fine smash. 30–15.

d. Marinade the mixture for several hours. Then melt a knob of butter and sauté the mixture quickly. Meanwhile, dice the vegetables and simmer gently for ten minutes. Add stock to the mixture if it becomes dry. Adjust seasoning, and serve immediately, garnished with salad.

e. YARD TO PROBE RIDDLE OF DEATH PLUNGE TOT

f. I wandered lonely as a cloud That floats on high o'er vales and hills, When all at once I saw a crowd, A host, of golden daffodils.

g. Mulligan's Way is the odds-on favourite at Sandsdown today. The going is soft, and that suits this filly down to the ground.

h. He suffered a cardiac arrest and was admitted to an intensive care unit. A coronary bypass was carried out, and his condition is now stable.

i. This is an 8 bit (64 K) machine, with an inbuilt VDU and dual disk drives.

Can you think of any other professions or fields of activity for which you know some specialized vocabulary?
Tell the other students!

Listening

1 | **T.22a** | You will hear five people talking about where they come from in Britain.
At first, they won't tell you exactly where this is. Try to guess from the clues they give you (and their accents, if you can!) which part of Britain they come from.
As you listen to each person, take notes under the following headings:
– place
– people
– climate
– dialect

2 | **T.22b** | You will now hear the same five people telling you which part of Britain they come from.
Put the numbers **1** to **5** in the correct place on the map, next to one of the squares.

3 There are ten dots on the map marked **a.–j.** Match them with one of the following towns.

Birmingham ( )   Cambridge ( )
Manchester ( )   Oxford ( )
Nottingham ( )   Bristol ( )
Cardiff ( )   Bournemouth ( )
Edinburgh ( )   Belfast ( )

4 What and where are the following?
– the West Country
– East Anglia
– Londonderry
– the Pennines
– the Highlands

5 Draw in the Welsh border and the Scottish border.

▶ **Language focus**

Read the Language study on *participles* (page 103) and do the practice exercises.

Vocabulary 2
Geographical expressions

Look at the map and answer the questions. The letters refer
to the places in the questions.

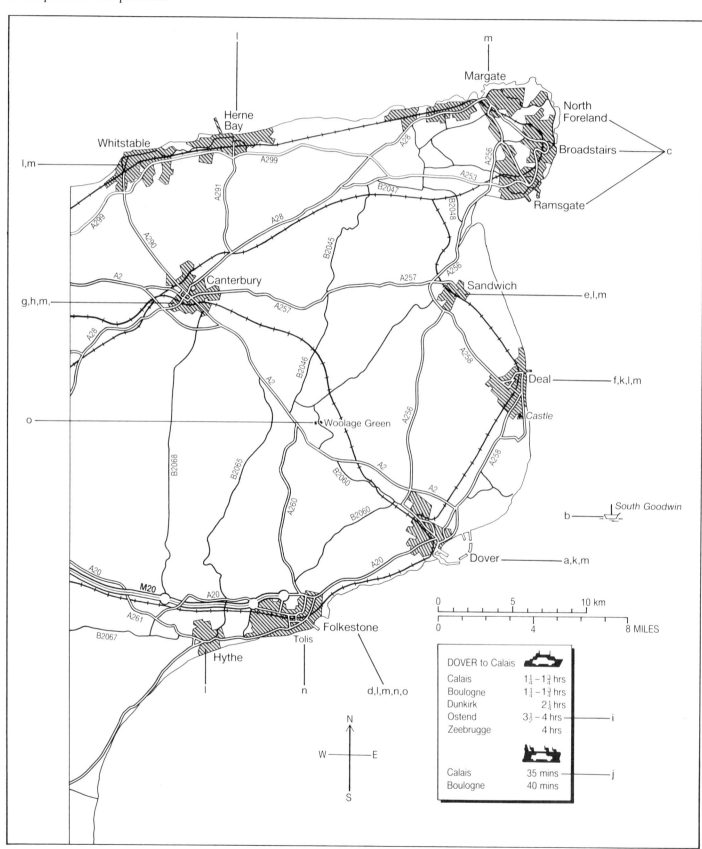

Fill in the gaps with one suitable word.

a. Dover is _____ the coast of south-east England.
b. The South Goodwin lightship is _____ the coast between Dover and Deal.
c. Broadstairs is exactly _____ between Ramsgate and North Foreland.
d. Folkstone is south-west _____ Dover.
e. Sandwich is about two miles _____ from the sea.
f. There is an ancient castle _____ the south of Deal.
g. Does the train from London to Dover stop _____ Canterbury?
h. There are a lot of attractive shops _____ Canterbury.

Here are the answers to two questions.
Look at the sailing times from Dover, and write the questions.

i. _____
   Between 3½ and 4 hours.

j. _____
   35 minutes.

Answer the following questions.

k. How far is it from Dover to Deal?
l. How do you get from Deal to Whitstable?
   (*Head north out of Deal on the A258 as far as . . .*)
   How do you get from Folkestone to Sandwich?
   How do you get from Hythe to Herne Bay?
m. Whitstable is seven miles north-west of Canterbury.
   Where is:
   – Sandwich in relation to Deal?
   – Dover in relation to Deal?
   – Margate in relation to Canterbury?
   – Folkestone in relation to Canterbury?

What do the following expressions mean?

n. Tolis is *a stone's throw* from Folkestone.
o. It's nine miles from Folkestone to Woolage Green *as the crow flies*.

Discussion

Home sweet home

Discuss the following questions in small groups.

1 Where do you consider your roots to be?
  Is it where you live now?
  If not, how often do you go back?

2 Close your eyes and think of *home*.
  What do you see?
  Are there any particular sights or smells that you associate with home? Any particular times of year?

3 Describe the part of your country that you come from in the same way as the people on the tape described their parts of Britain.
  What makes *your* part of the country special?

4 What do people from different regions in your country think of each other?
  For example, in England, those in the South think that Northerners only eat fish and chips, never wash, keep pigeons, work in coal mines, and have no taste. Those from the north think that Southerners don't know what hard work is, are afraid of getting dirty, have no sense of humour, are unfriendly, talk *posh*, and are all *sissies*. People who live in towns think that people who live in the country are *yokels*, who are illiterate and uncultured, and get drunk on cider.
  Are there similar prejudices and divides in your country?
  Why do you think they exist?

LANGUAGE STUDY

1 Relative clauses

The following sentences contain relative clauses. Say if they are examples of defining or non-defining relative clauses.

a. I met someone the other day who looks just like you.
b. Her name was Hellipop, which is a name I've never heard before.
c. She works for a company that organizes adventure holidays.
d. Some people she was talking to had been on a trip down the Amazon, which sounded very interesting.

▶ **Grammar reference: page 142.**

Practice

1 The following sentences contain some mistakes in the relative clauses. Find them and correct them.

a. All which you need to do is contact the police, that'll come immediately.
b. Someone that I really admire is Jimmy Savile, that spends all his time raising money for charities, which care for children.
c. Last night I went to a party that was unusual for me, because I don't usually go to them. I met Alison, who with I work, and she introduced me to her husband that I had never met before.

2 Put in the relative pronouns and the commas that are missing from the following sentences. If it is possible to omit the pronoun, add nothing.

a. The area of Britain _____ my family most likes to visit on holiday is Devon _____ is in the south-west of England, and _____ the weather is usually warm and sunny in summer.

b. We usually stay in a hotel _____ is run by a lovely Italian lady _____ English is almost indecipherable. There are signs in the hotel _____ nobody can understand _____ doesn't seem to matter, because everything runs very smoothly. The hotel is near the beach _____ has the highest tide in England.

c. Unfortunately, my children _____ usually eat anything _____ is put in front of them aren't terribly fond of the food _____ is served there. This is because the people _____ prepare the food most of _____ is Italian use too many herbs and spices for their liking. Everything _____ they cook is rather rich _____ suits my wife and I perfectly.

d. Also, the meal times are rather late for the children. They are used to eating at 5.30 _____ is when they are hungry after playing all day, but the restaurant doesn't open until 7.00.

e. That is one of the reasons _____ we decided to cater for ourselves this year. We stayed in a cottage _____ we saw advertised in the national press. The lady _____ cottage we rented is often abroad on business _____ is _____ she lets it out most of the year.

f. It was one of the nicest cottages _____ we have ever stayed at, and, of course, Devon is lovely. It is an area of England _____ is rich in history, and _____ offers great hospitality to its visitors.

3 Notice the possibilities when the verb in the relative clause takes a preposition.

The man	the police were **looking for**	has been found.
	for whom the police were **looking**	

In the spoken language, the first sentence pattern is the more common. The second sounds very formal. Decide whether the following sentences can be joined using both patterns, or whether only one is appropriate.

a. The man runs his own business. You were talking to him.
b. That's the man. I play tennis with him.
c. I'll give you the address. You should write to it.
d. Ministers have begun a project. Several EEC countries will take part in it.
e. The Board took a decision. The Chairman refused to accept any responsibility for it.
f. He was expressing political views. I couldn't agree with them.
g. Peter is a colleague. You can always count on his loyalty. (*Careful!*)
h. While travelling through Africa she succumbed to a tropical disease. She suffered from this for the rest of her life.

2 Participles

Present and past participles can be used in several ways.

a. As adjectives:
*a **broken** heart*
*a **blazing** fire*

b. As reduced relative clauses:
*He had a briefcase **containing** £1,000.* (that contained)

c. In adverb clauses:
*He stared out of the window, **wondering** what to do next.* (and wondered)
***Feeling** peckish, I went to see what was in the fridge.* (because I felt)

d. After certain verbs:
*I **spent** the whole summer **fishing**.*

Re-read the extracts from the three autobiographies and find examples of participles used in these ways.

▶ **Grammar reference: page 143.**

Practice

1 Complete the sentences with one of the following verbs in the correct form, either present or past participle.

want   write   employ   say   see   feel   miss

a. People _____ in the building trade have suffered many set-backs recently.
b. Firms _____ over fifty people have many legal obligations.
c. I got a letter from Jan this morning, _____ that she's expecting another baby.
d. A Van Gogh painting, _____ for over fifty years and _____ to be worth several million pounds, has been found in a Paris loft.
e. Shakespeare's first play, _____ when he was only twenty-six, was *King Henry VI, Part One*.
f. There was a lot of tension in the exam room, as all the students sat _____ as fast as they could.
g. Ronald Baines, _____ for questioning in connection with several robberies, has eluded the police for years.
h. Not _____ to get sunburnt, I sat in the shade on the beach.
i. _____ tired after a hard day's work, he fell into bed and went straight to sleep.
j. Jan Oppenheim, _____ by many to be the world's greatest opera singer, last night took Covent Garden by storm.
k. _____ that the weather was going to take a turn for the worse, we decided to stay at home.
l. _____ by millions every night, television advertisements are a powerful means of communication.

2 There is something odd about each of these sentences! Rewrite them to make them less ambiguous.
a. Rising majestically from the tropical vegetation, she gazed at the mountain with awe.
b. Walking along the beach, the sea looked warm and inviting.
c. Believed to be at least two hundred years old, I bought the painting and hung it in my living room.
d. Loosening his tie, she noticed he looked very tired.

REVISION

Nouns in groups

When nouns are put together, there are three common patterns. Most of the examples below are taken from the three autobiography extracts on pages 96–7.

a. The genitive with *-'s* or *-s'*:
Mother's prosperous days (line 5)
Daddy's tires (line 86)
a dogs' home

b. A noun followed by a prepositional phrase with **of**:
the . . . Houses of Parliament (line 11)
The last days of my childhood were also the last days of the village. (lines 29–30)
the days of the Romans (line 49)

c. Two or more nouns together, where the one(s) before the final one act as adjectives:
fruit shop (lines 7–8)
bus tickets (line 17)
village car park

Practice

1 Re-read the three extracts and find examples of the three patterns.

2 Combine the words in brackets in the following sentences, using one of the patterns. Sometimes more than one pattern is possible.

a. I always listen to my _____ (advice; parents).

b. I had to have a _____ (blood; test) to find out what was wrong.

c. Could you buy a _____ (wine; bottle) while you're at the shops?

d. Why is that flower in a _____ (wine; bottle)? Haven't you got a vase?

e. The _____ (decision; government) to close the hospital was met with incredulity.

f. Have you seen the _____ (keys; car) anywhere?

g. The _____ (disaster; announcement) left everyone stunned.

h. A _____ (salary; teacher) leaves little over for indulgences.

i. I need a good _____ (sleep; night). I'm exhausted.

j. The play is being shown at the _____ (theatre; Prince; Wales).

k. We're going to stay on my _____ (sister-in-law; farm).

l. _____ (shop; Mr Thomas) is open till nine o'clock.

m. Could you get my bag? It's in the _____ (back; car).

n. On the _____ (arrival; Queen), the crowd rose to its feet.

o. I like _____ (adventure; stories) but not _____ (films; war).

p. The _____ (post office; village) has closed down.

q. I want a copy of _____ (yesterday; newspaper). Have you got one?

r. Do you like my jumper? It's made of _____ (wool; lamb).

s. I hope you're hungry. We're having a _____ (lamb; leg) for supper.

t. Oh, what a pity! I had a _____ (chop; lamb) for lunch.

UNIT 10

Them and us

Discussion

It has often been said that Britain is a class-ridden society. It is certainly possible to make inferences about people's backgrounds from the way they behave, the car they drive, and so on.

With which social class in Britain do you associate the following?

Newspapers/magazines *The Times*   the *Sun*
the *Sporting Life*   *Country Life*   the *News of the World*

Favourite sports   football   horse racing   pigeon racing
rowing   fox-hunting   shooting   fishing   bowls   darts

Favourite drinks   Pimms   gin and tonic   bitter

Holidays   holiday camp   package holiday   tropical island

Car   Range Rover   Ford Escort   BMW

Evening entertainment   ballet   opera   working men's
club   gentlemen's club   bingo

105

Reading

Pre-reading task

You will read an article that appeared in the *Guardian* newspaper about a man called Rupert Deen, written by Polly Toynbee.
First, look at some of the letters that readers wrote to the newspaper in reaction to the article, a few days after it appeared.
Work in groups of three.

Read each letter and answer the questions.
1 Is it in favour of the article or attacking it? On what grounds?
2 What facts do you learn about Rupert Deen? What do the letter-writers think of him?
3 Having read the letters, what things do you want to find out when you actually read the article?

The amazing survival of the idle rich

Rupert Deen, Polly Toynbee discovered, was a wealthy hedonist, a relic from the age of Wooster. Not all our readers warmed to him . . .

THE PRESS and media recently made much of a man being sent to prison for refusing to work and labelled him 'super-scrounger.' In the light of Polly Toynbee's article on Rupert Deen, I take it he has inherited the title and now awaits magisterial censure.
Denham Ford,
46 Wellington Avenue,
Westcliff-on-Sea,
Essex SS0 9XB

HOW splendid to read Polly Toynbee's article on Rupert Deen! How refreshing to be away from energy crisis, USA economy, etc., etc.
We need the Ruper Deens of this world who unashamedly do what all the sane members of the human race would do if only they could afford it. And I bet he sends a few bob to Oxfam at Christmas!
Keith Lockett,
Urmston,
Manchester.

HAS Polly Toynbee nothing better to offer her women readers than the article on Ruper Deen which, at best, can be described as a total waste of space?
There are so many urgent and immediate issues relating to women and their position in society that need your coverage without resorting, surely, to writing about the apparently useless existence of people who obviously contribute nothing to society and its betterment.
Susan Alison Leach (Miss).
Social Worker.
Oxford.

AS I WAS reading Polly Toynbee's article I began to wonder whether or not I should write a letter asking the Guardian to justify wasting valuable print and space on this subject. However, as I read on to the final column, I realised that this character must surely stand as a salutary lesson to us all. His totally fascist and chauvinistic politics, manifest through his views on apartheid and women in particular are grotesque and damaging to any society.
This is an example of the product of a very particular social background; a person who lives in a very exclusive world, reads a very specific kind of newspaper and professes approval of Mrs Thatcher and the Conservative party.
Thank you for attempting to bring this state of affairs to more people's notice. I hope that other newspapers may have their consciences pricked and do the same.
N. Curry,
Brighton.

CAN Polly Toynbee really be thick? She must have realised she was being sent up something shocking by Rupert Deen. Why doesn't the Guardian give him his own column and he can do a tongue-in-cheek Nigel Dempster for us once a week.—Yours faithfully.
Norma Phillips (Mrs),
Tunbridge Wells.

(Guardian 23 August 1979)

THERE ARE different ways of being unemployed, some more pleasant than others. Rupert Deen is 40, and has never done very much to earn his living. He says his father
5 before him didn't do much either, except a bit of travelling. It was his grandfather who made a fortune out of Royal Dutch Oil.
I was put in touch with Rupert Deen by Richard Compton Miller, the London
10 gossip writer. I asked him if he could point me in the general direction of some people who didn't work for a living. He gave me quite a long list of names. But the only one who actually proved accessible was Rupert
15 Deen, who was tremendously welcoming and said of course I could come and interview him about his way of life.
He lives a luxurious bachelor life. He has never been married, and says he has no
20 intention of marrying. I was rather disappointed that he doesn't have a gentleman's gentleman. "I have Margaret from Kilburn to wash and clean for me," he said. "Of course if I wanted a gentleman's
25 gentleman I'd have one. I've always had everything I wanted, all my life. My childhood was a bit Spartan as you couldn't get things in the war, but otherwise I haven't denied myself much." I had
30 to ask how rich he was. Was he a millionaire, for instance? "It's frightfully sordid to talk about money," he said firmly.
He lives in a small Knightsbridge bijou
35 mews house, elegantly decorated with pictures of horses and hunting prints. He ushered me into his drawing room where his beautiful blonde girl friend, Amanda, and two Yorkshire farmers were drinking
40 Pimms. In the course of the interview they added their comments and expostulations, as a kind of chorus. Amanda was given to comments like "Oh Bear, *really!*" and "Oh Bear, *honestly!*" Rupert Deen is known to
45 his friends as Bear.
He started by describing for me a more or less typical day in his London life. "Well, I get up at 9.30. I go out and buy the newspapers. I get the Mail, the
50 Express, the Sporting Life, and the Financial Times. Over breakfast I read the Mail from cover to cover. Nigel Dempster is a great friend of mine. I skim through the Daily Express, and then I look at the
55 Financial Times. Next I have a bath and I read the Sporting Life. Between 11.0 and 12.0, as I complete my levee, I telephone my friends. I might do a bit of business phoning too, about horses or insurance."
60 Rupert Deen is a Lloyds underwriter — not exactly a strenuous career, an occupation closer to gambling on a large scale than to work. I asked how often he went into the office. "About two days a year,"
65 Amanda giggled. Rupert Deen said one or two days a week, when he was in town.
He sets off to lunch at 12.30. "About twice a week it's business of some sort. The rest of the time it's lunch with friends. I
70 usually go to Drones, Mimmo's, The Connaught, or the Savoy. Of course I go to the races about one day a week if it's not raining, so I wouldn't be eating in restaurants on that day; I'm in the city one

GUARDIAN WOMEN

The Upper Class

day." "I say," he added, "I hope you're commenting on my good looks, intelligence, and brilliant wit, what!"

He continued with the description of his day. "Well, then, exhausted by my tiring afternoon I'll have a bit of a rest, and get ready to go out to a dinner party or to the theatre, or films. Nothing too intellectual." He wouldn't say who his friends were, and whose dinner parties he went to. "One can't mention other people to the press," he said with surprising prissiness.

He was educated at Harrow. When he left there he went to the Ecole de Commerce at Neuchatel in Switzerland. Was that a university, I asked? "Well, kind of. I got a degree," he said. "They gave you a degree if you turned up for 22 days out of 100. I was there for a year." Did it teach him anything useful? He raised his thick eyebrows in a knowing look and said, "Not exactly academically, if you know what I mean. But you certainly built up quite a knowledge of the world."

He then went straight into Lloyds and stayed for eight years at something that was a more or less full-time job. "I just stood in queues and did what I was told," he said. "So I retired after eight years. I prefer retirement."

His year, he says, goes something like this: In May he goes to the South of France, to Monte Carlo and St Tropez. He comes back to England for Ascot in mid-June, and then Wimbledon. (Tickets, he says, are no problem). In July he goes racing at Newmarket and York, and often attends the Open Golf Championship. In August he goes to the second Test match, and shoots grouse every day after the Glorious Twelfth. In September he takes a house in St Tropez. He comes back from France, stopping in Paris for the Arc de Triomphe on the first Sunday in October. "Then I take a leisurely drive through Normandy, stopping to take in one or two studs on the way," he says. "I'm back in time to shoot one or two pheasants. Where? Oh, Hampshire, Lincolnshire, Norfolk, Scotland, everywhere."

What about November? "Oh well, November. That's my birthday. November 14, same day as Prince Charles." Does he know Prince Charles? "My lips are sealed. I said I wouldn't mention any names in this interview."

December he shoots, for even more days of the week, what he calls "Heavy shooting." The rest of the year he likes to travel to exotic countries. "I've been to Japan, Pakistan, the Khyber Pass, the Thar Desert. No, I don't mind the discomfort of sleeping out of doors, so long as one has plenty of servants. I go to South Africa occasionally. I thoroughly approve of apartheid. It works. We ought to have it here." He approves of Mrs Thatcher. "Her policies, I mean. I don't approve of her. I don't like a woman prime minister as I don't think women should have the vote, nor most men, for that matter. I think the vote should be given just to a few men, those who are well educated and who contribute to society, those who employ people, directly or indirectly." He said he definitely included himself.

I asked if he thought his way of life at all anachronistic? "Ana what? Come again? Not so much of the brainy talk." I explained, mentioning Bertie Wooster. He said, "Oh well, you see, I don't mind being a bit of a Bertie Wooster. I don't agree with the modern idea that you should work for the sake of it. Basically I'm a hedonist. I am extremely busy, you see, it's just that my energies go in a different direction to most people's." Did he ever feel that life should have some purpose? "No," he said.

(*Guardian* 13 August 1979)

Reading and inferring

Now read the article and answer the questions.

1 Why do you think Polly Toynbee wanted to interview someone who didn't work for a living?
2 What is a 'gentleman's gentleman'? What kind of work does Margaret from Kilburn do?
3 Is Rupert Deen a millionaire?
4 What impression does Polly Toynbee give of Amanda?
5 What is the busiest part of Deen's day?
6 How does Polly Toynbee describe his job?
7 What did he learn at the Swiss school?
8 What does a typical year consist of for Deen?
9 He gives restricted criteria for having the vote. Which do you think he qualifies under?
10 How honest do you think he was in the interview? The *Guardian* is a 'serious' newspaper, and Polly Toynbee is a 'serious' reporter. Do you think he was 'pulling her leg'?
11 How does Polly Toynbee want her readers to view Deen?
12 Which of the letters subsequently written to the *Guardian* do you think Polly Toynbee would most sympathize with? Which do *you* think was most appropriate?

What do you think?

1 Are there any aspects of Rupert Deen's life that you envy? Are there any of his opinions that you share?
2 Is it right that someone should have such a privileged life and do no work?
3 Which of the following describe Rupert Deen?

easy-going   sporting   liberal
sincere   ambitious   supercilious
radical   generous   charming
aristocratic   artistic

▶ Language focus

Read the Language study on *inversion to express emphasis* (page 112) and do the practice exercise.

Vocabulary 1

1 Adverb and verb collocations

Certain intensifying adverbs and verbs are often found together.

Examples
*I **thoroughly approve** of the scheme.*
*I **quite agree**.*

Put one of the following adverbs into each gap. Sometimes more than one might be possible.

sincerely	fully
seriously	strongly
completely	totally
firmly	distinctly
entirely	deeply
freely	greatly
absolutely	categorically

a. Good evening. First of all, I want to emphasize that my party _____ believes in democracy.

b. That is why we _____ hope you will vote for us at the next election.

c. There have been some smear campaigns by the opposition, but our Minister for Employment _____ denies the allegations that have been made against him.

d. He _____ admits that several mistakes were made during his tenure of office.

e. He _____ regrets that it was necessary to make three million people redundant to improve the employment situation.

f. But I _____ doubt whether the opposition could have done any better.

g. I _____ remember that in their last manifesto they said they would adopt similar measures.

h. They have _____ ignored the fact that world recession has hit every industrialized nation.

i. I am sure that this nation will _____ refuse to believe their empty promises when it goes to the polls next Thursday.

j. I _____ agree with our great Prime Minister that the road ahead will be tough.

k. I _____ admire his honesty and tenacity.

l. He _____ understands the needs of this great nation.

m. He _____ disagrees with people who aren't tolerant enough to see his point of view.

n. So I _____ advise you to vote for me. Together, we can secure the future.

2 Adverb and adjective collocations

Many intensifying adverbs and adjectives go together.

Examples
absolutely fascinating
totally destroyed

It is not always easy to know which can go together.

1 Sometimes there is a logical link between the adverb and the adjective.
Match an adverb in column **A** with an adjective in column **B**.

A	B
fully deeply bitterly perfectly	disappointed moved simple disturbed informed offended

2 Certain intensifying adverbs can only be used with *gradable* adjectives. (Gradable adjectives express qualities that can exist in different strengths.)
Which of the adverbs in column **A** and the adjectives in column **B** go together?
Sometimes more than one adverb is possible.

A	B
greatly terribly	relieved important simple annoyed impressed disappointed offended

3 Certain adjectives (called *limit* adjectives) already have very strong meanings. For example, **exhausted** means **very tired**. To intensify a limit adjective, we need an extreme adverb. This is why we *cannot* say *very **exhausted**.
Which of the adverbs in column **A** and the adjectives in column **B** go together?
Sometimes more than one adverb is possible.

A	B
absolutely totally utterly quite	delighted disgusted convinced appalled determined obvious amazed untrue

Practice

In pairs, write down some questions to ask your colleagues to which the reply will include one of the adverb/adjective collocations in Exercises 1-3.

Examples
A *What did you think of your exam results?*
B *I was **bitterly disappointed**.*
A *Are you going to take the exam again?*
B *Yes, I'm **quite determined** to pass.*

Remember you are expressing strong emotions, so make your voice sound extreme!

● Writing and speaking

You are going to prepare a speech.

1 Look again at the section on *ways of adding emphasis* on page 58 (in Unit 5) and at the Language study on *inversion to express emphasis* on page 112.

2 [**T.23**] You will hear a short political speech.
In pairs, note down the various ways in which the politician adds emphasis to what he is saying.

3 Now write your own speech.
You can choose one of the following topics, or one of your own.
– why English is the worst language to act as a world language
– the case for being a vegetarian
– why your school is the best
– dogs should not be allowed in towns
– there should be nothing on television for two days a week
– cigarettes should be banned in all public places
– the vote should be given to all people from the age of 16
– why privately owned vehicles should be banned from town centres
– people should retire at 50
– why your country should host the next Olympic Games
– the punishment should fit the crime
– chemical additives should be banned from the food we eat.

4 Deliver your speech to the rest of the class.
When you have finished, the class should take a vote to see if they support you or not!

Listening

Pre-listening task

You will hear an interview with Nigel Dempster, a journalist who writes the most famous gossip column in Britain for the *Daily Mail*.

First, discuss the following questions in groups.

1 Which people do newspapers like to gossip about in your country?
  Are they society people, pop stars, or film stars?

2 Why do people like to read gossip about the rich and famous?
  Is it envy?
  Is it to learn that they have similar weaknesses to ourselves?

3 It has been said that the Royal Family in Britain is like a soap opera.
  To what extent do you think this is a fair comparison?

4 What rumours have you heard recently about the Royal Family?

Listening for information

T.24 Now listen to the interview and answer the questions.

1 To what extent does Nigel Dempster answer the interviewer's first question?

2 In your opinion, does Nigel Dempster think his Diary has a serious purpose?

3 He quotes four kinds of stories that find their way into the Diary. Use your imagination to think of some concrete examples of each.

4 What is his attitude to the *Express*?
Why, do you think?

5 All journalists wield a lot of power.
What is the power that Nigel Dempster has over his 'subjects'?
Why does he describe them as subjects?

6 What is his point about the basic ingredient for gossip?
Do you agree?

7 How are stories about the Royal Family obtained?

8 What is his attitude to the Royal Family?

9 What is his attitude to the reporting on the Royal Family outside Britain?

What do you think?

1 Do you think such gossip columns serve a social purpose, or do they cater to baser instincts?

2 Randolph Hearst, the American newspaper publisher, said 'News is what someone, somewhere, does not want reported. All the rest is advertisement.' Can you think of any recent news stories which show the truth (or not) of this statement?

3 Randolph Hearst also said 'Dog bites man isn't news. Man bites dog is.'
What does this say about the kind of story newspapers look for?

4 Newspapers can twist stories to suit their own purposes. Consider the following stories:

An eighteen-year-old boy was in trouble with the police. Reporters asked his mother if there had been sex and drug parties at home. She was extremely shocked at the suggestion, and said 'No'.
The headline in the next day's newspaper was:

TIM'S MOTHER DENIES SEX AND DRUGS ALLEGATION.

A few years ago, the Pope was visiting New York. A reporter asked him a very silly question. 'Will you be seeing any prostitutes while you're here?'
By way of avoiding the question, the Pope asked a rhetorical question: 'Are there any prostitutes in New York?'
The newspaper next day splashed the story:

POPE'S FIRST QUESTION ON ARRIVING IN NEW YORK WAS

Do you know any similar stories?

5 If you were editor of a newspaper, which of the following stories would you decide to print? If you decided not to print, would it be because you thought people wouldn't be interested or for another reason?

An important member of the government is having an affair with his secretary. She's expecting his baby.

A highly-respected public figure of 75 was caught shop-lifting. She stole a tin of tuna.

A minor scandal about a public figure that happened twenty years ago.

The design of the bathroom suite belonging to a soap opera star.

▶ Language focus

Do the exercises on *formal and informal language* in the Language study (page 113).

Vocabulary 2
Synonyms in context

1 In the gap in the following sentences, put one word that has a similar meaning to the word in italics. Notice that sometimes the word class changes (e.g. adjective to noun).

Example
He **persisted** with the project despite all the problems, and finally his **perseverance** was rewarded.

a. Peter has the *annoying* habit of never arriving on time. It really _____ me.
b. My children *squabble* all the time. Their _____ goes on from morning till night.
c. Terrorists yesterday *attacked* an Army barracks. The _____ took place at 8.30 in the morning.
d. Acupuncture helped me a lot. It *eased* the pain in my back, and _____ the tension I've felt for so long.
e. The mountaineers pitched their tent just below the *top*. All being well, they would reach the _____ the next day.
f. Unfortunately, bad weather forced them to *retreat*. They _____ to the safety of the base camp.
g. After the accident I felt *shocked*, and the realization that I had nearly been killed left me _____ .
h. He is a very *cunning* opponent. He plays some _____ tricks.

2 Here is a list of twenty-four adjectives. Divide them into four groups consisting of three synonyms and three antonyms for the headwords below. Then write a suitable noun next to each adjective. The first one has been done.

urgent	impartial	immaculate
trivial	ancient	biased
impeccable	prejudiced	liberal
bigoted	faulty	antiquated
open-minded	faultless	vital
petty	current	essential
novel	flawed	antique
insignificant	up-to-date	second-rate

a. old

synonyms	antonyms
ancient castle	novel idea

b. fair

synonyms	antonyms

c. perfect

synonyms	antonyms

d. unimportant

synonyms	antonyms

LANGUAGE STUDY

1 Inversion to express emphasis

Certain expressions with a negative or restrictive meaning can be put at the beginning of a sentence for emphasis. This happens mainly in written English or in a very formal style of speaking, such as a public speech. Notice that the order of the subject and the verb is reversed. Inversion can also take place with certain conditional sentences. Compare the following sentences.

*I have **never** seen* such a badly behaved child!
***Never** have I seen* such a badly behaved child!

*One **rarely** finds* such a splendid example of his
***Rarely** does one find* work.

*I had **hardly** glanced at the report* when I was asked for
***Hardly** had I glanced at the report* my opinion.

*If you **should** find cause for complaint,* return the goods
***Should you** find cause for complaint,* immediately.

*If Holmes **hadn't** explained,* Watson would never have
***Had Holmes not** explained,* understood the case.

Emphatic structures must *sound* emphatic and formal! Practise saying them.

▶ **Grammar reference: page 144.**

Practice

Rewrite the following sentences, inverting the subject and verb, and using one of the patterns from the Grammar section.

a. The Director will never give in to public pressure.
b. As soon as the meeting started, fighting broke out in the audience.
c. Henry didn't suspect his brother of complicity in the crime for one moment.

d. I have never been so surprised in all my life.
e. You will not find craftsmanship of such quality anywhere.
f. I will never allow such practices to take place again.
g. He announced his discovery to the world only when he was certain of his results.
h. Good whisky is ready for consumption only after it has matured for ten years.
i. This government has deceived the public, and it has deceived itself.
j. This door should not be left open under any circumstances.
k. The values of our society are at risk, and the very survival of the nation is threatened.
l. This country has never been so threatened before.
m. Artists are rarely appreciated while they are still alive.
n. Children little realize that their world of innocence soon disappears.
o. I didn't intend to deceive you at any time.
p. If I ever told you a lie, I wouldn't be able to look you in the eye.
q. I respect her opinions, and I admire her character greatly as well.
r. If you require any further information, don't hesitate to contact me.
s. I haven't had to study so hard since I was at university.
t. If I hadn't witnessed the experiment with my own eyes, I would never have believed it could be done. (*two possible inversions*)

2 Formal and informal language

1 In the following extracts, styles have been mixed. Find the parts of each extract where the style is inappropriate, and rewrite them.

   a. Good evening. Here is the news. In the House of Commons a couple of hours ago, the debate about what's been going on in the National Health Service ended. The vote was close but the Government just got it. At one point, the Speaker of the House had to intervene as two Members of Parliament had a bloody great row about the financing of the Service. The Honourable Member for East Croydon reckoned that he had been unfairly treated, and accused the Prime Minister of telling fibs.

   b. Now listen, kids. I am not prepared to negotiate any further. Either you two tidy your room at this very moment in time, or there's no way I'll accompany you to the cinema, as was promised.

   c. A Dearly Beloved brethren. We have all come together to witness the marriage of James and Anne. James, how do you feel about taking Anne as your lawful, wedded wife?
      B Righto.

   d. Much research has been carried out to increase the fertility of the farm chicken. Several million pounds has been spent in this quest, and results have been promising. Consequently, lots and lots of tiny chick-chicks have come clucking into the world.

2 From the examples, discuss what makes a text more or less formal. Think of vocabulary and the complexity of the sentence.

3 In the following letter, select the item that is more formal.

26 May 1987

Dear Ms Denton

Thanks / Thank you | for your letter of 24 May. As I am sure you will | understand, / appreciate,

I am | most upset / very sorry | to | hear / learn | that you | were unable to / could not | locate my

suitcase. As I | said / pointed out | in my original letter, the suitcase contained

| a lot of / many | documents that I | need / require | for my | job. / work. | I have | had / been obliged

to | contact / get in touch with | my publishers to | get hold of / obtain | copies of documents that

your airline | lost. / mislaid. Naturally, / Of course, | I will | complete / fill in | the Claim Form,

but | I find it difficult / it is not easy | to | estimate / guess | the value of the documents.

About / Approximately | half of them are irreplaceable.

I | hope / trust | that in the meantime you | are still looking / continue to look | for my case.

Should you find it, / If you find it, | please contact me | straight away. / immediately.

I | look / am looking | forward to hearing from you.

Your sincerely,

James Burke

James Burke

4 Write a reply to the letter.

You are Ms Denton of the Lost Luggage Department. Mr Burke's suitcase has been found. It was accidentally routed to Moscow. Give details about how it will be sent to him. Apologize for any inconvenience. Offer him £200 compensation, and say that your airline will reimburse him for any expenses he has incurred.

Point out that your search for his case was hampered because his description of it was inaccurate. End with a 'sugary' comment about hoping that he will continue to use your airline!

REVISION

Pronouns – 'one', 'you', and 'they'

One, you, and **they** can all be used to refer to people impersonally. Here are some examples from the article about Rupert Deen.

One can't mention other people to the press. (line 84)
I don't mind . . . sleeping out of doors, so long as one has plenty of servants. (line 136)
I don't agree with the modern idea that you should work for the sake of it. (line 156)
They gave you a degree if you turned up for 22 days out of 100. (line 91)

One and **you** are used to mean 'people in general'. **One** is mainly written, and is (very) formal; **you** is informal.
They can be used to avoid the passive.

Example
I see they're knocking down that old building. What a pity!

This is more common in informal, spoken English than *I see that old building is being knocked down.*

They can also refer to unknown people who have the power or authority that we (ordinary) people do not have, and who we probably regard with mistrust. Hence the title of this unit, 'Them and us'.

Practice

In the following sentences, put one of the pronouns (or the possessive) into each gap.
a. Don't count _____ chickens before they hatch.
b. _____ said on the radio that we're in for a cold spell. Brr!
c. 'When _____ is in love, _____ always begins by deceiving _____, and _____ always ends by deceiving others. This is what the world calls a romance.' (Oscar Wilde)
d. Well, that was a turn-up for the books! It just goes to show _____ never can tell!

e. As soon as it snows in this country, all the trains stop. _____'d think _____'d manage to get *some* of them going, wouldn't _____?
f. What I've always said is that _____ should do to other people as _____ want/wants them to do to _____.
g. I had to go to court yesterday. _____ fined me fifty pounds for parking in the wrong place. Can you imagine!
h. Look at that 1930 Rolls Royce! _____ don't make them like _____ used to!
i. _____ always have/has to be careful with credit cards that _____ don't/doesn't go over _____ credit limit.
j. I hear _____'ve set up a way _____ can do all _____ shopping by television. Amazing what _____ can do these days!

115

UNIT 11

The brain

Problem solving

Problems are usually solved with the help of logic. Consider the following problems and try to solve them logically and as quickly as possible.

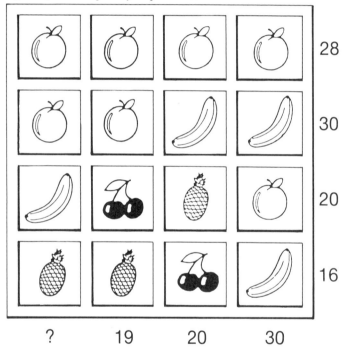

28
30
20
16

?   19   20   30

1 Work out the missing total for the left-hand column.

2 In this series, which number comes next?
    18   12   15   10   12   8   ?

3 Continue this series of letters
    BAD   CEF   DIG   FOH

4 20 men can dig 40 holes in 60 days, so 10 men can dig 20 holes in how many days?

5 *City* is to *man* as *nest* is to
    a. *bird*   **b.** *bee*   **c.** *ant*   **d.** *rabbit*

6 Which sport is played *at* the same as it is played *with*?

7 In this group which word does not belong?
    a. sadness   **b.** melancholy   **c.** sorrow   **d.** mourning

8 Someone had stolen the last chocolate cake. The three suspects were Paul, Ben, and Sam. They each made a statement:

Paul Ben stole the cake.
Ben That is true!
Sam I didn't take it!

As it happened, at least one of them told the truth and at least one of them lied. So, who in fact stole the cake?

Check the answers with your teacher.

Listening and pairwork

T.25 You will hear the beginning of an interview with Edward de Bono, a man who has done much to try and develop the skills of thinking and problem solving. He is particularly interested in 'lateral' (as opposed to 'logical') thinking and tells a story to illustrate the difference.
Listen to the introduction and the first part of de Bono's story about the worms.
Try to think of as many reasons as you can as to why there are only two holes.
Now listen to de Bono's answer and check your ideas with his solution.
Can you now explain the difference between logical and lateral thinking?

Consider these problems.

1 A man goes into a bar and asks for a drink of water. The barmaid gives him the drink and then suddenly screams. What possible explanations are there?

2 Lying on the ground in the centre of a field are a hat, a scarf, a pipe, some pieces of coal, and a carrot. What possible explanations could there be for this?

3 A man lives on the thirteenth floor of a block of flats. Every day he goes out to work, gets into the lift, and goes down to the ground floor. Every day when he comes home he gets into the lift and travels to the eighth floor, gets out, and then walks up the stairs to the thirteenth floor. Why?

Vocabulary 1

Idiomatic expressions

Study these dictionary entries for the words **mind** and **brain**.
Can you find the basic differences in meaning?
Work in pairs.

mind[1] /maɪnd/ n **1** [U] ability to be aware of things and to think and feel: *have the right qualities of mind for the job* ○ *have complete peace of mind.* **2** [C] (**a**) ability to reason; intellectual powers: *have a brilliant, logical, simple, etc mind.* (**b**) person who uses his reasoning or intellectual powers well: *He is one of the greatest minds of the age.* **3** [C] person's thoughts or attention: *Are you quite clear in your own mind what you ought to do?* ○ *Don't let your mind wander!* **4** [C] ability to remember; memory: *I can't think where I've left my umbrella; my mind's a complete blank!* **5** [U, C] normal condition of one's mental faculties; sanity: *be sound in mind and body* ○ *He's 94 and his mind is going,* ie he is becoming senile. **6** (idm) **absence of mind** ⇨ ABSENCE. **at the back of one's mind** ⇨ BACK[1]. **be in one's right mind** ⇨ RIGHT[1]. **be in two 'minds about sth/doing sth** feel doubtful about or hesitate over sth: *I was in two minds about leaving London: my friends were there, but the job abroad was a good one.* **be of one 'mind (about sb/sth)** agree or have the same opinion (about sb/sth). **be on one's 'mind; have sth on one's 'mind** (cause sb to) worry about sth: *My deputy has resigned, so I've got a lot on my mind just now.* **be ,out of one's 'mind** (*infml*) be crazy or mad: *You must be out of your mind if you think I'm going to lend you £50!* **be/ take a load/weight off sb's mind** cause one/sb great relief: *Paying my mortgage was an enormous weight off my mind!* **bear in mind that...** ⇨ BEAR[2]. [. . .] **have a mind of one's 'own** be capable of forming opinions, making decisions, etc independently. **have a (good) mind to do sth** (*infml*) have a (strong) desire to do sth:
□ **'mind-bending** *adj* (*infml*) strongly influencing the mind: *a mind-bending problem.* **'mind-blowing** *adj* (*infml*) (of drugs or extraordinary sights, experiences, etc) causing mental excitement, ecstasy, hallucinations, etc. **'mind-boggling** *adj* (*infml*) alarming; extraordinary or astonishing: *Distances in space are quite mind-boggling.* Cf BOGGLE SB'S MIND (BOGGLE). **'mind-reader** *n* person who claims to know what another person is thinking. **'mind-reading** *n* [U].
mind·less /'maɪndlɪs/ *adj* **1** not requiring intelligence: *mindless drudgery.* **2** (*derog*) lacking in intelligence; thoughtless: *mindless vandals.* **3** [pred] ~ **of sb/sth** (*fml*) not thinking of sb/sth; heedless of sb/sth: *mindless of personal risk.* ▷ **mind·lessly** *adv.* **mind·less·ness** *n* [U].

brain /breɪn/ *n* **1** [C] organ of the body that controls thought, memory and feeling, consisting of a mass of soft grey matter inside the head: *a disease of the brain* ○ *The brain is the centre of the nervous system.* ○ [attrib] *brain surgery.* **2** [U, C often *pl*] mind or intellect; intelligence: *He has very little brain.* ○ *She has an excellent brain.* ○ *You need brains to become a university professor.* ○ *He has one of the best brains in the university.* **3** (**a**) [C] (*infml*) clever person; intellectual: *He is one of the leading brains in the country.* (**b**) **the brains** [sing *v*] (*infml*) cleverest person in a group: *He's the brains of the family.* ○ *She was the brains behind the whole scheme.* **4** (idm) **blow one's brains out** ⇨ BLOW[1]. **cudgel one's brains** ⇨ CUDGEL. **have sth on the brain** (*infml*) think about sth constantly; be obsessed by sth: *I've had this tune on the brain all day but I can't remember what it's called.* **pick sb's brains** ⇨ PICK[3]. **rack one's brain(s)** ⇨ RACK[2]. **tax one's/sb's brains** ⇨ TAX. ▷ **brain** *v* [Tn] kill (a person or an animal) with a heavy blow on the head: (*fig infml*) *I nearly*

brained myself on that low beam.
brain·less *adj* stupid; foolish: *That was a pretty brainless thing to do.*
brain·storm /'breɪnstɔːm/ *n* **1** sudden violent mental disturbance. **2** (*Brit infml*) moment of confusion or forgetfulness; sudden mental aberration: *I must have had a brainstorm — I couldn't remember my own telelphone number for a moment.* **3** (*US infml*) = BRAINWAVE.
brain·storm·ing /'breɪnstɔːmɪŋ/ *n* [U] (*esp US*) method of solving problems in which all the members of a group suggest ideas which are then discussed: [attrib] *a brainstorming session.*
brain·wash /'breɪnwɒʃ/ *v* [Tn, Tn·pr] ~ **sb (into doing sth)** force sb to reject old beliefs or ideas and to accept new ones by the use of extreme mental pressure: (*fig*) *I refuse to be brainwashed by advertisers into buying something I don't need.* ▷ **brain·wash·ing** *n* [U].
brain·wave /'breɪnweɪv/ (*US* **brainstorm**) *n* (*infml*) sudden clever idea: *Unless someone has a brainwave we'll never solve this problem.*

pick[3] /pɪk/ *v* **pick sb's 'brains** ask sb questions in order to obtain information that one can use oneself: *I need a new French dictionary. Can I pick your brains about the best one to buy?* **pick a 'fight/**

▷ **rack** *v* **1** [Tn] torture (sb) on the rack. **2** [Tn esp passive] (of disease, pain or mental distress) cause agony to (sb): *racked with pain, fever, etc* ○ *A coughing fit racked her whole body.* ○ *a voice racked by sobs/weeping* ○ *racked by (feelings of) guilt, remorse, doubt, etc.* **3** (idm) **rack one's 'brain(s)** try hard to think of sth or recall sth: *We racked our brains for an answer.* ○ *I've been racking my brains (trying) to remember his name.*

Answer the questions. You will need to look at the two cross-references to **rack** and **pick** as well.

1. What is the difference between the following pairs, or groups, of words and expressions?
   a. mindless/brainless
   b. brainwave/brainwashing
   c. to have something on the brain/to have something on one's mind
   d. to have an excellent brain/to have a good mind to
   e. to have a brainstorm/mind-blowing/to be out of one's mind
   f. to rack one's brains/to pick someone's brains
   g. to be in two minds about something/to have a mind of one's own.

2. In the following sentences replace the words in italics with a word or expression from Exercise 1, making any necessary changes to fit the context.
   a. I've just had a *brilliant idea*!
   b. She's so clever that everyone in the class *asks her for ideas*.
   c. We really *aren't sure* whether we should buy that house or not. It's big and beautiful but it needs so much doing to it.
   d. You must be *mad* to give up such a well-paid job.
   e. I've *thought and thought about it* and I still can't remember where I put it.
   f. We looped the loop and nosedived towards the ground – it was the most *amazing* experience. And I don't even like flying!

Reading

Pre-reading task

1 How many synonyms or near synonyms can you think of for the word **mad**?
Check in your dictionaries and pool your ideas.
2 Which of the words and expressions you have collected are used to describe the medical condition?
Which can be used more informally?

Scan reading

You will read an extract from a book called *Mindwatching*, which describes an experiment conducted by David Rosenhan, a psychologist at Stanford University in California.

Read the extract quickly and decide which of the following was the main purpose of the experiment.

Was the aim to prove:
– that psychiatrists are too quick to admit people to mental homes?
– that psychiatrists and doctors are out of touch with their patients?
– that it is often very difficult even for psychiatrists to distinguish between the sane and the insane?
– that all supposedly sane people have elements of insanity?

Now read the extract in more detail and answer the questions.

[1] Rosenhan wondered what would happen if a number of entirely sane people attempted to gain admission to a mental hospital by pretending to have one of the symptoms of insanity. Would these
5 sane individuals be classified as insane? If they were admitted to the mental hospital, would the staff realize that a mistake had been made?
[2] The answers to these and other questions were obtained in a study in which eight normal people,
10 five men and three women, attempted to gain admission to twelve different psychiatric hospitals. They consisted of a young psychology graduate, a paediatrician, a psychiatrist, three psychologists, a painter, and a housewife. The twelve psychiatric
15 hospitals were located in five different states on the East and the West Coasts of America. They also varied considerably, ranging from relatively new to old and shabby, and from good staff-patient ratios to severe under-staffing.
20 [3] Each of the eight participants phoned the hospital asking for an appointment. Upon arrival at the admissions office, each of them complained of hearing voices (these voices were often unclear, but appeared to be saying 'empty', 'hollow', and
25 'thud'; they sounded unfamiliar but were of the same sex as the participant).
[4] The only important elements of deception were the claims about hearing voices and falsification of the participants' names and occupations; the
30 significant events in each participant's life were described as they actually happened. All of these sane people were judged to be insane, and all of them were admitted to hospital, apparently on the basis of their hallucinations. One of them was
35 diagnosed as suffering from manic-depressive psychosis; the others were diagnosed as schizophrenic.
[5] As soon as these pseudo-patients had been admitted to the psychiatric ward, they stopped
40 simulating signs of abnormality, although several experienced a brief period of nervousness and anxiety, because they felt they would immediately be exposed as frauds, which would be highly embarrassing.
45 [6] While they were in the psychiatric ward, the pseudo-patients indicated that they were fine and no longer experienced any symptoms. In general, they behaved in a friendly and co-operative way. The only unusual aspect of their behaviour was that
50 they spent a fair amount of time writing down their observations about the ward, its patients, and the staff. To begin with, these notes were written secretly, but as it gradually became clear that no one took much notice, the note-taking was done
55 quite openly.

7 The hierarchical structure of the various psychiatric hospitals was such that those of greater professional status had the least to do with their patients (and pseudo-patients). The average daily
60 contact of the pseudo-patients with psychiatrists, psychologists, and doctors was 6.8 minutes. In view of this general lack of careful observation by those in authority, it is not surprising that the pseudo-patients were not released very quickly. The actual
65 length of hospitalization ranged from 7 to 52 days, with 19 days being the average.

8 The fact that all the pseudo-patients were released within a few weeks of admission may suggest that the psychiatric staff discovered that the pseudo-
70 patients had been sane all the time. However, this was not the case. All the pseudo-patients were discharged with a diagnosis of 'schizophrenia in remission', indicating that the deception had not been detected.

75 9 Interestingly, several of the real patients became suspicious about the pseudo-patients. The first three pseudo-patients were placed in wards containing a total of 118 patients, 35 of whom voiced their doubts. They said things like, 'You're
80 not crazy. You're a journalist, or a professor. You're checking up on the hospital.' However most of them were reassured by the pseudo-patients' insistence that they had been sick before they came into hospital, though they felt fine once
85 they had been admitted. Nevertheless a few of the bona-fide patients continued to voice the opinion that the pseudo-patients were sane.

10 If we accept these findings at face value, they suggest that the distinction between the sane and
90 the insane is so blurred that it is entirely possible for the sane to be mistaken for the insane, at least by psychiatrists. Rosenhan wondered whether he could show the opposite effect, namely the insane being regarded as sane. He used as his testing
95 ground a research and teaching hospital. The staff there had heard about the study just described, and had informed Rosenhan that they would not have proved so gullible.

11 The first thing that Rosenhan did was to tell the
100 staff of this hospital that one or more pseudo-patients would attempt to gain admission at some time during the following three months. Each member of staff was asked to observe all patients who presented themselves for admission or in the
105 ward and say whether they thought they were pseudo-patients or genuine patients.

12 Judgements were obtained on a total of 193 patients admitted for psychiatric treatment. Forty-one genuine patients were judged with great
110 confidence to be pseudo-patients by at least one member of staff. Nineteen patients were suspected

of being frauds by one of the psychiatrists and another member of staff. In fact, none of Rosenhan's pseudo-patients sought admittance
115 during this time. Apparently, then, mental hospital staff do sometimes think that people committed to their care are sane.

13 Rosenhan's main conclusion, which is tremendously important if it is true, was as follows:
120 'It is clear that we cannot distinguish the sane from the insane in psychiatric hospitals.' Part of the problem may be that, under normal circumstances, doctors and psychiatrists are more inclined to call a healthy person sick than a sick person healthy. It is
125 obviously dangerous for a doctor to fail to take appropriate action when a sick person asks for treatment. A psychiatrist who refuses to hospitalize someone who has suspicious symptoms and asks to be hospitalized may face legal action if the patient
130 subsequently commits suicide or murder, so it is natural for him to err on the side of caution.

Comprehension check

1 Which paragraph(s) do the following summaries refer to?
   a. how the pseudo-patients behaved while they were in the hospital
   b. how we know that the deception was not detected
   c. the reasons for the original experiment
   d. the supervision of patients in the hospital
   e. the kind of people who were selected for the experiment
   f. the reaction of the real patients to the pseudo-patients
   g. how the pseudo-patients deceived the experts to gain admittance
   h. Rosenhan's conclusion
   i. the results of the second experiment
   j. the reasons for the second experiment
   k. how the second experiment was set up.

2 Work in groups of three.
   Without looking back at the passage, make notes under the summary headings, using them in the right order.

3 Still in groups, work together to produce a summary of the extract, using appropriate linking words to join your ideas.

What do you think?

1 Are you surprised at the results of these experiments?
2 These experiments took place in the USA. Do you think that attitudes to psychiatry are different there from in your own country? If so, how? Why?
3 Would you agree to take part in such an experiment if it were held in your country?

Vocabulary

The following are dictionary definitions of words or phrases in the text. Find these words. The definitions are presented in the same order as the words appear.

a. to be in bad repair or condition
b. dull sound, as of a blow on something soft
c. person or thing that deceives
d. real or genuine
e. what something seems to be from appearances
f. unclear and confused
g. easily deceived or cheated.

▶ Language focus

Read the Language study on *hypothesizing* (page 122) and do the practice exercises.

Listening

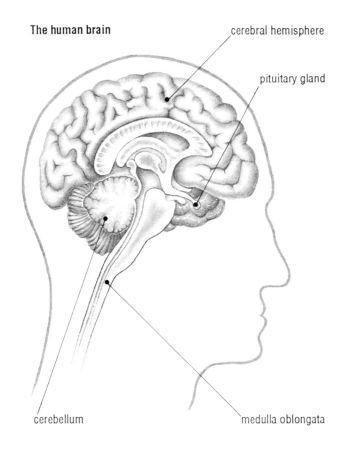

The human brain

cerebral hemisphere

pituitary gland

cerebellum

medulla oblongata

Pre-listening task

Work in pairs.
What do you know about the workings of the brain?
How does the human brain differ from that of animals?

Do you think the following statements are true or false?
Write **T** or **F** in each box.

T/F

1 The brain of a young child is more receptive than that of an adult. ☐

2 If the brain is regularly used and stimulated we can continue to learn the older we get. ☐

3 If you don't challenge your brain for as long as twenty years you will never be able to use it properly again. ☐

4 The only permanent cause of brain deterioration is disease or physical damage. ☐

5 People who are good with their hands are not usually very brainy. ☐

6 The human brain has increased in size over the years. ☐

7 Very soon the human brain will be so large that our bodies will become top-heavy. ☐

8 Scientists believe that if human beings live permanently in the weightlessness of space, the human form will change. ☐

Listening and checking

T.26 Listen to an interview with Tony Buzan, who has written several books on the brain and how to use it more effectively.
Check your true/false answers, and amend them if necessary.

What do you think?

1 Did anything that Tony Buzan said surprise you?
2 Do you know anything about research that is being done on the functioning of the brain?

▶ Language focus

Read the Language study on the *Present Subjunctive* (page 123) and do the practice exercise.

Speaking and writing

1 Work in groups of three.
  Look at the cartoon and decide on a title to suit the story.
  Decide on names for the characters, then work together
  to tell the story.
  Try to incorporate as naturally as possible some of the
  following expressions and structures: **wish**; **if only**; **would
  rather**; **it's time**; **it's about time**; conditional sentences;
  structures which take the present subjunctive.

  Begin like this:
  For many years, Mr . . . had been suffering from . . .

2 Write the story, incorporating appropriate linking words.
3 When you have finished, read your story to the rest of the
  class.

Vocabulary 2
Nouns formed from multi-word verbs

Compound nouns, consisting of a verb and a particle, are one of the fastest growing areas of vocabulary in English. Sometimes their meaning is related to the corresponding multi-word verb, and sometimes not.

Examples
*There was a **walk-out** at the factory* (Workers walked out.)
*The company's **output** increased by ten per cent.* (NB: but **to put out** does *not* mean to produce.)

Sometimes the words are written as one word, and sometimes they are hyphenated.
You need to check them in a dictionary.
Sometimes the particle comes first, and sometimes the verb comes first, but the stress is almost always on the first word:

'walk-out   'output   'bypass   'take-over

Practice

Complete the sentences with a compound noun formed from the particle which heads each group, and a verb from the following list.

black	cover	draw	hand	shake
break	cry	fall	look	stand
come	cut	flash	set	tip

The particle may come before or after the verb.

back
a. Your plan has many advantages, but unfortunately there is one major _____. It would be far too expensive.
b. Government _____ in the medical profession have caused severe staffing problems in many hospitals.
c. Her hopes of winning a gold medal suffered a serious _____ when she was injured at the beginning of the season.
d. It is only towards the end of the film that we learn the hero's motives through several _____ to his childhood.

out
e. The meeting was long and stormy, and the _____ was the resignation of the director.
f. I was knocked on the head in the accident, and I had a _____ that lasted about ten minutes. I don't remember anything that happened.
g. There was a public _____ when it was discovered that the government had been selling arms to the rebels.
h. 'You don't need to take notes,' said the teacher. 'I've got a _____ to give you with all the information.'
i. He always used to be a miserable sort of person, but after his illness, when he nearly died, his whole _____ on life changed and he began to appreciate what it had to offer.

down
j. He had a promising career, but gambling was his _____. In a few years he had lost every penny he owned.
k. The earthquake caused a complete _____ of communications in the country, which greatly hampered rescue operations.

up
l. When the new director was appointed, there was a complete _____ of the whole organization as he tried to streamline our operations.
m. The government tried to hide the facts of the awful mistake they had made, but their _____ didn't work, and gradually all the details of the disaster came out.

by
n. The school always has two teachers on _____ to step in should anyone be ill or late.

off
o. The criminal that the police had been looking for since May was arrested at a house near Glasgow following an anonymous _____ from a member of the public.

LANGUAGE STUDY

1 Hypothesizing

1 The following sentences all contain verbs in the Simple Past, but they do not always refer to real past time. Read through them and decide which refer to the *real, factual* past.
   a. Suppose the brain grew too heavy for the human body to support!
   b. He would wave whenever he walked past the house.
   c. I couldn't swim until I was fourteen.
   d. If I could afford it, I'd buy it.
   e. It's an hour since we had a break.
   f. Isn't it time you had a holiday?
   g. Did you fall in love at first sight?
   h. I'd rather you didn't tell anyone about this.
   i. He behaves as if he owned the place.
   j. If only he weren't so rude!
   k. I wish you didn't have to go.
   l. You didn't say if you had to go.

   What do the sentences that *don't* refer to the past have in common?

2 The following sentences all contain verbs in the Past Perfect, but they do not always refer to the real past-in-the-past.
   Read them through and decide which refer to the *real* past-in-the-past.
   a. I wish you hadn't said that. It was very cruel.
   b. I knew I'd seen her somewhere before.

c. Had I realized how upset she was, I would have apologized.

d. Suppose the atom bomb had never been invented! Just think!

e. She said I hadn't told her the truth.

f. I would rather you had told the truth.

g. You look as if you'd seen a ghost!

h. He looked as if he'd had a good time.

What do the sentences that *don't* refer to the past-in-the-past have in common?

▶ **Grammar reference: page 144.**

Practice

1 Finish the following sentences in such a way that each means the same as the sentence above it.

a. It's such a pity, I always forget people's names.
I wish . . .

b. It's a shame you live so far from us.
I wish . . .

c. It worries me that you smoke so much.
If only . . .

d. Don't tell lies! It's very upsetting.
If only . . .

2 How many correct and natural sentences can you make from this table?

I wish	I	remembered	his birthday.
		would remember	
He wishes	he	could remember	my birthday.
		had remembered	

3 Put the verb in brackets in an appropriate tense to express either fact or non-fact as appropriate. Where there is no verb (_____), insert an auxiliary verb.

A This hotel is horrible. I wish we (a) _____ (not come) here. I (b) _____ never _____ (see) such a dirty hotel in my life! If only the bathroom (c) _____ (be) clean, I (d) _____ (can) have a bath, but it (e) _____ (be) filthy in there. I (f) _____ even _____ (not wash) my socks in it!

B I know, but it (g) _____ (get) late, we (h) _____ (drive) all day, and I (i) _____ (want) to stop. We might not have found another hotel for miles! Then where (j) _____ we _____ (stay)? This is better than nothing. At least we can get something to eat. It's time we (k) _____ (go) down to the restaurant. It closes soon. We (l) _____ (find) somewhere nicer tomorrow, I (m) _____ (promise).

A All right. If it (n) _____ (be) so late, I (o) _____ (suggest) we (p) _____ (go) into town to look for somewhere else to eat, but if we (q) __ __ __, we might not find anywhere. It's quite late already.

B I wish you (r) _____ (stop) moaning about everything I (s) _____ (decide) to do. You (t) _____ (be) so indecisive, if it (u) _____ (be) up to you, we (v) _____ (never decide) to do anything!

A All right! Let's go. I'm hungry.

2 The Present Subjunctive

The Present Subjunctive is formed with the base form of the verb (which is the infinitive without **to**). It is used in **that** clauses after verbs, adjectives, or nouns that express a necessity, plan, or intention for the future. Notice that the subjunctive is the same whether the sentence is present or past.

Examples
They demanded | *that he **consider** his situation carefully.*
She suggests

It is important | *that she **be admitted** to hospital*
The proposal was | *immediately.*

The Present Subjunctive can be avoided by using **should** in the **that** clause.

Examples
*They demanded that he **should consider** his situation carefully.*
*The proposal was that she **should be admitted** to hospital immediately.*

▶ **Grammar reference: page 145.**

Practice

Finish the following sentences so that each means the same as the sentence above it. Do this in two ways, one with the Present Subjunctive and one with **should**.

a. 'Why don't you study maths at evening class?' she said to him.
She suggested that he . . .

b. 'Let's finish the meeting on time,' he said to them.
He proposed . . .

c. 'Take the prisoner below deck and tie him up!' shouted the captain.
The captain commanded . . .

d. 'If I were you, I'd have the beef,' said the waiter.
The waiter recommended . . .

e. 'The minutes of the meeting must be read,' said the chairperson.
The chairperson insisted . . .

f. The contract must be signed by all parties.
It is important . . .

g. The candidates must have a thorough medical examination.
It is essential . . .

h. 'I would like a full inquiry to take place,' said the Prime Minister.
The Prime Minister requested . . .

123

REVISION

Informal speech

1 Match lines from column **A** with lines from column **B** to form two-line dialogues.

A	B
1 What a horrible day!	a. I know. I wasn't born yesterday.
2 I'm going to do it whether you like it or not!	b. We have our ups and downs.
3 I paid the tax bill just in time.	c. Just a few bits and bobs.
4 How do you get on with her?	d. I blew it.
5 You look very chuffed.	e. You dare!
6 Can you lend me a fiver?	f. Serves you right!
7 How did you manage to finish the job so quickly?	g. You might as well. You've got nothing to lose.
8 Could you mend this, Dad and get me a drink of juice?	h. You can say that again!
9 No, no. This is how you do it.	i. Hang on! I've only got one pair of hands!
10 How was your exam?	j. It's a good job too.
11 Did you buy anything?	k. Piece of cake!
12 I'll ask her what her politics are.	l. Not half! It was great.
13 My stomach hurts. I've eaten too much.	m. I wouldn't. It's a touchy subject.
14 Do you think I should try again?	n. No way! Sorry.
15 Did you enjoy the party?	o. Yes, I've just had some good news.

1 _____   4 _____   7 _____   10 _____   13 _____
2 _____   5 _____   8 _____   11 _____   14 _____
3 _____   6 _____   9 _____   12 _____   15 _____

2 Work in pairs.
   Write a short dialogue, incorporating some examples of informal speech.
   When you have finished, read it out loud to your colleagues.

UNIT 12

The meaning of life

Discussion

Work in groups to answer the questions.

1 Link each of the pictures with one of the religions listed below.

Christianity   Judaism
Islam   Buddhism
Hinduism
an ethnic religion (not a world religion, i.e. belonging to a restricted area)

In which part of the world do you think each of the pictures has its origin?

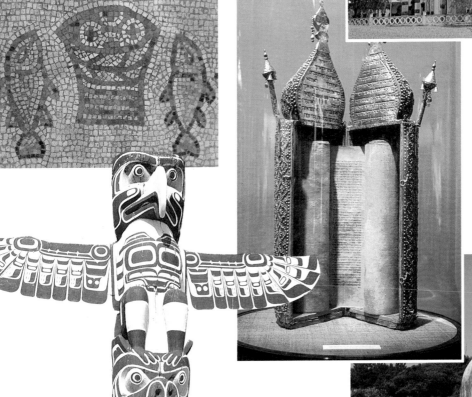

2 Which religion:
   a. has the largest number of adherents in the world?
   b. has the second largest number of adherents?
   c. divides families into four castes which rarely mix?
   d. began in India in approximately 1500 BC?
   e. began as a breakaway from Hinduism in approximately 500 BC?
   f. has a fish as one of its symbols?
   g. believes that Adam, Abraham, Jesus, and Muhammad were all prophets?
   h. believes in Brahman, the Absolute?
   i. believes in Allah?
   j. believes that on the Day of Judgement, men and women will be raised from the dead and will appear before God to be judged and assigned to Heaven or Hell?
   k. believes it is the only true religion?

3 Are the following statements true or false?
   a. Fundamentalist Christians in America reject Darwin's theory of evolution, and maintain that the world was created as described in the Old Testament.
   b. The Koran is the oldest surviving example of religious literature.
   c. Hinduism says that, at death, the soul passes into another body until released from the continuous wheel of rebirth.
   d. Moses led the Hebrews out of Egypt in about 100 BC.
   e. Jehovah's Witnesses will not accept blood transfusions.
   f. Mormons believe that Jesus Christ visited America after his resurrection.

4 What do different religions have in common?
   Think of the following:
   – belief in a deity
   – a doctrine (a set of beliefs)
   – a code of conduct (how people should act and behave)
   – the use of sacred stories
   – rituals and ceremonies
   – hierarchies

5 What ethnic religions do you know of?

Reading

Pre-reading task

1 Here is the first part of an article that you will read from the *Guardian* newspaper.
   Check that you understand the following words:

   brink   comatose
   tantalizing trauma
   glimpse   after-effects

   Now read the first part of the article.

On the brink of tranquillity

People who are unexpectedly brought back to life frequently claim to have enjoyed a tantalising, and encouraging, glimpse of the condition to come. David Lorimer investigates the Near Death Experience

IT IS now 10 years since Dr Raymond Moody's *Life After Life*, the first survey of the Near Death Experience, became a best-seller. Research now shows that there is a continuation of conscious
5 experience in some 40 per cent of cases where a person's physical body is comatose after an accident, surgery or other life-threatening trauma. The subjective existence of the NDE is no longer in doubt. Nor are the sometimes dramatic after-
10 effects.

2 Have you heard any stories about people who have had Near Death Experiences?
   Do you expect the experiences described in the article to be pleasant or frightening, or both?

3 The first sentences of eight paragraphs have been removed from the article.
   They are given here, but in the wrong order.
   In pairs, say what you think the order might be.
   a. In stage four, the light gradually enlarges until the experiencer emerges into it.
   b. Many are at first distressed and disappointed to find themselves back in the physical body with its pain and limitations.
   c. Professor Kenneth Ring of the University of Connecticut has described a widely accepted sequence of stages in the experience.
   d. A small number of negative NDEs has also been recorded.
   e. The final and deepest stage is 'entering the light', into a transcendental environment of surpassing beauty.
   f. Material values and status matter less; there is more emphasis on being rather than having.
   g. Perhaps the most pervasive after-effect of the NDE lies in the changed attitude to death and the possibility of an afterlife.
   h. At this point, the experiencer may have the impression of seeing his or her earthly life in review, discovering that nothing has been erased.

Reading and matching

Now read the article.
Decide which sentence begins which paragraph, and see if your order was correct.

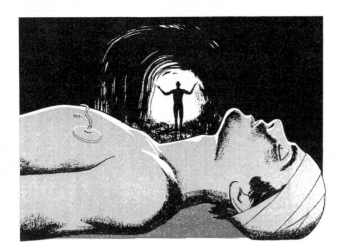

1 . . . . The first stage (they occur with diminishing frequency) is characterised by an overwhelming sense of peace, calm, and wellbeing, as well as freedom from bodily pain, which may have been acute. In the second stage, the experiencer feels detached from the physical body, which is often seen below and in a slightly different light.

The detachment is emotional as well as physical: the self no longer identifies with what it sees as a physical instrument to be discarded when worn out. There is a sensation of weightlessness; mental processes are very clear and the senses of sight and hearing extremely acute. Hearing seems to be telepathic: "I heard him say, or rather, saw him think." Experiencers are often able to describe in some detail events which actually took place while they were "unconscious".

Sometimes these two stages are bypassed and the experiencer finds herself or himself moving rapidly down a dark tunnel towards a light. Some researchers interpret this as the transition into another mode of consciousness.

2 . . . . There's a feeling of love, joy, beauty, and peace; the light exudes compassion and understanding, and may be felt as a presence or being with whom the experiencer feels at one, which some call an encounter with the "Higher Self."

3 . . . . Not only life experiences, but also the effects of thoughts, feelings and actions on others are now felt as if they were at the receiving end. The moral implications of this are momentous: it implies that we are so linked to each other that we undergo the reverberations of all we think, say, feel or do. For the experiencer, awareness and control of thoughts, feelings and actions become a central concern.

4 . . . . There may be meetings with dead relatives and loved ones, who usually make it clear that the experiencer's time is not yet up and that they must return to earth. Sometimes the return is symbolically presaged by a door, boundary or river which they are not allowed to cross. People return for two main reasons: either their purpose has not been fulfilled or they must meet the needs of family and dependants.

5 . . . . "Death is the hardest thing from the outside and as long as we are outside of it," wrote C. G. Jung, after his own NDE in 1944. "But once inside, you taste of such completeness and peace and fulfilment that you don't want to return."

He found his illness gave him a glimpse behind the veil into what he called the truly real life; he was horrified at the prospect of returning to "this fragmentary, restricted, narrow, almost mechanical life, where you were subject to the laws of gravity and cohesion, imprisoned in a system of three dimensions and whirled along with other bodies in the turbulent stream of time."

For Jung, death, far from being the irreversible extinction of consciousness, heralded an expansion and intensification of experience. It was our physical reality which now seemed unreal, limited and robot-like: a complete revolution of perspective and assumptions.

6 . . . . In *Return From Death* (Routledge and Kegan Paul), the first comparative survey to be published in this country, Margot Grey has found it possible to discern five stages which correspond to the positive ones: fear and a feeling of panic; out-of-the-body experience with an urge to return to the physical body; entering a black void; sensing an evil force which tries to drag you down; and entering a hell-like environment.

7 . . . . Experiencers — as distinct from people who have been close to death but have not experienced continuation of consciousness — lost their fear of death and are convinced of the existence of an afterlife, whatever the researchers conflicting interpretations.

They tend to find they have an enhanced appreciation of beauty, silence, the present and the small things of life. Their concern for others is greater; they have more insight and understanding, more tolerance and acceptance; they become more sympathetic listeners. They are less concerned with impressing others, and have an increased sense of self-worth.

8 . . . . Some record the development of paranormal and healing abilities. There is a quest for meaning and intellectual or spiritual understanding.

The change in religious or spiritual orientation can also be significant. Typically, there is an emphasis on the spiritual life and unconditional love, with less stress on formal aspects of religion. People feel closer to God, especially if they have had a mystical encounter. There is an openness to eastern religions and the idea of reincarnation, a belief in the essential unity of all faiths, and an intense desire for a universal religion which would dissolve the barriers that human beings have erected against each other.

Perhaps the most intriguing aspect of Margot Grey's book has to do with the "planetary visions" — ostensibly precognitive glimpses of coming world events. Whatever one's interpretation of the evidence, there is a surprising consensus on what is to come: widespread earthquakes and volcanic activity, a pole shift, erratic weather patterns, drought and food shortages, economic collapse, social disintegration, diseases of unknown origin, and possibly nuclear or natural holocaust or catastrophe.

Such calamities are seen as the inevitable result and reflection of a universally flagrant and ignorant violation of natural and spiritual laws, a necessary shake-up and purification which will bring a new sense of unity and cooperation. The severity of the disasters is said to depend on the extent to which human beings work to acquire the qualities that the NDE itself brings: unconditional love and spiritual values.

So the NDE is not a peripheral phenomenon of merely private interest. It points to a living universe and a spiritual view of humankind, towards personal survival of death, and towards the breakdown and renewal of our civilisation. The crisis is an opportunity.

(*Guardian* 19 December 1985)

Comprehension check

1 In lines 8–10 it says 'The subjective existence of the NDE is no longer in doubt.' What *is* in doubt?
2 Describe briefly the characteristics of the five stages. Which of them describe something physical, and which mental?
   Which sound pleasurable and which frightening?
3 What is the one experience which may constitute objective proof of the NDE?
4 How can an experiencer say 'I . . . saw him think' (lines 29–30)?
5 'The moral implications of this are momentous . . .' (lines 52–3). Why?
6 How does the experiencer learn that his/her time is not yet up?
   What are the two main reasons for returning? What *doesn't* dictate whether a person dies or not?
7 What did Jung find horrific about life? What did he call 'truly real life'? Why, do you think?
8 What are some of the changes that come over experiencers when they return to life?
9 What are some of the barriers that we have erected against each other?
10 What are 'planetary visions' (line 150)? What sort of world do they predict?
11 Explain the ideas expressed in the final paragraph.

What do you think?

1 Many of the experiences sound like dreams. Have you ever had a similar dream?
2 In what ways are the events described in the article reflected in religious beliefs that you know about?
3 Have you heard of any mediums or spiritualists who claim to be able to communicate with the dead?

▶ Language focus

Read the Language study on *nouns with a special meaning in the plural* and *they referring to a singular person* (page 131) and do the practice exercises.

Vocabulary 1
Noun collocations

There are many nouns which typically go with particular uncountable nouns.

Examples
a lump of sugar/coal
an item of news
a piece of advice

1 Put one word into each gap to express a unit. Sometimes there are several possibilities.
   a. a _____ of chocolate/soap
   b. a _____ of meat
   c. a _____ of water (a small amount)
   d. a _____ of celery
   e. a _____ of garlic
   f. a _____ of salt (a tiny amount)
   g. a _____ of soda in my whisky
   h. a _____ of thunder
   i. a _____ of lightning
   j. a _____ of dry weather
   k. a _____ of wind
   l. a _____ of fog
   m. a _____ of fresh air
   n. a _____ of applause
   o. a _____ of fun
   p. a _____ of dust
   q. a _____ of glass (intact)
   r. a _____ of glass (in my finger)
   s. a _____ of blood (for analyis)

2 What nouns can you think of to complete the following phrases? Use your dictionary.
   a. a stroke of _____
   b. an act of _____
   c. a state of _____
   d. a round of _____
   e. a grain of _____
   f. a fit of _____

3 Work in pairs.
   Write questions to ask your colleagues which will elicit the use of some of the above collocations.

   Examples
   A *What do we need from the butcher's?*
   B *A nice joint of meat for Sunday.*

   A *How much chilli sauce should I put in?*
   B *Just a dash.*

Artist's impression of our galaxy, the Milky Way, as it might be seen from a spacecraft. Our solar system (see inset) is about 25,000 light years from the galactic centre.

Listening

Pre-listening task

Discuss the following questions.

1 It has been said that we need religion to explain our world to us. Would you agree?

2 Different religions have different explanations of the creation of the world. Which ones do you know about? Why did Darwin's theory of evolution challenge the theological view?

3 'My suspicion is that the universe is not only queerer than we suppose, but queerer than we *can* suppose.'
(J. B. S. Haldane, scientist)
What scientific explanations of the universe do you know of?

4 You will hear an interview with Dr Carl Sagan, the cosmologist.
Here are the opening words of the interview. Check you know all the words.
'We've examined the universe in space, and seen that we live on a mote of dust, circling a humdrum star, in the remotest corner of an obscure galaxy.'

5 Here are some further words from the interview. Check that you understand them before you listen.

Darwin's conclusions are *disquieting*.
There is *compelling* evidence that man is evolved from apes and other *primates*.
It is *elevating* to think we are connected to all living things.

The universe is *expanding*. Will it one day *contract*? Will the galaxies *plummet* towards each other? Will everything be *ground* to ashes?
Before the Big Bang, all the *matter* in the universe was *confined* to an extremely small volume.
Is creation a *plausible* explanation for the origin of the universe?
Theologians *blanch* when asked where God came from.

Listening for information

T.27   Listen to the interview and answer the questions.
1 Why, according to Dr Sagan, do some people find Darwin's views *disquieting*?
2 What is it that he finds *elevating*?
3 What is the *cosmic movie* that he refers to? What does it tell us about the origins of the universe?
4 What is the *key question*?
5 'There's no beginning,' says Dr Sagan emphatically. This may bring to mind the opening words of the Old Testament. Do you know them?

▶ Language focus

Read the Language study on *the use of -ever for emphasis* and *the use of -ever to express surprise* (page 131) and do the practice exercises.

Vocabulary 2
Synonyms and their associations

Here is a text which was supposedly found in the Old Saint Paul's Church, Baltimore, dated 1692. (There has been doubt about its authenticity because of the modern feel of the language in it.)

It is called 'Desiderata', which means 'things that are desired or missing'. Read it through quickly. In what ways does it avoid expressing the views of one particular religion?

Now read it again, and decide which of the words on the right best fills each gap.

DESIDERATA

GO PLACIDLY AMID THE NOISE AND HASTE, and remember what peace there may be in silence. As far as possible without surrender be on good terms with all persons. Speak your truth quietly and _____ and listen to others, even the _____ and ignorant: they too have their story.

clearly, articulately, unambiguously
gloomy, dull, dim

Avoid loud and _____ persons, they are vexations to the spirit. If you compare yourself with others you may become vain and _____ ; for always there will be greater and lesser persons than yourself. Enjoy your achievements as well as your plans.

touchy, argumentative, aggressive

bitter, spiteful, twisted

Keep interested in your own career however _____ ; it is a real possession in the changing _____ of time. Exercise caution in your business affairs; for the world is full of _____ . But let this not blind you to what virtue there is. Many persons _____ for high ideals and everywhere life is full of heroism.   Be yourself. Especially, do not _____ affection. Neither be cynical about love, for in the face of all aridity and disenchantment, it is perennial as the grass.   Take kindly the counsel of the years, _____ surrendering the things of youth. Nurture strength of spirit to _____ you in sudden misfortune. But do not distress yourself with imaginings. Many fears are born of fatigue and _____ . Beyond a wholesome discipline, be gentle with yourself.

humble, trivial, insignificant

hazards, fortunes, opportunities
intrigue, strategies, trickery
strive, struggle, endeavour

forge, fake, feign

willingly, gracefully, elegantly
protect, guard, shield

loneliness, solitude, isolation

You are a child of the universe no less than the trees and the stars. You have a _____ to be here. And whether or not it is clear to you, no doubt the universe is _____ as it should. Therefore be at peace with God, whatever you conceive Him to be; and whatever your labors and aspirations, in the noisy confusions of life keep peace with your soul.   With all its _____ and drudgery and broken dreams, it is still a beautiful world. Be careful. Strive to be happy.

role, right, privilege

unfolding, proceeding, progressing

pretence, sham, swindle

You will now hear a recording of the original. Compare the words that you chose with the original. Do you think any of your words were better? Why does this text sound modern rather than about three hundred years old?

LANGUAGE STUDY

1 Nouns with a special meaning in the plural

Sometimes, a countable noun has a special meaning in the plural.

> **min·ute**¹ /'mɪnɪt/ n **1 (a)** [C] one sixtieth part of an hour, equal to 60 seconds: *It's ten minutes to/past six.* ○ *I arrived a couple of minutes early/late.* [. . .] **4 minutes** [pl] brief summary or record of what is said and decided at a meeting, esp of a society or committee: *We read (through) the minutes of the last meeting.*

Practice

For each of the following words, write two sentences, one using the word in the singular and one in the plural, to show two different meanings.

a. fruit	**f.** custom	**j.** air
b. sight	**g.** ground	**k.** manner
c. pain	**h.** work	**l.** damage
d. honour	**i.** spirit	**m.** surgery
e. charity		

2 'They' referring to a singular person

Notice the following sentence from the text about Near Death Experiences.

There may be meetings with dead relatives and loved ones, who usually make it clear that the experiencer's time is not yet up and that they must return to earth.

They is used here to avoid saying **he** or **she**.

Practice

In the following sentences, put **they**, **them**, **their**, or **themselves**.

a. If anyone phones me, tell _____ I'm out, but get _____ number and I'll phone _____ back.

b. There's someone waiting for you in reception. I think _____ want to ask you some questions.

c. A When I called for help, nobody came.
   B Didn't _____? That's awful.

d. Someone's been through the house with mud on _____ shoes.

e. Has everyone got _____ ticket?

f. It was a great party. Everyone enjoyed _____.

g. Everybody has to hand in _____ essay tomorrow.

h. Someone's been smoking in here, haven't _____?

i. Everyone knows _____ have a right to speak _____ own mind.

3 The use of '-ever' for emphasis

Whatever, **whoever**, **whichever**, **whenever**, **wherever**, and **however** are used to express *It doesn't matter what/who/which*, etc.

Examples
*Well, I like it **whatever** you might think.*
***Whatever** the weather, I get up at dawn and go for a walk.*
*Take **whichever** one you want.*

They can also express the idea of ignorance, indifference, or something not precisely specified.

Examples
*Give this to Mary, or Marie, **whatever** her name is.*
*I'll ring you at 8.00 or 8.30, **whenever** I get the time.*

Practice

Fill each gap with one of the above words formed with **-ever**.

a. _____ thinks that the earth is flat is a fool.

b. I don't want to be disturbed. _____ calls, and _____ they want, tell them I'm out.

c. Hang the picture _____ you like, I don't mind.

d. _____ hard I try, I can never remember people's names.

e. _____ my wife cooks, she gets distracted, so the meat or the vegetables, _____ it is she's cooking, gets burnt.

f. She can't decide whether to study economics or politics, but I'm sure she'll do well _____ she chooses.

g. Pick up the children. Megan, Kate, Dave – maybe Beth will be there. _____ many there are, bring them back here for tea.

h. You've got to get the money somehow, but for goodness' sake don't pay too much interest, _____ you get it.

i. Could _____ leaves the room last turn all the lights out?

j. _____ you go, and _____ long you are away, you never forget your own home town.

4 The use of '-ever' to express surprise

It is also possible to use **-ever** with interrogative words to express surprise.

Examples
***Whoever** is that woman talking to your sister?*
***However** did you manage to save so much money so quickly?*
***Whatever** did you do that for?*

The same meaning can be expressed more informally using **on earth**.

Example
*What **on earth** is that?*

Practice

Think of informal, emphatic questions to ask about the following situations. Be very careful with your intonation.

Example

A Have you heard about the man who's going to row single-handed across the Atlantic?

B *Whatever* does he want to do that for?
*What **on earth** is he going to eat all that time?*

a. Bill and Sheila are taking their nine children caravanning in Siberia.

b. A wine connoisseur paid £20,000 for an 1812 bottle of claret.

c. You and your husband/wife have just sat down to dinner when two friends turn up unexpectedly, wanting food and somewhere to stay the night.

d. Peter has a family to support, but he gave up a well-paid job and now refuses to get out of bed.

e. Malcolm has brought a python back from Sumatra. He says he's going to keep it as a pet.

REVISION

Review of input

Here is another letter from Serge, the student in Edinburgh. We hope that your English has improved more rapidly than his! There are about sixty mistakes, of grammar, vocabulary, punctuation, and style. Find the mistakes and rewrite the corrected letter.

Edinburgh
20 March

Dear Anna

Thanks for your letter. Obviously I was sorry to hear of the fall of your aunt. I hope her to feel better soon. She must get on now. Precisely how old is she? It should be horrible for her to fall and not able to get someone helping her. If she doesn't live by her own, people won't be so worry, but the old are so stubborn and want there independence. Give to her my regards when you're next seeing her, and say her I think she's absolutely brave!

You have classes every week at nightschool, haven't you? You say you have four three hours exams next week. Good luck at them. Only you can do your best — you can't do more than it. You say you're working hard — I'm mostly impressed! You were never used to work for your exams. You said you needn't have, because always you found exams so easily. Anyway, try doing your best this time!

Since I've written to you lastly, I had an accident. Nothing serious. I went to a very eccentric party giving by Alan, about whom I told you in my last letter. At first I didn't go, because I was feeling tired, but at the end I changed my mind and went. Alan introduced me to his girl friend I never met before. She was terribly delightful, but the others all were rather odd, and I couldn't have thought of anything to talk to them about. If Alan isn't a close friend, I wouldn't go to the party. After all, what happened is that I tripped a table over and knocked me out! I don't know how did it happen. I couldn't have too much to drink, because I just only arrived when it happened. I was taken to the hospital for a X-ray, because they were worried in case I broke my arm that was swelled. When I had come round, I was laying on a hospital's bed. I felt fine after a few hour's rest and went home. I sent Alan some bunch of flowers to apologize the trouble I caused – did I do right? What would you do in my situation? Did you do the same like I did?

It's time for you to come to see me. Spring will come, and the flowers must be out soon. Should you require me to investigate train times, I'll do it for you.

Keep in touch. Write soon.

Best wishes,

Serge

133

GRAMMAR SECTION

UNIT 1

Noun phrases

1 Plural expressions in compound adjectives

When expressions of measurement are used as adjectives (and come before the noun), they are normally singular.
*a ten-**pound** note   a three-**metre** drop*
*a forty-five **minute** tape   a six-**month**-old baby*
*a five-**star** hotel   a hundred-**watt** bulb*

2 Compound nouns

Nouns combine freely to form compound nouns. The first noun classifies the second, telling us more about it. A **horse-race** is a kind of race; a **race-horse** is a kind of horse.

The main stress usually occurs in the first noun, but not always.
'lipstick   'photocopy   'graveyard   'seafood
'fireplace   'earthquake   'crossword puzzle
but *apple 'pie*
In some cases, both patterns are possible.
week'end   'weekend

Very common compounds, especially those which consist of two short words, are written as one word.
breakfast   grandchildren   briefcase   teacup

Some are written with a hyphen.
letter-box   air-conditioning   baby-sitter   birth-control

Some are written as two words.
coffee cup   drug addict   telephone bill   tax cuts

There are no fixed rules governing this, and some words are found in several forms. Even dictionaries disagree! The best advice is to refer to a good learner's dictionary when in doubt, and to be consistent in using the form you choose.

3 Information before and after a noun

Here are some further examples of how information about a noun can be added both before and after it.

Before the noun	Noun	After the noun
both my	grandparents	on my mother's side
the first few	years	of my life
an old people's	home	on the edge of the countryside
a	boy	delivering newspapers
the	people	invited to the wedding

Avoiding repetition

1 When a verb is used with an auxiliary, it is possible to use the auxiliary on its own when repeating the idea contained in the verb, for example in answers to questions.

A ***Will** it **rain** this afternoon?*
B *Yes, I think it **will** (rain this afternoon).*

A ***Should** I **revise** for this test?*
B *Yes, I think you **should** (revise for the test).*

A *If I were rich, I'd **give up** work.*
B *I **wouldn't** (give up work). I'd buy a farm.*
These are called short answers.

2 Where there is no auxiliary verb, **do/does/did** is used to avoid repeating the verb.
A *I **adore** Italy.*
B *I **do**, too.*
A *I **thought** the film was wonderful.*
B *I **didn't**. I loathed it.*

3 To know which auxiliary verb (or **do/does/did**) to insert, it is necessary to reconstruct the part of the sentence that is missing, and to carefully consider the meaning and the time of the events in the sentence.
A *I didn't see the film last night.*
B *You **should have**. It was great.*
B is giving advice about a past event.
A *You must see the Renoir exhibition. It's superb!*
B *I **have**.*
(Present Perfect because the action is relevant to the present.)
A *I wish you'd lock the house when you leave.*
B *I **did**.*
(Past Simple because the action happened at a specific time in the past.)

'A' or 'an'?

1 We need to put **an** before any noun that begins with a vowel-sound.
an apple / ən æpl /

2 A word that begins with a vowel when written does not necessarily begin with a vowel-sound when spoken.
a uniform / ə juːnfɔːm /

3 A word that begins with a consonant when written may begin with a vowel-sound when spoken.
an hour / ən aʊə /

4 In abbreviations, if the pronunciation of the letter begins with a vowel-sound, then **an** is used.
an MA / ən em eɪ /

'The' – / ðə / or / ðɪ / ?

The rules regarding the pronunciation of **the** follow the same pattern as for **a/an**.

The pronunciation is / ðɪ / before *any* vowel-sound.
the apple / ðɪ æpl /
the hour / ðɪ aʊə /
the MA / ðɪ em eɪ /
But, remember,
the uniform / ðə juːnɪfɔːm /

UNIT 2

Narrative tenses

1 The Past Simple

The Past Simple is used to narrate past events in chronological order.
*Alice **left** her family home in the morning and **moved** to the big city. What a busy day it **was**! She **sat** and **looked** at the cosy living room around her. At last the house **was** hers. She **gazed** out at the London skyline with awe.*

2 The Past Perfect

The Past Perfect is used to express an action that happened *before* a definite time in the past. A writer can use it to re-order the events of a narrative for dramatic effect.
*Alice sat and looked at the cosy living room around her. At last the house was hers. What a busy day it **had been**! She **had left** her family home in the morning and **had moved** to the big city. She gazed at the London skyline with awe.*

Notice that **had** need not be repeated if the subject of both verbs is the same.
*She had said goodbye to her mother and (had) **caught** the train to London.*

It is not always essential to use the Past Perfect. If it is clear that the events described in the time clause took place before the one in the main clause, the Past Simple can be used.
*After she **said** goodbye to her mother, she **caught** the train to London.*

If it is important to show that the first action was completed before the second one began, the Past Perfect must be used.
*When she **had raised** sufficient capital, she **put in** an offer on the house.*

For reasons of style, it is unwise (and unnecessary) to have too many verbs in the Past Perfect one after another. Once the time aspect of 'past-in-the-past' has been established, the Past Simple can be used as long as there is no ambiguity.
*The furniture suited the room perfectly. She had been to auction rooms looking for just the right period pieces, and had found some excellent examples of Regency workmanship. She **bought** them at good prices, and **didn't pay** more than five hundred pounds for anything.*

3 The Past Continuous and the Past Perfect Continuous

The Past Continuous and the Past Perfect Continuous (as with all continuous tenses) express ideas of activity in progress or repeated activity.
*She **was wearing** a green velvet dress.*
*She **was hoping** the phone would ring.*
*She **had been arranging** and **rearranging** the rooms for weeks.*

4 The future-in-the-past

Sometimes, in a narrative, a writer (or speaker) wants to express the future as seen from a specific point in the past. This is called the 'future-in-the-past'.

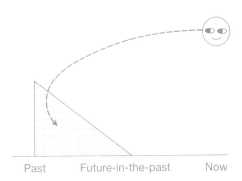

Past   Future-in-the-past   Now

This is expressed by **was going to** (+ verb) or the Past Continuous.
*Alice smiled as she thought of the evening to come. She **was meeting** Peter, and together they **were going to see** a play at the Adelphi Theatre.*

Would (+ verb) is also used to express the future-in-the-past, but is restricted to a literary style and is rarely used in spoken English.
*She looked around the room, wondering where to put the pictures. She **would hang** her favourite water-colour above the fireplace, but **would have to think** carefully about the others.*

The uses of these three forms are exactly parallel to the use of the Present Continuous **is going to** (+ verb), and **will** to refer to the real future.
*I'm **meeting** Peter tonight.* (planned arrangement)
*We're **going to see** a play.* (planned intention)
*I'll **hang** the water-colour above the fireplace.* (spontaneous intention)
*I'll **have to think** carefully about the others.* (**will** as future auxiliary)

Was/were to (+ verb) also expresses the future-in-the-past, and has the idea of **was/were destined to**. This, too, is restricted to a literary style.
*Little did she realize that the evening **was to turn out** very differently.*

As

Below are some of the many uses of **as** in English.

1 In comparisons, both **as** and **like** are used, but **as** is a conjunction and is followed by a clause, and **like** is a preposition and is followed by a noun.
*I cook **as the Italians do**, with lots of fresh pasta, vegetables, and herbs.*
*He worked on the farm **as his father had done** before him.*
*He can run **like a hare**.*
*You're **like a child**, sometimes.*
*It's **like cream**, only with fewer calories.*

In comparison **as** can also be used before a prepositional phrase.
*In 1986, **as in 1985**, there was a drop in the birth-rate of developed countries.*

2 **As** is used to state the role, job, or function of a person or a thing.
*We all work together **as a team**.*
*She worked **as a waitress** over the summer.*
*He used an old plastic bag **as a wastepaper basket**.*

3 **As** is commonly used after certain verbs. For example:
*You have been **described as** 'the best Prime Minister who never was'.*
*He is **regarded as** a bit of a misfit.*
*Do you **see** this job **as** something you want to do for a long time, or not?*
*I have always **thought of** myself **as** being middle-of-the-road in my views.*

4 **As . . . as . . .** expresses equality; **not as/so . . . as . . .** expresses inequality.
*She's **as tall as** me.*
*She's **not so tall as** her father was,*
*and she isn't **as dark as** him.*

There are many common expressions with the **as . . . as . . .** pattern.
*I worked **as hard as** I could.*
*I will reply **as soon as** possible.*
*You can go **as long as** you promise to come back.*
*They've got a flat in London **as well as** a cottage in the country.*

5 **As** is used in a similar way to **because** to give the reason for something; however, it places less emphasis on the reason than **because**:
*I bought her some flowers **as she had been very kind to me** since the death of my mother.*
***As the weather was so bad**, we stayed in and played cards.*

6 **As** is used to talk about actions that take place at the same time.
***As the sun rose**, little by little the extent of the damage was revealed to us.*

***As the door swung open**, she saw the body slumped over the table.*

Future forms

It has often been said that English does not have a future tense as many other languages do. Instead, there are several forms which express future events, and which one the user selects depends on *how he or she sees the event* as much as its certainty or nearness to the present.
The main forms are given here in order of frequency:

1 **'Will'**

Will can function as an auxiliary of the future in simply predicting a future event.
*The Queen **will** open the new hospital next Thursday.*
*Tomorrow **will** be warm and sunny everywhere.*

Will can also function as a modal auxiliary which expresses ideas of willingness and spontaneous intention.
***Will** you help me for a minute?*
*What a lovely shirt! **I'll** buy it.*

2 **'Going to'**

Going to expresses a premeditated intention.
*I'm **going to** decorate the bathroom this weekend.*
*The Government is **going to** reorganize the entire Civil Service.*

Going to is also used to predict a future event for which there is some evidence now.
*Great news! I'm **going to** have a baby!*
*They're looking very angry. I think they're **going to** start throwing stones.*

3 **The Present Continuous**

The Present Continuous is used to express an arrangement, usually for the near future.
A *What **are** you **doing** tonight?*
B *I'm **going out** for a meal.*

It is wrong to use the Present Simple in this sense, for example:
* *What do you do tonight?*
* *Do you go to the party on Saturday?*

The Present Continuous cannot be used to express an event that has not been arranged by human beings. We cannot say:
* *It is raining tomorrow.*
* *The sun is rising at 5.00 tomorrow morning.*

4 **The Present Simple**

The Present Simple is used to express a future event which is seen as being certain because of a timetable or calendar.
*What time **does** the film **start**?*
*My train **gets in** at 11.00.*
*The Cup Final **takes place** on April 13.*

5 The Future Continuous

The Future Continuous expresses an activity that will be in progress around a specific time in the future.
Don't phone at 8.00 – I'll be having supper.
This time tomorrow I'll be flying to Hong Kong.

The Future Continuous also expresses an action that will occur in the natural course of events, independently of the will or intention of anyone directly concerned.
In a few minutes we will be landing at Heathrow Airport.
(Of course the pilot has not just decided this!)
Hurry up! The bus will be leaving any minute!

The Future Continuous is often used to express a casual or polite question about someone's future plans. The speaker is trying not to impose his/her will in any way. This is related to the use of the Future Continuous described above, i.e. that it can express an action that will occur independently of the will or intention of the people concerned.
Compare:
Will you bring Kate to the party? (Perhaps a request.)
Will you be bringing Kate to the party? (I'm just asking.)
Will you be using the car tonight? If not, could I have it?

6 The Future Perfect

The Future Perfect expresses an action that will have finished before a definite time in the future.
I'll have finished my work by the time you get back.
Most of the leaves will have fallen by the end of November.

UNIT 4

Modal auxiliary verbs

Modal verbs are a very rich and subtle area of the English language. They can all refer to the certainty, possibility, or probability of an event, and they can all refer to future time.

Modal auxiliary verbs, present and future

The main modal verbs that express present and future probability are given here in order of degrees of certainty, **will** being the most certain and **might/could** being the least certain.

1 'Will'

Will and **won't** are used to predict a future event which is seen as certain.
I'll be on holiday next week.
I won't do any work at all.

Will and **won't** are also used to express what we believe or guess to be true *about the present*. They indicate an assumption based on our knowledge of people and things; their routine, character, and qualities.

Is that the phone? It'll be John. He said he'd ring around now.
A *I wonder what Meg's doing now?*
B *It's 7.00. I suppose she'll be getting supper ready.*
Don't take the meat out of the oven. It won't be ready yet.

2 'Must'

Must is used to assert what we infer or conclude to be the most logical or rational interpretation of a situation or events. As we do not have all the facts, it is less certain than **will**.
The negative of this use of **must** is **can't**.
He walked across the Sahara Desert! He must be mad!
You must be joking! I simply don't believe you.
She can't have a ten-year-old daughter! She's only twenty-five herself!

3 'Should'

Should expresses what may reasonably be expected to happen. It also carries the meaning that we *want* whatever is predicted to happen, and is therefore not used to express negative or unpleasant ideas. It suggests a conditional: *If everything has gone/goes according to plan, then x should happen.*
Our guests should be here soon (if they haven't got lost).
This homework shouldn't take you too long (if you've understood what you have to do).
We should be moving into our new house soon (as long as all the arrangements go smoothly).

4 'May'

May expresses the possibility that something will happen or is already happening.
We may go to Greece for our holidays. We haven't decided yet.
We may not have enough money to go abroad this year.

5 'Might'

Might, like **may**, expresses possibility, but in a more tentative way.
It might rain. Take your umbrella.
I might not be back in time for supper, so don't wait for me.

6 'Could'

Could is used in a similar way to **might**.
You could be right, but I doubt it.
The American film could be worth seeing, but it didn't get very good reviews.

Could not is not used to express a future possibility. The negative of **could** in this use is **might not**.
You might not be right.
It might not be interesting.

Couldn't has a similar meaning to **can't** in 2 above, only slightly weaker.
She couldn't have a ten-year-old daughter! She's only twenty-five herself!

Modal auxiliary verbs in the past

All the modal verbs given above can be used with the perfect infinitive to express varying degrees of certainty about the past. Again, **will/would** is the most certain and **might/could** is the least certain.

*You say you stayed in a hotel near the lake? That **would have been** my parents' hotel! What a coincidence!*

*It **won't have been** Peter you met at the party last night. He was ill in bed.*

*It **must have been** Simon. He looks very like Peter.*

*It **can't have been** a very interesting party. No one seems to have enjoyed it.*

*Where's Henry? He **should have been** here ages ago!*

*He **may have got** lost.*

*He **might have decided** not to come.*

*He **could have had** an accident.*

Other uses of modal auxiliary verbs

Here is some further information about modal verbs and the different senses in which they are used. Often the past form is very different from that used in the present.

1 Obligation

Must is used to express strong obligation. The past is expressed by **had to**.

*You **must** try harder!*

*I **had to** work hard to pass my exams.*

Should is used to express milder obligation. The past is expressed by **should have** (+ past participle).

*You **should** rest.*

*You **should have listened** to my advice.*

2 Permission

May is used to express permission. The past is expressed by **was allowed to**.

May I ask you a question?

*I **was allowed to** do whatever I wanted when I was young.*

3 Ability

Can is used to express general ability; the form in the past is **could**.

*I **can** swim.*

*I **could** swim when I was 6.*

To express a particular ability on one occasion in the past, **could** is not used. Instead, **was able to** or **managed to** is used.

*I **was able to** go to university when I was 16.*

*The prisoner **managed to** escape by climbing onto the roof.*

4 Willingness

Won't expresses a refusal, by either people or things. The past is **wouldn't**.

*The car **won't** start.*

*He was angry because she **wouldn't** lend him any money.*

5 Characteristic behaviour

Will is used to express characteristic behaviour. The past is expressed by **would**.

He'll sit for hours staring into the fire.

*My grandma **would** always bring me a little present when she came to visit.*

6 Past forms of 'need'

Need has two past forms. **Needn't have** (+ past participle) expresses an action that was completed but that wasn't necessary.

*You **needn't have bought** any butter. We've got lots.*

Didn't need to (+ infinitive) expresses an action that was not necessary, but we do not know if it was in fact completed or not. The context usually makes this clear.

*I **didn't need to do** any shopping because I was eating out that night.*

UNIT 6

Adjective order

Generally speaking, value adjectives (which indicate personal opinion) come first, followed by size, age, shape, colour, origin, and material.

Compound nouns (e.g., **washing machine**; **coffee pot** – see Unit 1 'Noun phrases') are never separated.

The table below gives several examples of noun phrases with adjectives in this order.

Determiner	Value	Size	Age	Shape	Colour	Origin	Material	Compound	Noun
two	lovely				black		leather	riding	boots
a	priceless		nineteenth-century			Impressionist			painting
their		huge		circular				swimming	pool
my						Swedish	wooden	salad	bowl
the	dirty		old				metal	garden	seat
one		tiny		L-shaped				utility	room
Jane's	pretty					Victorian		writing	desk
his	charming				whitewashed			country	cottage

UNIT 7

Verb patterns in reported speech

For reference, here are four common patterns used in reporting speech, with examples of verbs that frequently occur in these patterns. Note that some of the verbs can be used in other patterns as well.

Verb + object + infinitive
I advised him to look for a job.

advise	order
ask	permit
beg	persuade
challenge	remind
encourage	request
forbid	tell
force	urge
invite	warn

Verb + **that** + clause
She admitted that she had made a mistake.

add	explain
admit	insist
accept	point out
agree	promise
argue	protest
complain	warn
deny	

Verb + **-ing**
He denied stealing the money.

admit	deny

Verb + infinitive
She agreed to do it.

agree	refuse
offer	threaten
promise	

Suggest

Suggest is not used with an object + infinitive. It can be followed by an **-ing** form or **that** + clause.
He suggested having a long break to recuperate.
He suggested that I (should) have a long break to recuperate.

Conditional sentences

English tense usage can be divided into two categories: tenses used to refer to fact, and those used to refer to non-fact. Fact is what is considered to be real or quite possible; non-fact is what is supposed or wished for, which is either unreal or improbable.

Fact	*I **work** in a restaurant, but I **don't earn** much.*
	*If I **find** a better job, I'**ll take** it.*
Non-fact	*I **wish** I **had** a lot of money.*
	*If I **had** a lot of money, I **would open** my own restaurant.*

Tenses used to refer to fact are related to real time. For example, a past verb form refers to the past.
*I **had** a lovely holiday in Spain last year.*

Tenses used to refer to non-fact are not related to real time. Generally speaking, this unreality is expressed by shifting the verb form 'backwards' (for example, from present to past).
*If I **had** a car, I could visit my friends.*

Here the past verb form does not refer to the real past, but to the 'wished for' present and future. It has the effect of distancing the meaning from reality. It is important to understand this difference between fact and non-fact when discussing conditional sentences. (The use of tenses for non-fact is dealt with further in Unit 11.)

1 Type 1

Type 1 conditional sentences are based on fact in real time. They express a possible condition and its probable result.
*If it **rains**, I'**ll get** wet.*
*If he **doesn't come** soon, we'**ll miss** the bus.*

Will is not usually used in the condition clause. However, it can appear when **will** expresses willingness (or in the negative, refusal), or insistence.
*If you'**ll wash** the dishes, I'**ll put** them away.*
(If you are willing to . . .)
*If Peter **won't** give you a lift, I will.*
(If Peter isn't willing to . . .)
*If you **will** smoke, of course you'll get a cough.)*
(If you insist on smoking . . .)
When **will** expresses insistence, it is stressed and never contracted.

Should and **happen to** can be used in the condition clause to suggest that something may happen by chance, but is unlikely.
*If you **should** come across Pearl, tell her to give me a ring.*
*If you **happen to** find my book, pop it in the post to me.*

There are several other links with meanings similar to **if** that can introduce Type 1 conditional sentences.
***Provided/providing** I have the time, I'll give you a hand to fix it.*
***Supposing** you miss the plane, what will you do?*
*I'll come tomorrow **unless** I hear from you before.*
(If I don't hear from you . . .)

2 Type 2

Type 2 conditional sentences are not based on fact. They express a situation which is contrary to reality in the present and future. This unreality is shown by a tense shift 'backwards':

Present ——————————→ Past
will (+ verb)   **would** (+ verb)

They express a hypothetical condition and its probable result.
If I were taller, I'd join the police force.
(In reality I am not, and never will be, tall enough to join the police force.)
If you saw a ghost, what would you do?
(I don't believe in ghosts, so I don't think you will ever see one.)

The difference between Type 1 and Type 2 conditional sentences is not related to time. Both can refer to the present or the future. By using a past verb form in Type 2, the speaker suggests that the situation is less probable, or impossible, or imaginary.
Compare the following.
If it rains this weekend, I'll . . .
(Said in England, where rain is common.)
If it rained in the Sahara, the desert would . . .
(This would be most unusual.)

If there is a nuclear war, we will . . .
(I am a pessimist. Nuclear war is a real possibility.)
If there was a nuclear war, we would . . .
(I am an optimist and I think nuclear war is very unlikely to happen.)
If you come to my country, you'll have a good time.
(Possible.)
If you came from my country, you'd understand us better.
(Impossible – you don't come from my country.)

Were is often used instead of **was**, especially when the style is formal. It is also commonly used in the expression **If I were you** . . . when giving advice.
If he were more honest, he would be a better person.
If I were you, I'd cook it for a little longer.

The Type 2 conditional can make a suggestion sound less direct and hence more polite.
Would it be convenient if I called this evening around 8.00?
Would you mind if I opened the window slightly?

Would is not usually used in the condition clause. However, as with **will**, in Type 1, it can appear when it expresses willingness. Again, it makes a suggestion sound more polite.
I would be grateful if you would give this matter your serious attention.

Were to can be used in the condition clause to suggest that something is unlikely to happen.
If you were to find that your husband had been unfaithful, what would you do?

3 Type 3

Type 3 conditional sentences are not based on fact. They express a situation which is contrary to reality in the past. This unreality is shown by a tense shift 'backwards':
Past ——————————→ Past Perfect
would (+ verb)   **would have** (+ verb)

If I had known his background, I would never have employed him.
(I didn't know his background and I did employ him.)
If I hadn't seen it with my own eyes, I wouldn't have thought it possible.
(I did see it with my own eyes, so it must be possible.)

4 Type 2 and Type 3 mixed

It is possible for each of the two clauses in a conditional sentence to have a different time reference, and the result is a mixed conditional.
If we had brought a map with us, we would know where we are.
If we had brought is contrary to past fact (we didn't bring a map).
We would know is contrary to present fact (we don't know).

If I didn't love her, I wouldn't have married her.
If I didn't love her is contrary to present fact (I do love her).
I wouldn't have married her is contrary to past fact (I did marry her).

Care needs to be taken when the Type 2 conditional refers to the future.
I would come to the party next Saturday if I hadn't arranged to go to the theatre.
This conditional is sometimes 'unmixed' to regularize the tense sequence.
I would have come to the party next Saturday if I hadn't arranged to go to the theatre.
This sentence sounds a little odd, however, as the verb action (**come to the party**) is in the future, whilst the 'regularized' verb form (**would have come**) usually refers to the past.

UNIT 8

Time clauses in the past

1 The Past Simple and the Past Perfect

Both the verb in the main clause and the verb in the time clause can be in the Past Simple if the sentence contains the idea that the second action is the result of the first, or that it happened immediately afterwards.
When she saw the photograph, she burst out laughing.
As soon as I got home, I had a bath.
I held her hand until the doctor came.

*By the time we **got** home, we **were** all very hungry.*
*Once she **had** the necessary information, she **left.***

If it is important to show that the first action was completed *before* the second one began, the Past Perfect must be used for the action that happened first (see page 135).
*When she **had seen** all the photographs, she went home.*
*As soon as I **had read** the letter, I threw it away.*
*He didn't leave the house until he **had checked** that all the windows were closed.*
*By the time we got home, the programme we wanted to watch **had ended.***
*Once the sun **had gone down**, the air turned cold.*

2 'As', 'while', and 'when'

As, **while**, and **when** are used, often with the Past Continuous, to express an activity that was in progress when another action took place.
*As/while/when we **were walking** in the park, we saw a squirrel.*

To express two activities in progress at the same time, **while** is often used with either the Past Simple or the Past Continuous.
*While I **did**/**was doing** the crossword, my wife **read**/**was reading** a book.*
When and **as** are not very common in this type of sentence.

As can be used to talk about two developing or changing situations.
*As she **grew** older, she **began to doubt** many of her parents' ideas.*

Remember that **as** can also mean **because** (see page 136).
*We had to walk **as** it was too late to catch a bus.*

3 'After' and 'before'

Participle clauses are common with **after** and **before**.
***After resting for several days**, she felt much better.*
***Before opening the letter**, he examined the postmark to see where it was from.*

Time clauses in the future

Time conjunctions

Time conjunctions are not usually followed by **will**.
*I'll give you a ring **when I get** home.*
*As soon as I **am** seventeen, I'm going to buy a car.*
*I'll stay up **until** the film **ends**.*
*The meal will be ready **by the time** you get home.*

The Present Perfect

As with the Past Perfect in time clauses in the past, if it is important to show that the first action is completed before the second one begins, the Present Perfect is necessary.
*When you**'ve read** my book, could you give it back to me?*
*As soon as I**'ve finished** it, I'll give it to you.*
*I'm going to sit here until I**'ve learnt** all the irregular verbs.*

*By the time you**'ve washed** your hands, the meal will be on the table.*

Punctuation

1 Commas

Commas are used to separate items in a list.
We had wine, whisky, brandy, and port.
It is not necessary to separate the last two items with a comma (i.e. here 'brandy and port'). Both styles are acceptable, but whichever one you choose, be consistent.
Commas are not used before **that**, **if**, **what**, **where**, etc. in reported speech, or after verbs of saying and thinking.
He said that he was going.
I wonder if he knows.
I don't know what he wanted.
I don't think that's a very good idea.

Commas are often used after clauses with **if**, **when**, **after**, etc. when these come first in a sentence. When they come after the main clause, it is more usual not to have a comma.
If you're ready, we can start.
We can start if you're ready.

Commas are necessary with non-defining relative clauses, but not with defining relative clauses (see page 142).
Churchill, who lived to the age of 91, enjoyed brandy and fine cigars.
The Prime Minister who led the country during the Second World War was Churchill.

2 Direct speech

Notice the use of quotation marks, commas, full stops, question marks, and exclamation marks in the following sentences.
John said, 'The trouble is, I can't afford it.'
'The trouble is, I can't afford it,' said John.
'Where are you going?' asked Mary.
'Look out, Peter!' shouted Anne.

3 Apostrophes

Apostrophes are used to show the possessive.
John's car
the boys' playroom (more than one boy)
Dr James's consulting room
a week's holiday (of one week)
two weeks' holiday (of two weeks)

They are used to show where letters have been missed out in contracted forms, or where numbers have been missed out.
I can't help you. (cannot)
It doesn't work. (does not)
I met her in '72. (1972)
17 September '87. (1987)

They can be used in the plural of dates.
the 1920's

4 Other punctuation marks

Semicolon

Semicolons show a longer pause than a comma. The two sentences are grammatically independent, but their meaning is closely connected.
The Home Secretary was in favour; The Prime Minister didn't agree.

Colon

Colons are used before a list.
She has five children: James, Henry, Elizabeth, Kate, and Joseph.

Brackets

Brackets are used to separate extra information, or a comment, from the rest of the sentence.
Cleanliness (as my mother used to tell me) is next to godliness.

Hyphen

Hyphens are used after certain prefixes in some compound nouns (see page 134), in some compound adjectives, and in adjective phrases that consist of more than two elements.

anti-American   semi-automatic   pre-revolutionary
pre-exist   under-rehearsed
air-conditioning   tape-recorder
hard-hearted   broad-shouldered
a well-to-do area   a make-or-break situation

Hyphens are also used when expressions of measurement, amount, and quantity are used as adjectives before a noun (see page 134).
a ten-pound note   a three-hour film.

UNIT 9

Relative clauses

It is important to distinguish between defining and non-defining relative clauses. Defining relative clauses are an essential part of the meaning of a sentence and therefore they *cannot* be left out. They define exactly who or what we are talking about.
There's the woman you were telling me about.

Non-defining relative clauses add extra information of secondary importance, and *can* be left out of a sentence.
Mrs Bottomley, who was an extremely mean person while she was alive, has left all her money to a cats' home.

Non-defining relative clauses are mainly found in written English, where sentences are carefully constructed. In spoken English, they sound rather formal, and can easily be expressed by simpler sentences.

Did you know Mrs Bottomley has left all her money to a cats' home? It's incredible, really. She was an extremely mean person while she was alive.

Defining relative clauses

Here are the main forms used. The forms in brackets are possible but not as common.

	Person	Thing
Subject	who (that)	that (which)
Object	– – (that)	– – (that)

Notice that English likes to drop the relative pronoun when it defines the object of the clause.
*The doctor **who helped me most** was Dr Clark.* (subject)
*The doctor **I found most helpful** was Dr Clark.* (object)
*The treatment **that helped me most** was acupuncture.* (subject)
*The treatment **I liked best** was acupuncture.* (object)

Notice that there are no commas before and after defining relative clauses when written, and no pauses when spoken.

That is usually used after the following: superlatives, **all**, **every(thing)**, **some(thing)**, **any(thing)**, **no(thing)**, and **only**.
*He wrote some of **the best poetry that's ever been written**.*
***All that's needed** is a little more time.*
*Don't take **anything that's valuable**.*
***The only thing that matters** is that you're safe.*

Prepositions can come either before relative pronouns or at the end of the relative clause. In spoken English, it is much more common to put the preposition at the end (and to drop the pronoun).
*This is the book **I was talking to you about**.*
*The people **I work with** are very kind.*
*The hotel **we stayed at** was a little disappointing.*

A second relative introduction by **and** or **but** usually takes a **wh-** pronoun, not **that**.
*Someone **that I greatly admire**, but **who I've never met**, is Professor Keats.*

Non-defining relative clauses

Here are the main forms used. The form in brackets is possible but not as common.

	Person	Thing
Subject	, who	, which . . . .
Object	, who	, which . . . .
	(, whom . . . ,)	

*Mr Jenkins, **who has written several books**, spoke at the meeting last night.* (subject)
*Peter Clark, **who the Prime Minister sacked from the Cabinet**, has become the chairman of Redland Bank.* (object)
*My favourite drink is whisky, **which is one of Britain's most profitable exports**.* (subject)
*I gave him a sandwich, **which he ate greedily**.* (object)

Notice that there are commas around non-defining relative clauses when written, and pauses before and after them when spoken.

Prepositions can come at the end of non-defining relative clauses, but in a formal style they are usually put before the relative pronoun.
*The lecturer spoke for two hours on the subject of Weingarten's Theory of Market Forces, which none of us had ever heard **of**.*
*The privatization of all industry, **to** which this government is deeply committed, is not universally popular.*

'Which'

Which can be used in non-defining clauses to refer to the whole of the preceding clause.
*He passed the exam, **which** surprised everyone.*
*The lift isn't working, **which** means we'll have to use the stairs.*

'Whose'

Whose can be used in both defining and non-defining relative clauses to refer to possession.
*There's the woman **whose** son was killed recently. (defining)*
*ABC Airways, **whose** fares across the Atlantic were lower than anybody else's, has just declared itself bankrupt. (non-defining).*

'What'

What is used as a relative pronoun instead of **the thing that** in some sentences.
*Has she told you **what's** worrying her?*
*I have to do **what** I believe is right.*

'When' and 'where'

When and **where** can be used to introduce both defining and non-defining relative clauses. In defining relative clauses, **when** can be left out.
*Can you tell me the exact time **(when)** you hope to arrive?*

Where cannot be left out unless we add a preposition.
*That's the hotel **where** we're staying.*
*That's the hotel we're staying **at**.*

In non-defining relative clauses, **when** and **where** cannot be left out.
*We go swimming after 5.00, **when** everyone else has gone home.*
*He shops in Oxford, **where** his sister lives.*

'Why'

Why can be used to introduce defining relative clauses after the word **reason**. It can be left out.
*Do you remember **the reason why** we are arguing?*

NB We can also say:
*Do you remember **why** we are arguing?*
where the clause beginning with **why** is the object of the verb.

Participles

1 As adjectives

Present participles describe an action which is still happening.
*He dives into the sea to save the **drowning** child.*
*They watched the **burning** forest.*

Past participles describe the result of an action that has happened.
*She looked at the **broken** chair.*
*The **completed** statue looked very lifelike.*

2 As reduced relative clauses

When participles come after a noun, they are like reduced relative clauses.
*I met a woman **riding** a donkey. (who was riding)*
*The cash **stolen** in the raid was never recovered. (that was stolen)*

3 In adverb clauses

Participle clauses can describe actions that are going on simultaneously.
*She sat by the fire **reading** a book and **sipping** a mug of coffee.*
*He went to the party **dressed** as a monkey.*
Participle clauses can describe actions that happen consecutively.
***Opening** his suitcase, he took out a revolver.*
***Released** from its cage, the lion prowled around.*

If it is important to show that the first action has finished before the second begins, the perfect participle is used.
***Having** finished lunch, we set off.*

Participle clauses can express the idea of **because**.
***Being** a mean person, he never spent more than he had to. (Because he was a mean person, . . .)*
*Not **knowing** what to do, I waited patiently. (Because I didn't know . . .)*
***Weakened** by years of bad health, she could hardly sit up in bed. (Because she had been weakened . . .)*

NB Notice that in all participle clauses, the subject of the clause and the subject of the main verb must be the same.

4 After certain verbs

Many verbs can be followed by an **-ing** form.
*I **spent** the evening **decorating**.*
*He **spends** his money **gambling**.*
*Don't **waste** time **thinking** about what might have been.*
*Let's **go swimming**.*
*He **keeps on asking** me to go out with him.*
*I **can't stand getting up** in the dark.*

UNIT 10

Inversion to express emphasis

1 Inversion can take place after negative adverbials such as **never**, **nowhere**, **not for one minute**, **not since**, **not until**, **never again**, **rarely**.
Never had he eaten such a huge meal.
Nowhere will you come across a more hospitable nation.
Not until I reached home did I allow myself to consider the result of my actions.
Rarely do you meet a man of such integrity.

2 Inversion can take place in certain established sentence patterns.
Hardly had the two strangers arrived when the majority of the guests departed.
No sooner had we sat down to dinner than there came an explosion from the kitchen.
Little did anyone realize the seriousness of the situation.

3 Inversion takes place after expressions with **only** and **no**.
Only when I myself became a parent did I realize the value of my parents' advice.
Not only did she write short stories, but she was also a painter of talent.
Only after years of practice could I perform the delicate manoeuvre.
At no time was I ever informed.
In no way can this government deny its guilt.
On no account will I compromise my ideals.

4 Inversion can be used instead of **if** in conditional sentences (see page 139).
Should you ever come to London, I'll show you around.
(Type 1 – *If you should ever come . . .*)
Were he to realize the danger he was in, he would not proceed with this plan.
(Type 2 – *If he realized . . .*)
Had you arrived earlier, you would have seen a most remarkable sight.
(Type 3 – *If you had arrived . . .*)

UNIT 11

Hypothesizing

As we saw in Unit 7 (page 139), English tense usage can be divided into fact and non-fact. There are certain constructions (including conditional sentences) that have a hypothetical meaning, and the unreality that they express is shown by shifting the verb form 'backwards'.
I wish I knew the answer (but I don't know it).
If only I hadn't behaved so badly (but I did behave badly).

1 Hypothesizing about the present and future

Present and future time reference
The Simple Past tense form is used for present and future time reference. Notice that **were** is used instead of **was**, especially in formal style.
I wish I were taller!
If only he were here now!
Supposing/suppose you had a million pounds? What would you do?

Present state versus present action or event
When we hypothesize about a present state, the Simple Past tense form is used.
I wish you lived nearer.
If only I had a car!

When we hypothesize about a present action or event, **would** is used.
I wish you'd help more in the house.
If only she wouldn't wash her socks in the bath!

Would here expresses willingness in the first sentence, and annoying habit in the second.

'I wish'/'if only'
Notice that it is unusual to say **I wish/if only I would (n't)** . . . because we can control what we want or do. However, we can say **I wish/if only I could** . . .
I wish I could remember where I put my glasses.
If only I could give up smoking.

We can say **I wish/if only . . . would** to refer to a definite time in the future, but only if we think that the action will probably not happen.
I wish she'd come with me tomorrow.
If only you'd fix the car this weekend, we could go for a drive.

If it is possible that our wish *will* be realized, then a different structure such as **I hope** is needed.
I hope it doesn't rain tomorrow.

Fact versus non-fact
Notice the difference between fact and non-fact in the following pair of sentences.
He looks as if he is French.
(Fact – it is perfectly possible that he is.)
He looks as if he were French.
(Non-fact – we know he isn't.)

The same distinction is found with other **as if/as though** structures.
Why is that girl smiling at me as though she knew me?
He looks after her as though she were his sister.
He behaves as if he owned the place.

'It's time'
It's time can be followed by an infinitive.
It's time to go to bed.
It's time for us to go.

When we want to say that it is time for someone else to do something, the construction **it's time** + past tense form is often used.
It's time you got your hair cut.

'Would rather'
Would rather can be followed by an infinitive (without **to**).
I'd rather have red wine, please.
When **would rather** is followed by another person, the construction **would rather** + person + past tense form is used.
I'd rather you kept this a secret.
She would rather you paid by cheque.

2 **Hypothesizing about the past**

Past time reference
The Past Perfect tense form is used for past time reference.
I wish she hadn't been so unkind.
If only the police had looked in the attic, they would have found him!
Supposing/suppose we had missed the plane? What would we have done?

'Would rather'
Would rather + the Past Perfect is possible, but it is more usual to express the same idea using **wish**.
I'd rather | *you had said nothing.*
I wish

Fact versus non-fact
Notice the difference between fact and non-fact in the following sentences.
He looked as if he was tired.
(Fact – this is probaby how he felt.)
He looked as if he had seen a ghost.
(Non-fact – very improbable.)

3 **Would like**

Would like can be used with a perfect infinitive to talk about things we wish we had done.
I would like to have lived in the eighteenth century.

This can also be expressed by **would have liked** followed by either an ordinary infinitive or a perfect infinitive.
I would have liked to live | *in the eighteenth*
I would have liked to have lived | *century.*

The same forms can be used to refer to the present and the future if it is contrary to fact.
I would like to have stayed in | *tonight, instead*
I would have liked to stay in | *of going out.*
I would have liked to have stayed in

The Present Subjunctive

1 **After verbs, adjectives, and nouns**

The Present Subjunctive is used in **that** clauses after verbs, adjectives, and nouns that express a necessity, plan, or intention for the future (or the future-in-the-past).
She insisted that he help her.
The judge demands that the prisoner tell the truth.
NB The subjunctive is the same whether the sentence is present or past.

Verbs that follow this pattern are: **order**, **command**, **insist**, **demand**, **request**, **ask**, **recommend**, **propose**, **suggest**, and others with similar meanings. Remember that they must be followed by a **that** clause.

Adjectives that follow this pattern are: **important**, **vital**, **essential**, **necessary**, **desirable**, and others with similar meaning.

Nouns that follow this pattern are related to the verbs listed above: for example, **order**, **request**, **proposal**, **suggestion**.

2 **Alternatives to the subjunctive**

The Present Subjunctive is not very common in modern British English, and is used mainly in formal style. It can be avoided in all the above examples by using **should**.
She insisted that he should help her.
The judge demands that the prisoner should tell the truth.

The subjunctive is sometimes avoided by using an indicative form in its place.
She insisted that he helped her.
The judge demands that the prisoner tells the truth.

However, this is not always possible, and it is better to use **should** if you wish to avoid the subjunctive.

3 **The Past Subjunctive**

There is a Past Subjunctive in English, but it is only visible with the form **were** to express non-fact.
If I were rich, I'd give all my money to you.
I wish he were here now.

Tapescript section

UNIT 1

Tapescript 1a

Interview with Mr Ian Beer, Head Master of Harrow School

I = Interviewer
B = Mr Beer

I Let me ask you first, er, Harrow School and schools like it are known as 'independent' schools, and until recently they were referred to as 'public' schools. Why is it that a private school was known as a public school?

B You must remember that the vast majority of the independent schools were founded well before any government in this country made state education available to all. Therefore, before 1900, all these independent schools were available to the total public. Admittedly they had to pay fees. And that is where the name 'public' came from. Once the government began to legislate to give all children in the land a state education then the public schools, which were indeed private, changed their name to being 'independent', in other words, independent of government control.

I Has Harrow School changed in the past hundred years?

B I think that if a foreigner came to Harrow Hill and looked at the boys in the High Street, and the masters, they would think it hadn't . The boys wear straw hats, they wear the old what is called a 'bluer' - a blazer kind of garment - during the week, they wear tails on a Sunday, the senior boys wear top hats. All the masters have to teach in suits and wear gowns. I have to wear my mortar board to raise my hat to the boys as they raise their hat to me. And there is a traditional formality along the High Street. Once you dive into the classroom, or into a boarding house, or into my study, you would find that the place had changed at a deeper level very very much indeed; the curriculum of course has changed fundamentally, science was not taught here in the last century; er ... that Fox Talbot, who started photography in this country, started his experiments in this very house, but was banned by the headmaster as he did not want chemistry to be taught. So today you will find Latin and Greek is taught as it was in 1570, but you will also find craft design technology, Russian, computer sciences, and a lot of very modern teaching techniques in all subjects.

I You have 770 boys here between the ages of thirteen and eighteen. Erm ... what about discipline? How do you control them?

B Well, we're rather a village on the hill. There are 770 boys, there are over 200 people employed here, who live on the hill with their families, and we try and run it as a little village. We do not, as a lot of er ... other people I know think, we do not beat any boys here. Erm, we try and encourage them to treat other people as they would be treated. We're very fussy about courtesy. And the normal kinds of ill discipline, which you would find in any family of young boys growing up and spreading their wings, are usually things which are anti-social. And so we try and punish them by making them do something back for the community. If you had been here this morning, you would have found a senior boy with a group of naughty boys at quarter to seven in the morning. They would be clearing up all the litter over the main public streets of Harrow Hill in order to keep our environment clean and tidy.

I As this is a boarding school, let's talk a bit about the extra-curricular activities. What ... what do you do with the children when they're not in class?

B We here feel strongly that we educate 'the whole man'. And therefore, because they're here twenty-four hours of the day, it gives us the opportunity of , erm, carrying out our academic teaching in the formroom, and then in the afternoons and evenings we devote our time to such activities as teaching acting, music, art, technology, all the kind of games you could possibly think of, society life - debating societies, science societies, philosophy societies, er ... chapel services, communion services. In other words we try here, I come back to the word I used earlier, we are really a village, (laugh) and we have total village life.

Tapescript 1b

Radio programme on independent schools

P = Presenter
W = Patricia Wilby

P Hello, and welcome to today's *Worldly Wise*, the programme that investigates current issues and tells you, the consumer, all about them. Today our attention turns to independent schools, the alternative system for those that can afford it. Most people believe that independent schools offer their pupils advantages that state schools don't. Some think this is unfair. Others will go to the edge of ruin to get the 'best' education for their children. What are the independent schools like these days? Are they still as they were depicted in so many books and films? We sent Patricia Wilby to investigate.

W In 1980 Eton abolished fagging - that is younger boys as servants to older, more senior ones - after the Head had at last persuaded two-thirds of his housemasters that this was an outdated institution. Winchester, for the first time in its history, sent more boys to provincial universities than it sent to Oxbridge. Bradford Grammar School decided that boys of thirteen and fourteen should be compelled to study science. And the Head Master of Oundle was able to assert that, although the practice had not been formally abolished, boys had not been beaten 'for many years'. Public schools are not what they were. For a start, you're not supposed to call them 'public' schools any more. They prefer the term 'independent' school, suggesting initiative and enterprise instead of snobbery and prejudice. Over the past fifteen years, they have set out to bury the image of institutions that were socially divisive, obsessed with the classics, disdainful of industry because it meant money was earned, not inherited, and where success on the sports field was more important than success in the exam room. The modern public school will point out that engineering is the largest single destination for its leavers. It will show you computer terminals, science laboratories, and craft workshops. It will introduce you, if at all possible, to pupils whose backgrounds are far from aristocratic.

Yet what is remarkable about this revolution is not so much that it has happened, but that it has happened so recently. And if much has changed, what critics regard as the most important things have not. The majority of the nation's Cabinet Ministers, top civil servants, ambassadors, High Court judges, military leaders, bishops, and bank directors went to public schools. They still account for about half the entrants to Oxford and Cambridge.

Although most Western countries have independent school sectors, the British public school system is unique in the extent to which it is set apart from the rest of the nation. This isolation is possible because, by comparison, the private sector in Britain is remarkably small. Around five per cent of the nation's schoolchildren go private, while in the United States the figure is ten per cent, and in France thirty per cent. But the most significant change of all is the importance that is now attached to academic achievement. In the top schools, the focus is firmly on A levels. GCSEs are regarded as a distraction, and pupils might take one or two when they are fifteen. It is academic success that is going to keep top people where they think they belong - at the top.

P And that was a special report by Patricia Wilby. Next week we'll be looking at the state of state education. Until then, good-bye.

UNIT 2

Tapescript 2

Interview with Graham Greene

I = Interviewer
GG = Graham Greene

I The main problem about interviewing Graham Greene is that there is so much one could ask him about, so many things he's done, places he's visited during his seventy-eight years, as well as writing more than twenty of this century's most ingenious, inventive, and exciting novels. In appearance, he's tall and slim, with that slightly apologetic stoop that tall people sometimes have. A modest, affable man, who seemed at first a little nervous of my tape-recorder. 'Every novelist', he once wrote, 'has something in common with a spy. He watches, he overhears, he seeks motives, and analyses character. And as he does so, there's a splinter of ice in his heart.' That's an essential quality, according to Graham Greene.

GG You've got to be cold, and you mustn't get emotionally involved with your characters.

I So you have to preserve a distance from your characters?

GG You've got to preserve a distance. I mean, they're going to come out of your guts, as it were, and you've got to cut the umbilical cord very quickly.

I What about the kind of ice in the heart that you need when you're listening to other people's conversations, or observing the way they're reacting . . .

GG Yes . . . actually, I used that phrase about er . . . when I was young and I was in hospital for appendicitis, and there was a small boy who had broken his leg at football, and he died in front of one's eyes. And then the parents arrived, they'd been summoned to the hospital, and arrived too late, and the mother broke down, and wept by the bed, and used the kind of banal phrases that a bad writer would use in a book. And then, I mean, the fact . . . all the other people in the ward put on earphones over their ears, and I'm afraid I didn't. I . . . I just . . .

I You listened because you felt it was something you could use.

GG . . . because it was something I could use.

I Do you observe yourself closely, too, your own emotions? Are those important for a writer to use?

GG Erm . . . I probably do without knowing it, because I went through psychoanalysis when I was sixteen, and that probably gave me a habit of . . . of observing.

I How much do you use your own experience, then, I mean, places you've been to, people you've met, in your writing?

GG Not people, much. I mean (mumble) except perhaps a very tiny, minor character, or somebody who passes across the stage, as it were, without any speech. But er . . . the main character has to be imagined, and therefore some of one must be in him, but he's a kind of composite figure, like we're composite figures of our fathers and grandfathers and great-grandfathers.

I Graham Greene's flat at Antibes in the South of France contains several abandoned, unfinished novels. Greene says that as he writes a novel, the narrative is outside his conscious control. He hands over that control to the story and the characters, and he never knows, therefore, until he's at least a quarter of the way into a book, whether it will actually grow into a complete novel or not.

GG As a rule, one knows the beginning, and the middle, and the end. The great thing is to let the characters dictate . . . certain extent. They, they, they probably won't dictate any change in the end, because in the end is one's beginning, as it were. But er . . . it's a very pleasant sensation when one gets up from a day's working - 'Well, I never though that er . . . I never thought of that !'

I *Ways of Escape* is the title of your second autobiographical book.

GG Yes.

I You said that a large part of your life, writing and travelling, is escape. Escape from what?

GG Boredom.

I Is that boredom with the world or with yourself?

GG B . . . with both, probably. (laughs)

I I find it hard to understand in a way how someone who has a great curiosity about people, and who also has the means and the opportunity to travel, can nevertheless be bored.

GG Well, I think one is born with a capacity for boredom. I've . . . I experienced it first, terribly, at the age of sixteen. And er . . . even . . . even danger doesn't destroy boredom . . . for instance, during the Blitz, one could be afraid for about an hour or so, but then one became bored . . . became increasingly boring. And once when I was . . . I think it comes in *Ways of Escape,* when I was caught in crossfire on the Suez Canal, one was afraid for a while. One was for about two hours or more on a sandbank, and then one got more and more bored. So I think . . . it is a disease, really.

I But you have sought danger as a way of . . .

GG Yes.

I . . . relieving boredom.

GG Yes, but then unfortunately the danger (laugh) becomes boring!

Tapescript 3

Extract from a spy story

Angus Pym woke up on the dot of six o' clock, as he always did, no matter where he was or what he had been doing the previous day. His first thought was the realization that he was still wearing shirt and trousers, and when his eyes fell on the reports piled up around him on the bed, the events of the previous evening came back to him. He had gone to his club for supper, had just finished his steak tartare and was looking forward to a splendid zabaglione when his meal was rudely interrupted by a call from M, his controller.

After an ice-cold shower, Pym thought carefully about which suit to put on. He was seeing M at nine o' clock that morning, and he wanted to make a good impression. Glancing at himself in the mirror, he noticed that he had put on weight recently. He would have to pay more attention to his diet in the future.

An hour later, as he was driving through the rush-hour traffic on his way to meet M, Pym carefully considered the contents of the files. So Zircon, the organization which sought to control the free western world, was back in business? Its founder, Leon Biarrowitz, was dead. Pym knew this, because he had personally arranged his death. But who controlled Zircon now? Doubtless M would tell him.

UNIT 3

Tapescript 4

'Mad Dogs and Englishmen' by Noël Coward

In tropical climes there are certain times of day
When all the citizens retire
To take their clothes off and perspire.
It's one of those rules that the greatest fools obey
Because the sun is far too sultry
And one must avoid its ultry violet ray.
The natives grieve when the whitemen leave their huts
Because they're obviously, definitely nuts!

Mad dogs and Englishmen go out in the midday sun.
The Japanese don't care to,
The Chinese wouldn't dare to.
Hindus and Argentines sleep firmly from twelve to one.
But Englishmen detest a siesta.
In the Philippines they have lovely screens
To protect you from the glare.
In the Malay States there are hats like plates
Which the Britishers won't wear.
At twelve noon the natives swoon,
And no further work is done.
But mad dogs and Englishmen go out in the midday sun.

It's such a surprise for the Eastern eyes to see,
That though the English are effete
They're quite impervious to heat.
When the whiteman rides every native hides in glee,
Because the simple creatures hope he
Will impale his solar topee on a tree.

It seems such a shame when the English claim the earth
That they give rise to such hilarity and mirth.

Mad dogs and Englishmen go out in the midday sun.
The toughest Burmese bandit
Can never understand it.
In Rangoon the heat of noon is just what the natives shun
They put their Scotch or Rye down and lie down.
In a jungle town where the sun beats down
To the rage of man and beast,
The English garb of the English *sahib*
Merely gets a bit more creased.
In Bangkok at twelve o' clock
They foam at the mouth and run
But mad dogs and Englishmen go out in the midday sun.

Mad dogs and Englishmen go out in the midday sun.
The smallest Malay rabbit
Deplores this foolish habit.
In Hong Kong they strike a gong
And fire off a noonday gun
To reprimand each inmate who's in late.
In the mangrove swamps where the python romps
There is peace from twelve to two.
Even caribous lie around and snooze,
For there's nothing else to do.
In Bengal to move at all is seldom if ever done.
But mad dogs and Englishmen go out in the midday sun.

Tapescript 5

Interview with Quentin Crisp

P = **Presenter**
C = **Quentin Crisp**
I = **Interviewer**

P This is part of an interview with Quentin Crisp which was broadcast on LBC (London Broadcasting Company) radio. The interviewer asked Quentin Crisp why he had always felt different and apart from other people.

C I really never had any option to do anything else. I was never going to be able to join the human race, and I realized that very early. When I was a child I was an object of scorn. I don't ever remember not being laughed at, by my brothers and my sister, my parents when I was a child, by the other boys at school, as you can well imagine, when I went to school, and by the people with whom I worked when I went out into the world. So that it seemed I either had to try and make a go of being myself or accept complete failure as being a real person.

I It sounds as though it was . . . very miserable childhood. Was it?

C It was a miserable childhood, but one must be careful. I wasn't beaten, I wasn't shut in dark cellars for days on end. You hear now of such terrible things happening to children that you have to be careful when you say 'I had a rotten childhood'. It was, in a sense, my own fault. I was unable to learn how to be with other people in the sense of being *like* other people.

I When did that first hit you, when did you first realize that that's how you felt?

C Well, I suppose mostly at school, when my appearance, which was just like, to me, I was just like everybody else. I mean, they wouldn't have allowed me to grow my hair long, er, because as you know a public school is just like being in prison. But it still made no difference. People were saying 'Why on earth do you say these things? Why do you stand like that? Why do you look like that?' I mean, it never stopped.

I Do you think this was with you from birth, I mean, if the rest of your family was so completely conventional and ordinary, how did you learn to be like that?

C I don't know how it happened, because, yes, my mother and father were middle-class, middle-brow, middling people, and my sister was just like a human being all her life. My brothers were sort of part-time hooligans. When my . . . one of my nieces went all the way to Chile to . . . er . . . see her cousin and see my brother, when she came back, she said 'Oh, he's a hooligan'. And I said 'He can't be, he's been with the same firm for thirty years'. And she said 'Well, he went to a board meeting wearing rope-soled sandals and one of his daughter's jumpers'.

I But . . . I mean . . . did . . . have you kept in touch with your family? Did you feel that you were rejected by your family, or did you reject your family?

C They were very good. They . . . my father died when I was twenty-two, more or less in self-defence, I think. My mother lived until I was in my fifties, and of course, if you live long enough, you become the same age as your parents. If you're three and your mother is thirty, she might be from another planet. If you're fifty-three and your mother is eighty-three, what the hell, you're just two little old people. So I got to know my mother, and indeed I knew her better than I knew my sister, in a sense.

P The interview goes on to discuss Quentin Crisp's career as a writer, which, although successful, did not bring in much money.

I Would you have liked more money though? I mean, would you . . . what would you have done with it if you'd had it?

C If I'd had a great deal of money, I wouldn't have lived very differently. I would have lived in one room - I never know what people do with the room they're not in - I would have lived in a larger room, and it would have been made so that everything was very easy for me to do. I like the process of living to be reduced to an absolute minimum. But otherwise and that, I would have lived in America earlier, I could have gone there, and I should say if I was rich I would have been welcome come what may. Otherwise and that, I would have lived in one room, I would have done whatever people found for me to do, and when I wasn't doing it, I would have done a hell of a lot of nothing. I'm very good at doing nothing.

I One of the stories about you is that you lived in this room in Chelsea for thirty-seven years without ever cleaning it. Is that true?

C That's true. There's no need to clean your room. All that's a dream invented by your mother. Er, all . . . everyone who sees you in your room says 'You can't go on living like this. You'll get some terrible disease . . .' erm, and so on. It's all quite untrue. I'm still here, nearly eighty, and I've never cleaned any room I've lived in.

UNIT 4

Tapescript 6

Six people's childhood memories

1 I used to like to do well just to see the look of pleasure on my dad's face. He'd say 'Pet, it's like a tonic to me when you do well - I don't know how I have such clever children!' But I never felt

I was being pushed too hard. If I did badly he'd just say 'Well what'll it matter a hundred years from now that you failed your Geography exam!'

2 Whatever I did was just never quite good enough. I wasn't very strong as a child - I used to get attacks of asthma, so I couldn't do PE or games. Well, anyway, when I was twelve I was so thrilled because I was put in the second eleven for cricket. I was so sure he'd be pleased. D'you know what he said? 'Second team? When I was your age I was in the first for cricket, rugby, *and* hockey.' I felt so crushed, I just crawled away and cried - in private of course!

3 Our house was always open to whoever came round. You'd never know how many people would sit down to a meal. My parents were always inviting people in, and my sisters and I brought friends from school. They used to love coming to our house because they were made so welcome. There were no petty rules, and as long as we tidied up they didn't mind what we did. We called a lot of my parents' friends 'Uncle' or 'Aunt' so-and-so. We never used to know who were our real relations! But what was so nice for us kids was that we grew up surrounded by a lot of adults, not just our parents, so we heard what they had to say, and they listened to our opinions as well.

4 I think it started out of sheer boredom - I mean - they gave me every material benefit, pocket money any time I asked; I had my own brand-new BMW when I was seventeen. I wanted for nothing except their time - I mean - they were always so busy, always getting dressed up to go somewhere, and so wrapped up in each other. I really don't know why they had children. They always said I was a mistake! Anyway I started hanging about with this bunch of 'yobbos' and they said 'Try it' - and I thought 'Why not? Who cares?'

5 They finally split up when I was four. It's one of my earliest memories - my dad sitting me on his knee and saying, 'Mummy and daddy have decided to live in different houses and I want you to decide which house you want to live in.' Can you imagine asking a child of four? I hadn't a clue what to say, but my very much bigger brother was standing behind him mouthing, 'Say mum, say mum.' So I did, and I never saw my dad again except once when I was about ten - from the top of a double-decker bus. At least, I think it was him - I'm sure it was, that time - only I still keep thinking I see him all over the place. I've had three step-dads - it's not the same.

6 She was like a sea of calm, nothing ruffled her, she always had time. Me and the others would be scrapping about something, and she'd say 'OK, OK, let's calm down, let's go back to the beginning and sort it out - so we did, and it was sorted out!' I remember this schoolfriend of mine, she fell off her bike and completely smashed her front teeth. She didn't cry because she was hurt, but because her mother was so particular about her appearance. She said 'She'll kill me, she thinks I have such lovely teeth!' I thought 'Gosh - how weird, I couldn't bear it if my mother was like that!' In fact this friend came to my mum first and she rang and told her mum what had happened. Fancy not being able to go to your own mum!

Tapescript 7

Extract from a talk by Dr Spock, the pediatrician

I think in previous centuries, and still in the first half of the twentieth century, parents felt they had to intimidate their children, just the way I was intimidated, scolded all the time, made to feel evil, threatened with loss of love, and maybe some kind of punishment. I used to be scared of my parents, I was scared of the policeman on the block, I was scared of my teachers, I was scared of barking dogs, I was scared of bullies. Now I think that it was Freud and Dewey particularly who changed that point of view. Freud said in so many words, it isn't by disciplining or intimidating your children, it's by loving them, then they love you, and they want to be worthy of you, and they want to grow up to be mature people like you. In other words it's the love between parent and child that makes them mature, and become responsible. And I think it was Dewey who said, you don't have to force children to learn, they're wild to learn. I think both of these philosophers gave parents more trust in their children. I think my job was to translate this into ordinary language and apply it to ordinary home situations. And that what the book really says is, not only trust yourself as a parent, it says, trust your children. They will want to grow up responsible. So I think many fewer parents tried to intimidate their children in the last twenty-five years. And I think that's why their children are that independent. So when the Government says, 'Don't reason about the war, go off and fight it because we tell you to', young people say, 'Wait a minute, maybe you're not right. Maybe it isn't the right war.' And I think that when universities say to youths, 'Never mind your ideas about how you should be taught, we're in this business, you take it from us.' And I think young people said, 'Well, maybe it is our business. We're the ones who are here for the education.' So I think that I had a small part in translating Freud and Dewey.

Tapescript 8

'How to live to be 100 or more' by George Burns

People keep asking me, 'George, you're 88, how do you do it? You make films, you do television, you give concerts, you record albums, smoke cigars, drink Martinis, go out with pretty girls - how do you do it?'

It's simple. For instance, a Martini. You fill the glass with ice; then pour in some gin and a touch of dry vermouth, add an olive, and you've got yourself a Martini.

Today you don't have to worry about getting old; you have to worry about rusting. So I also do exercises and walk a lot. Walking is even easier than making a Martini. I take one foot and put it in front of the other foot; then I take the other foot and put it in front of the other foot, and before I know it I'm walking. And you don't even need an olive. Every morning, I walk a mile and a half. My advice is to walk whenever you can. It's free; you feel better and look trim.

If you want to live to be 100 or older, you can't just sit around waiting for it to happen. You have to get up and go after it.

There's no point in kidding yourself. When you get older you slow down, you wear out a little. But right now I'm 88, and there isn't a thing I can't do today that I couldn't do when I was 18. Of course, I was pathetic when I was 18. I wasn't so hot when I was 25 either. I saved everything for now. I hate to brag, but I'm very good at 'now'.

Here are my other secrets for long life:

Think positive. If you ask me what is the single most important key to longevity, I would have to say it's avoiding worry, stress, and tension. And if you didn't ask me, I'd still have to say it . Worry, stress, and tension are not only unpleasant but can shorten your life.

My attitude is, if something is beyond your control, there's no point worrying about it. And if you can do something about it, then there's still nothing to worry about. I feel that way when the plane I'm on is bouncing around in turbulence. It's not my problem. The pilot gets a lot of money to fly that plane; let him worry about it.

I can honestly say I was not even uptight about my heart bypass several years ago. It was beyond my control. It was the doctor's business.

When I came round from the anaesthetic, I heard the surgeon say, 'George, you did great. You're just fine.'

I said, 'Doctor, I wasn't the least bit concerned.'
'Really?' he said. 'I was a nervous wreck.'

Even that didn't bother me. Then he handed me his bill, and I passed out.

Stay active. I know that for some people retirement works out fine. They enjoy it. I also know that for a great many others it presents lots of problems.

To me the biggest danger of retirement is what it can do to your attitude. When you have all that time on your hands, you think old, you act old. It's a mistake. I see people who, the minute they get to be 65, start rehearsing to be old. They practise grunting when they get up, and by the time they get to be 70 they've made it - they're a hit - they're now old!

Not me. When you're around my age you've got to keep occupied. You've got to do something that will get you out of bed. I never made any money in bed. Yes, find something that will make you get out of bed - like an interest, a hobby, a business, a pretty girl - there we are, back in bed again. At my age at least let me talk about it.

Challenge yourself. When my wife Gracie retired in 1958, I could have retired too. Even today I don't have to do what I'm doing. I don't have to travel round giving concerts, making movies, doing television specials, recording country-music albums, being a sex symbol.

I firmly believe that you should keep working as long as you can. And if you can't, try to find something that will interest you. Don't wait for it to happen; make it happen. Remember, you can't help getting older, but you don't have to get old.

I look to the future, because that's where I'm going to spend the rest of my life.

I feel sorry for people who live in the past. I know it was cheaper then, but you can't keep looking in a rear-view mirror - unless you enjoy having a stiff neck. If you really think your life is over and you have no place to go, I advise you to take very short steps. It'll take you longer to get there.

I don't live in the past; I live in a house in Beverly Hills. It's more comfortable. Actually, you may not believe this, but I don't waste time looking through scrap-books of my career or rereading my old reviews - they were painful enough to read the first time. I find it's best to fall in love with what you're doing today. The things I did yesterday I was in love with yesterday. But that romance is over. I'm very fickle.

There's an old saying, 'Life begins at 40.' That's silly - life begins every morning when you wake up. Open your mind to it; don't just sit there - do things. Swim the English Channel; find a cure for the common cold; be the first to go over the Niagara Falls in

a rocking chair. You see, the possibilities are endless.

If all else fails, try doing something nice for somebody who doesn't expect it. You'll be surprised how good you feel. The Scouts have the right idea. Many's the time I've helped a young lady across the street and over to my place. You should see all my badges.

The point is, with a good positive attitude and a little bit of luck, there's no reason you can't live to be 100. Once you've done that you've really got it made, because very few people die over 100.

Tapescript 9

A short conversation

W = Woman
M = Man

W We had a lovely time at Jim and Chris's last night.

M Did you? That's nice.

W Jim always cooks such wonderful meals.

M Does he? I didn't realize he could cook.

W He's just finished a Cordon Bleu cookery course at night school.

M Has he? Well, I hope we get invited for dinner soon!

W They said they were going to invite you and Sarah next weekend.

M Are they? That's great - I'll look forward to that.

UNIT 5

Tapescript 10

'They' by Siegfried Sassoon

The Bishop tells us: 'When the boys come back
They will not be the same; for they'll have fought
In a just cause; they lead the last attack
On Anti-Christ; their comrades' blood has bought
New right to breed an honourable race.
They have challenged Death and dared him face to face.'

'We're none of us the same!' the boys reply.
'For George lost both his legs; and Bill's stone blind;
Poor Jim's shot through the lungs and like to die;
And Bert's gone syphilitic: you'll not find
A chap who's served that hasn't found *some* change.'
And the Bishop said: 'The ways of God are strange!'

Tapescript 11

The Christmas Truce, 1914

Part 1
(gunfire in the background)

A Hey, listen!

B Yeah, they're coppin' it down Railway Wood tonight.

A Nah, not that. Listen. (singing in the background) What is it?

C Singin' innit?

B It's those Welsh bastards in the next trench.

C That's Jerry, that is.

B Yeah, it is Jerry. It's comin' from over there.

D Sing up, Jerry! Let's 'ear yer!
('*Heilige Nacht*' in the background)

C Oh nice, weren't it? (clapping)

E (from afar) Tommy? Hello Tommy!

B Eh! 'E 'eard us!

C 'Ello?

E *Fröliche Weihnacht!*

C Eh?

B What?

E Happy Christmas!

ALL Oh! 'Appy Christmas!

F Hey, yeah, it's Christmas!

Part 2

I = Interviewer
GW = Graham Williams
HS = Harold Startin

I That scene from the West End musical of the 1960s '*Oh What a Lovely War!*' is a pretty accurate illustration of the kind of thing that happened in several places on the Western Front on that Christmas Eve of 1914. Listen to the account of someone who was actually there. Graham Williams, a rifleman with the London Rifle Brigade, was on sentry duty that night.

GW On the stroke of 11 o' clock, which by German time was midnight, 'cos they were an hour ahead of us, lights began to appear all along the German trenches, and er . . . then people started singing. They started singing *Heilige Nacht*, (stutter) *Silent Night*. So I thought 'Well, this is extraordinary!' And I woke up all the other chaps, and all the other sentries must have done the same thing, to come and see what was going on. They sang this carol right through, and we responded with English Christmas carols, and they replied with German again, and when we came to *Come All Ye Faithful*, they joined in singing, with us (mumble) singing it in Latin, *Adeste Fideles*.

I So by the time you got to that carol, both sides were singing the same carol together?

GW Both singing the same carol together. Then after that, one of the Germans called out, 'Come over and see us, Tommy. Come over and see us!' So I could speak German pretty fluently in those days, so I called back . . . I said, 'No, you come over and see us!', I said, '*Nein, kommen . . . zuerst kommen Sie hier, Fritz!*' And nobody did come that time, and eventually the lights all burned out, and quietened down and went on with the usual routine for the night. Next morning I was asleep, when I woke up I found everyone was walking out into no-man's-land, meeting the Germans, talking to them, and . . . (mutter) wonderful scene . . . couldn't believe it!

I Further along the line in the perfect weather, Private Harold Startin of the Old Contemptibles was enjoying that morning too. He couldn't speak any German, but that didn't stop him making friends.

HS We were 'Tommy' to them, and they were all 'Fritz' to us. (mumble) They couldn't have been more cordial towards you, all sharing their goodies with you. They were giving us cigars (laughs) about as big as your arm, and tobacco.

I Were you frightened at first? Were you suspicious at all? Because these were people . . .

HS No!

I . . . that you'd been trained to hate, weren't they?

HS No! There was no hatred, we'd got no grudge against them, they'd got no grudge against us. We were . . . we were the best of pals, although we were there to kill one another, there were no two ways about that at all. They helped us bury our dead, and we buried our dead with

149

their dead. I've seen many a cross with a German name and number on and a British name and number on. 'In death not divided.'

I Did you do other work during the truce as well? Was it just burying the dead, or were there other things . . .

HS Oh, there was strengthening the trenches, borrowing their tools . . .

I You actually borrowed German tools to strengthen your trenches?

HS We borrowed German tools. They . . . then . . . they'd come and help you strengthen your defences against them.

Part 3

I = Interviewer
HS = Harold Startin

I Not only was the truce more extensive than anyone has realized before, it also lasted much longer than has been believed until now. In some areas, the war started up again on New Year's Day, but in the part of the line where Harold Startin was, the truce lasted a lot longer than that.

HS Ours, it went on for six weeks. You can read in the history books about Sir John French, when he heard of it, he were all against it. But our truce went on for six weeks. And the Württemberg Regiment, they got relieved before we did, and they told us they thought it we' the Prussian Guards goin' to relieve them, and (stutter) if it was, we should hear three rifle shots at intervals, and if we only heard three shots we should know that the Prussian Guards, that we' opposite us then, and we'd got to keep down.

I Because they would be fiercer than . . .

HS Yes!

I . . . than the Württembergers?

HS Yes!

I Can you remember particular Germans that you spoke to? Over six weeks you must have made friends?

HS I spoke to one, Otto comes from Stuttgart, as 'as been over to England to see me.

I So you made friends during the truce and kept in touch after the war?

HS Made friends during the truce, and friends after.

Part 4

I = Interviewer
MB = Malcolm Brown

I By early February 1915, the truce was over. Two people, Malcolm Brown and Shirley Seaton, wrote a book about the Christmas Truce, determined that this should be an event that should not be forgotten.

MB This was the f . . . the first year of the first total war, a war which has become legendary for its viciousness and brutality. And we think it's really rather remarkable that in that war, there occurred, beyond question, the greatest instance of friendship and fraternization between opposing warring forces. And though at the time, that event disappeared over the horizon as the great battles of 1915, '16, '17 came on, now when one looks back on it, one can see that this was, as it were, the lighting of a light, the shi . . . er, er . . . a shining light, the making of a gesture, the laying down of a sort of a first glimmer of protest against the concept that nations should be locked in massive and total war together.

Goodbyee!
(Soldiers' song from the 1914-1918 war.)
Goodbyee! Goodbyee!
Wipe the tear, baby dear, from your eyee!
Though it's hard to part, I know,
I'll be tickled to death to go.
Don't cryee! Don't sighee!
There's a silver lining in the sky.
Bon soir, old thing! Cheerio! Chin-chin!
Au revoir! Toodle-oo! Goodbyee!

Tapescript 12

Emphatic Structures

See page 58.

UNIT 6

Tapescript 13a

Pygmalion : Extract 2

See page 67.

Tapescript 13b

Pygmalion : Extract 3

Higgins [*brusquely, recognizing her (Eliza) with unconcealed disappointment, and at once, babylike, making an intolerable grievance of it*] Why, this is the girl I jotted down last night. She's no use: I've got all the records I want of the Lisson Grove lingo; and I'm not going to waste another cylinder on it. [*To the girl*] Be off with you: I don't want you.

The Flower Girl Dont you be so saucy. You aint heard what I come for yet. [*To Mrs Pearce, who is waiting at the door for further instructions*] Did you tell him I come in a taxi?

Mrs Pearce Nonsense, girl! What do you think a gentleman like Mr Higgins cares what you came in?

The Flower Girl Oh, we are proud! He aint above giving lessons, not him: I heard him say so. Well, I aint come here to ask for any compliment; and if my money's not good enough I can go elsewhere.

Higgins Good enough for what?

The Flower Girl Good enough for ye-oo. Now you know, don't you? I'm come to have lessons, I am. And to pay for em too: make no mistake.

Higgins [*stupent*] Well!!! [*Recovering his breath with a gasp*] What do you expect me to say to you?

The Flower Girl Well, if you was a gentle-man, you might ask me to sit down, I think. Dont I tell you I'm bringing you business?

Higgins Pickering: shall we ask this baggage to sit down, or shall we throw her out of the window?

The Flower Girl [*running away in terror to the piano, where she turns at bay*] Ah-ah-oh-ow-ow-ow-oo! [*Wounded and whimpering*] I wont be called a baggage when Ive

offered to pay like any lady.
Motionless, the two men stare at her from the other side of the room, amazed.

Pickering [*gently*] What is it you want, my girl?

The Flower Girl I want to be a lady in a flower shop stead of selling at the corner of Tottenham Court Road. But they wont take me unless I can talk more genteel. He said he could teach me. Well, here I am ready to pay him - not asking any favour - and he treats me as if I was dirt.

Mrs Pearce How can you be such a foolish ignorant girl as to think you could afford to pay Mr Higgins?

The Flower Girl Why shouldnt I? I know what lessons cost as well as you do; and I'm ready to pay.

Higgins How much?

The Flower Girl [*coming back to him, triumphant*] Now youre talking! I thought youd come off it when you saw a chance of getting back a bit of what you chucked at me last night. [*Confidentially*] You had a drop in, hadnt you?

Higgins [*peremptorily*] Sit down.

The Flower Girl Oh, if youre going to make a compliment of it -

Higgins [*thundering at her*] Sit down.

Mrs Pearce [*severely*] Sit down, girl. Do as youre told. [*She places the stray chair near the hearthrug between Higgins and Pickering, and stands behind it waiting for the girl to sit down*].

The Flower Girl Ah-ah-ah-ow-ow-oo! [*She stands, half rebellious, half bewildered*].

Pickering [*very courteous*] Wont you sit down?

Liza [*coyly*] Dont mind if I do. [*She sits down. Pickering returns to the hearthrug*].

Higgins Whats your name?

The Flower Girl Liza Doolittle.

Higgins How much do you propose to pay me for the lessons?

Liza Oh, I know whats right. A lady friend of mine gets French lessons for eighteen pence an hour from a real French gentleman. Well, you wouldnt have the face to ask me the same for teaching me my own language as you would for French; so I wont give more than a shilling. Take it or leave it.

Higgins [*walking up and down the room, rattling his keys and his cash in his pockets*] You know, Pickering, if you consider a shilling, not as a simple shilling, but as a percentage of this girl's income, it works out as fully equivalent to sixty or seventy guineas from a millionaire.

Pickering How so?

Higgins Figure it out. A millionaire has about £150 a day. She earns about half-a-crown.

Liza [*haughtily*] Who told you I only —

Higgins [*continuing*] She offers me two-fifths of her day's income for a lesson. Two-fifths of a millionaire's income for a day would be somewhere about £60. It's handsome. By George, it's enormous! It's the biggest offer I ever had.

Liza [*rising, terrified*] Sixty pounds! What are you talking about? I never offered you sixty pounds. Where would I get—

Higgins Hold your tongue.

Liza [*weeping*] But I aint got sixty pounds. Oh—

Mrs Pearce Dont cry, you silly girl. Sit down. Nobody is going to touch your money.

Higgins Somebody is going to touch you, with a broomstick, if you dont stop snivelling. Sit down.

Liza [*obeying slowly*] Ah-ah-ah-ow-oo-o! One would think you was my father.

Higgins If I decide to teach you, I'll be worse than two fathers to you. Here! [*he offers her his silk handkerchief*]

Liza Whats this for?

Higgins To wipe your eyes. To wipe any part of your face that feels moist. Remember: thats your handkerchief; and thats your sleeve. Dont mistake the one for the other if you wish to become a lady in a shop. *Liza, utterly bewildered, stares helplessly at him.*

Mrs Pearce It's no use talking to her like that, Mr Higgins: she doesnt understand you. Besides, youre quite wrong: she doesnt do it that way at all [*she takes the handkerchief*].

Liza [*snatching it*] Here! You give me that handkerchief. He give it to me, not to you.

Pickering [*laughing*] He did. I think it must be regarded as her property, Mrs Pearce.

Mrs Pearce [*resigning herself*] Serve you right, Mr Higgins.

Pickering Higgins: I'm interested. What about the ambassador's garden party? I'll say youre the greatest teacher alive if you make that good. I'll bet you all the expenses of the experiment you cant do it. And I'll pay for the lessons.

Liza Oh, you are real good. Thank you, Captain.

Higgins [*tempted, looking at her*] It's almost irresistible. She's so deliciously low - so horribly dirty —

Liza [*protesting extremely*] Ah-ah-ah-ah-ow-ow-oo-oo!!! I aint dirty: I washed my face and hands afore I come, I did.

Pickering Youre certainly not going to turn her head with flattery, Higgins.

Mrs Pearce [*uneasy*] Oh, dont say that, sir: theres more ways than one of turning a girl's head; and nobody can do it better than Mr Higgins, though he may not always mean it. I do hope, sir, you wont encourage him to do anything foolish.

Higgins [*becoming excited as the idea grows on him*] What is life but a series of inspired follies? The difficulty is to find them to do. Never lose a chance: it doesnt come every day. I shall make a duchess of this draggle-tailed guttersnipe.

Liza [*strongly deprecating this view of her*] Ah-ah-ah-ow-ow-oo!

Higgins [*carried away*] Yes: in six months - in three if she has a good ear and a quick tongue - I'll take her anywhere and pass her

off as anything. We'll start to-day: now! this moment! Take her away and clean her, Mrs Pearce.

Tapescript 13c

Pygmalion: Extract 4

See pages 68-9.

Tapescript 14

A monologue

Quite honestly, I don't know how you've put up with it for all these years. Personally, I would have left after a few weeks. After all, it's not as though it was your fault, I mean to say, he was the one that was so keen on it in the first place. Actually, he had to work really hard to persuade you, if I remember rightly. Frankly, I think you should remind him of that a bit more often. You are still speaking to each other presumably? I wouldn't blame you if you weren't! Seriously though, enough is enough. Admittedly he wasn't to know, but he should have made it his job to find out! After all, he always prides himself on his thoroughness! Ideally, he should have had it surveyed properly. Of course it costs a bit, but it's always worth it. Obviously he trusted his own judgement. Well, all I can say is it certainly let him down badly this time! Let's hope he's learnt a lesson from it ! Next time - and I hope it's soon for your sake - maybe he'll listen to you. Surely he will? Incidentally, do you know the Turners are thinking of moving to the same estate? As a matter of fact, Jane was telling me they've already viewed a couple of properties. In all fairness we'll just have to warn them. Perhaps you should get Jack to tell them!

Tapescript 15

Dialogues for completion

See page 72.

UNIT 7

Tapescript 16a

Interview with Joanna Bogle, of the National Viewers' and Listeners' Association

I = Interviewer
JB = Joanna Bogle

I Joanna Bogle is a member of the National Viewers' and Listeners' Association, which aims to monitor the output of both television and radio. Joanna believes quite firmly that TV stations should recognize more fully the power and influence of television, and exercise stricter control over programme content. I asked her what kind of thing she personally found offensive on television.

JB Well . . . this would be difficult to say. First I don't think one wants to say so much personally as what our association would find offensive and it's not only offensive but harmful. I do think that I personally find a great deal of the exploitation of sex and sexuality offensive. Perhaps this is particularly as a woman. And I find it very irresponsible too

because we are now recognizing that some of the revolting attitudes towards sex and towards women which became popular . . . have become popular over the last couple of decades have had a number of seriously sad side effects, not least the tragedy of AIDS and so on. So I personally am offended by that, but I would say that the association is probably slightly more concerned, particularly about violence, - violent language, violent activity, and the idea that sloshing out at somebody, engaging in really savage, barbaric er . . . er . . . activity is a normal thing even a praiseworthy, heroic, manly thing to do. I'm thinking, for instance, of films like *Sebastiane*, and *Jubilee*, that disgusting film where policemen were seen erm . . . being the victims of cannibalism and somebody was roasted alive on a spit . . . ugh . . .

I Was this shown on television?

JB Er . . . Yes this was shown on Channel 4. I regard that as unacceptable . . . grossly violent, sadistic er . . . with the most horrible and depraved of overtones. I think there's a case for saying that some things don't really have a place on the small screen at all, and belong to the private cinema club for those who really like that kind of thing.

I But don't people realize the difference between fantasy and reality?

JB Ah . . . I don't actually think people do know the difference between fantasy and reality, not that that always matters it can even be quite amusing. On BBC radio, the programme *The Archers*, the popular everyday tale of farming folk, they wanted to write a new baby into the story at one point . . . they'd had a young couple getting married and er . . ., a couple of years later they thought 'time to introduce a baby into the script' and they decided against it because they didn't have the staff at the BBC at the time to cope with the flood of little white knitted woolly things that would be arriving for this non-existent baby! They had to wait until they'd got the secretaries and so on to cope with it! So people do believe in it. It's ridiculous, people write to *Coronation Street* for the imagined wedding anniversaries and birthdays and funerals and so on that crop up. Fantasy is . . . is . . . very difficult to remove from reality.

I What evidence is there that, um, the violence or indeed sexual behaviour that is seen on television is reflected in behaviour . . . I mean isn't it the other way round?

JB This of course is the big debate and it is true that television both reflects and influences. I think we've all had the experience of being enormously inspired by magnificent music or a stirring speech or a call to courage. We've all been moved by some impressive event on television and certainly we can even see within a whole country that you can create a mood or a climate by the way in which you present an . . . an activity, and I think that it's rather silly to imagine that people who are uplifted by er . . . a lovely piece of pageantry or by stirring music are not depraved by something that's disgusting. Clearly we're both. It is true tha . . . that the mixture between what influences you and wha . . . and how *you* influence the screen is . . . is a blurred area and everybody in the mass media knows this, but I would say that by and large one of the major influences on all our lives is television, and people wouldn't spend thousands of pounds on advertising on it if it didn't influence people -

'Persil washes whiter' says the voice over and over again and millions of housewives are absolutely convinced that it does and they go out and buy the product. So I think the influence is mostly that way round.

Tapescript 16b

Interview with Kate Adie, a BBC journalist

I = Interviewer
KA = Kate Adie

I   What evidence is there that, er, television influences behaviour?

KA There is quite a lot of evidence that it influences behaviour in a manner of life-styles, images, popularity of fashion. Whether it's a deep influence on behaviour is question-able, because it could be seen as both a force for good and a force for evil, and many of the grey areas in between, and it's certainly not one nor the other, because television, for example, has endless images of heroism, of good, of . . . of grandeur, of charity, of loving, which . . . and we have a world which certainly doesn't emulate that one hundred per cent of the time. Also television has images of violence, of unpleasantness, of evil, of cruelty, and . . . again you find that in society, but not one hundred per cent. I'd almost reverse the remark and say that I think that television is a reflection of the society in which you live, as long as that television is free to be that reflection.

I   When you say 'free to be that reflection', in what ways is it constrained from doing that?

KA I suppose we take the view in this country, where television has . . . on the whole been run by people of a certain amount of education, and a certain social background for many years, that television has, on the whole, been what a certain group of people think other people ought to have. It certainly hasn't been a straightforward television being people . . . what people would like to have. Television being what people would like to have, in other words, a lowest common denominator . . . er attitude to television, would for example, er, introduce a great deal of pornography onto television. You would also have a much larger percentage of . . . low-challenging pro-grammes. By that I mean pap, really non-chal-lenging, unintelligent, soap opera, quiz pro-gramme . . .

I   You recently made a television documentary on the subject of violence on television. To what extent did this change your views?

KA I'm going to sound a very obstinate, ignorant hippopotamus and say . . . you know, not a great deal, because I work most of the time in this area. I work . . . I spend a lot of my time seeing with my own eyes the sort of subject which is extremely difficult to put on television, which I was making the programme about, about violence. I see quite a bit of death and cruelty and . . . of unkindness and violence and brutality. All of these things. And I have to make regular judgements about what I feel can be shown on television, and I by no means have ever believed that everything can be shown. I see no evidence, I hear no evidence of real harm done to people by the mere showing of violent acts on television, with the rider that, of course, there are always people who will be watching who are uniquely susceptible.

I   So you're saying that there are certain people who may be influenced?

KA Of course there are.

I   But they (unclear) . . . majority.

KA There are . . . they . . . of course there are people who are influenced by anything.

I   In the course of your work you deal with issues that contain real violence. There's also a lot of fictional violence on television. Do you feel that viewers can understand the difference between fantasy and reality?

KA Most can. First of all I think it's up to the television erm . . . companies, for a start, to bear some responsibility for saying 'This is fictional; this is a fantasy', and to say 'This is reality'. I think television companies have a responsibility on one side, on the other side I think that most viewers do distinguish. Some don't. There are hordes of people, you know, in this country, who . . . are . . . are deeply in search of Coronation Street in Lancashire. They actually . . . you know . . . people go and try to find the Archers. They want to know where Ambridge is. They spend their lives crawling round Yorkshire looking for Emmer-dale Farm. All of these fictional places.

I   What do you personally find offensive on television?

KA I find gratuitous violence extremely offensive. I don't like violence. I don't like it in real life. I am actually physically sickened when I see people fighting. I do not like it. Erm . . . I . . . I also find horror where there is a sort of . . . where the human body is chopped up, squashed, generally exploded and extruded. I find this appalling. I don't like it myself. I would not stop other people watching it.

Tapescript 17

A poem on English pronunciation

See pages 80-1.

Tapescript 18

The meeting

B = Alice Barron
D = James Dunlop

B   Well, James, the best I can do for a pay rise this year is five per cent. Sorry. You see, it can't be more because, well . . . quite simply, profits have been lower than expected.

D   Five per cent! But at the beginning of the year you said it would be at least eight per cent! Do you realize that the rate of inflation this year is running at ten per cent? Most of the work-force can hardly afford to pay their bills.

B   James, I know very well that the situation is difficult. I'm not having a rise at all. I'm really sorry it can't be more this time round. But the company must have capital for research and development. Without that, there'd be no future. The company would have to close.

D   I don't believe that ! We've got orders for the next twelve months. You're just trying to keep the pay rise as low as possible. Well, there'll be trouble, you see. You could have a strike on your hands.

B   That really would be a terrible thing to happen. Look, why don't you explain the situation to the staff, and then come back to me?

D   All right, but only if you say you're prepared to negotiate a settlement and not just impose a figure.

B   Well, all right, I'll see what I can do.

UNIT 8

Tapescript 19

'Little Red Riding Hood and the Wolf' by Roald Dahl

See page 86.

Tapescript 20

Sounds

1 A lion roaring
2 A door creaking
3 A church bell chiming
4 Fingers tapping on a table
5 Someone crunching an apple
6 A car horn blaring
7 Someone gasping in amazement
8 A boot squelching in mud
9 A stone plopping into water
10 The click of a camera
11 A door banging
12 Someone groaning in pain
13 A wolf howling
14 A fire crackling
15 Someone shrieking in terror
16 A squeaky toy
17 A sandbag thumping onto the floor

Tapescript 21

Interview with Barbara Cartland

I = Interviewer
BC = Barbara Cartland

I   Your first novel was published in 1923, and since then you've written over four hundred and fifty books. In fact, you hold various world records. Can you tell me a bit about that first?

BC Yes. At the moment I hold the world record for the amount of books I've sold, which we say is forty-five million, but we don't really know, because when I went to I . . .Indonesia the other day, the children kept coming up for autographs, and I said 'What's all this? I don't publish in Indonesia!' What a surprise! I found they'd plagiarised every book, including the last two from America, and every publisher printed them! So er . . . my son spoke to the ambassador and he said he could do nothing limply, so I'm . . . I'm in Indonesian, I'm in . . . I found a book of . . . mine written in Thai, which they hadn't paid on, and all these Indians always plagiarise everything. So I mean I've no idea how much I really sell, it's absolutely extraordinary! And it's very interesting because, as you know, I'm very pure, and my heroine is never allowed to go to bed until she has the ring on her fingers, and erm . . . I sell more than anybody else. And what I've done is also . . . that is the amount of books I've sold, according to the *Guinness Book of Records* I'm the best-selling author in the world . . . and I've also done the record number of books every year. For the last eleven years I've done an average of twenty-three, and nobody's argued (laughs). They ke . . . they keep saying, 'You know, you've done more than anybody else.' So I presume there it is. And now at the moment I'm just starting on Monday, I shall be starting my er . . . eight-eenth this year, so I shall have broken the world record again.

I Amazing! How do you set about organizing your writing day? I mean, to write so much you must be very organized about it.

BC Oh, I'm very organized. I have five secretaries. But what I do is, every day that I'm at home, like today, you see, (mumble) until you could come at four o'clock, I erm . . . I write between six and seven thousand words. Yesterday I did eight thousand by mistake, which was between ten-past one and half-past three. And I lie on the sofa, and I shut my eyes, and I . . . just tell the story. I make very few corrections, actually, I only cut the paragraphs if they're too long. And erm . . . the thing is that when I want a plot, I . . . I say a prayer. I say 'I want a plot. Don't give me two 'cos it's terribly inconvenient' (laughs) and er . . . the plot is there ! I mean, I can't explain why, but instantly I have a plot. And then I read twenty to thirty history books for every novel I write for the simple reason that I'm used enormously in schools and universities, especially in America, and so everything has to be correct. I mean I take an enormous amount of trouble. I ring up the Indian embassy if I've got a train going at a certain date, 'cos I write in the past, you see, and say, 'Had the trains got as far as Peshawar?' If they hadn't, I don't put it in, you see. And I do all those little things. And the other day I was doing one er . . . going to er . . . to Holland, you see, to Rotterdam, and I found out exactly when they . . . where they went from in England, what it cost and how long it took. I mean, person . . . they don't all know . . . but the Americans love it, because they say they have a history lesson and a geography lesson in everything I write, and I enjoy it because I like to be . . . to have perfection.

UNIT 9

Tapescript 22a

A variety of accents

1 Hello there! I come fer (from) a large town, and it's on a very big river, and the big river goes out to the sea, and once upon a time the place where I come fer used to build ships, and these ships went all over the world. And people went everywhere. You could get ships to Ireland, you could get ships to your Far East, you could get ships to England. But no' anymore, because the industry's all gone now. There's nae mair (no more) o' that stuff.
Now the town is broken up into two pieces. You've got the East End, and that's where all the poor people come fer, and you've got the West End. That's where . . . the university is. You've got all the posh people down that way. You get people like . . . talk in funny ways. They talk posh. 'You ken when I mean?' But, where I come fer, it's all high-rise blocks and motorways. In the old days - do you know what I mean? - there was the Gorbals and there was tenement flats, and aye! Folks were rough, you ken? But underneath all that, it was friendly. You know? You get people upstairs, you get your friends down the close, and everybody going together. And what can you say about the weather? Well, you ken, there's a great word for it when it's kind of raining and a wee bit damp. It's drich. And it looks drich. I'll tell you, it looks drich.

2 Well, I live in a very large city. It's a port, and it's on the River Mersey. It's very close to Wales, and in fact locally it's known as the capital of Wales, but that's a joke, really.
It's got several landmarks. One is known as the Liver Building, and that's right on the river. It's a great big building with two towers, and on each tower there's an enormous bird, which is called the Liver bird. There's also . . . we've got two cathedrals, and they're at opposite ends of a long street, which is called Hope Street. One's a Catholic cathedral, and it's very modern - looks like, you know, a rocket that's about to take off. And the other one is traditional.
The industry, of course, being a port, is mainly shipping and the docks. There's a lot of unemployment in our city and it causes a lot of bother. It's a depressed area, really. The attitude of people from other parts of the country is . . . isn't very friendly towards us. I mean, there is the north - south divide. There's no getting away from it. And they all think we're lazy layabouts and good-for-nothings, and they think we deserve to be out of work, but it's not . . . it's not like that at all. I mean . . . it's really awful.
People often laugh at our acccent, but it's become very famous throughout the entire world because of four very special musicians, called the Beatles. Erm . . . it's an accent where we talk through our noses, I think, a lot of the time. I think that might be the damp from the river! But erm . . . It's called Scouse.

3 Well, there be two parts to where I come from. There be the moors, and they can be bleak, wild places, with mists and howlin' winds, and you can see the smugglers as are used to be. And then we go' (got) lush, green countryside, with palm trees and plants and flowers as you don' see elsewhere, 'cos you don' ge' (get) no frosts where I comes from. Heh . . . it be often wet, though, with grey sea mists and drizzle comin' off the cliffs.
Where I comes from is famous for clotted cream . . . and pasties. Now there be a meal an' arrf (and a half). Men use' take pasties into the fields for lunch - potato, carrot, p'raps some meat, all wrapped in pastry. You don' ge' good 'uns now, though.
We be warm folk, we look after usselves, we ain' so keen on forrners (foreigners) from up country, though. We li' (like) takin' arr (our) time over things, there be no poin' rushin' 'bout. If summun (someone) say 'I do it drekkly (directly) f'ree (for you), m' dear', it mean I do it in the nex' three month'. Heh. We have arr (our) own accent, course we do. We say 'Oh arr!' for 'Oh yes!' We say 'How you seemin'?' 'I urrai (I'm alright).' An' we say 'Time furra touchpipes' - that's 'time furra break, time furra rest'. An' we might have some crib, that's sum'n (something) to eat mid-mornin'. Ooh, arr. We have us own ways.

4 I come from a very big county. Erm . . . there's a huge variety of scenery in it. There's hills and dales, and there's er . . . sweeping sort of bleak moors as well er . . . and some sort of rugged coastline. At one time, there was a huge amount of industry there - manufacturing, textile and steel industry, but now of course, a lot of those have closed down, and other industries have come in. The people up there have a sort of a . . . a double reputation. They . . . they're both meant to be er . . . warm-hearted and hospitable, but at the same time you hear they're very suspicious of strangers. And where I come from, we call them 'comers-in'. And you're a comer-in even if you've been living in the town for twenty years or so. Erm . . . the weather is . . . is very mixed. It can be er . . . very . . . very good weather and very . . .

very wet. It's er . . . usually associated with being very wet up there.
Erm . . . the accent. There's a bit of a cliché erm . . . that people use when they're talking about the accent of this county . . . erm . . . they say 'There's trouble at t'mill'. Now, that 't' (of) course stands for 'the' - trouble in the mill - but in actual fact, it's never actually sounded, so you'd say 'trouble in mill, trouble in . . . trouble in mill.' Erm . . . there's odd words, like 'lakin'', that's messin' about, playin' about, lakin' about. And you might say 'I'm off whoam now' - 'I'm goin' 'ome.' And there's a motto for this county, which sums up another characteristic of the county people, which is meant to be a sort of meanness erm and . . . also a sort of knowingness. Anyway, the motto is 'See all, 'ear all, say nowt; eat all, sup all, pay nowt; and if thou ever does owt for nowt, always do it for thissen.'

5 Where I live there's this huge river called the Tyne, and now . . . this river is famous for its bridge - it's got the most er . . . wonderful bridge ever built in this country. It's er . . . a big, metal bridge, you know. It's been there for, oh, a long time. It was one of the first metal bridges ever built, I think. And er . . . it's called the Tyne Bridge, you know, and it's . . . it's famous. And er . . . it's one of the great landmarks of er . . . this town. And erm . . . on one side it's called Tyneside, you know. It's funny that, because both sides are Tyne side, really, but anyway just one side is called Tyneside, and you're actually a Tynesider if you live there. And I would say the main industry is er . . . coal, you know, you've got mines all over the place. A lot of people, you know, from up there emigrate because the weather is dreadful up there. It's all cold and rainy, you know. And er . . . a lot of people got to places like well, Canada or America, you know. Now, with regard to the accent, as you can hear, it's a bit strange, but, you know, it can be even stranger. If you're a real Geordie, you say things like er . . . instead of 'I'm going home', you say things like 'I'm gannin yem; I'm gannin yem, hinny'. And nobody understands what you're saying, if you come south, you know.

Tapescript 22b

'Where I'm from'

1 I'm fer Glasgow.
2 I'm from Liverpool.
3 I be from Cornwall.
4 I'm from Huddersfield, in the West Riding of Yorkshire.
5 I come from Newcastle.

UNIT 10

Tapescript 23

A political speech

Ladies and er . . . Gentlemen. I would like to talk to you for a moment about the current er . . . situation. Never before has this country faced such a crisis point and what is needed is courage and honesty. Should we fail to deal with the situation firmly, the consequences could be er . . . absolutely disastrous for us all . It is at moments such as this that the true character of a nation shines through, but I seriously believe that the right action taken now will resolve the problems that have faced us so menacingly. (Applause) What we must all realize is that the way ahead is hard, and sacrifices must be made, but on no account and in no circumstances must our resolve be shaken. It is quite obvious that those who do not firmly believe, as I do, that this is so, are mistaken. Were we to act as they suggest, we would face a situation from which we might never recover, and this must not be allowed to happen. (Applause) I sincerely hope that you will join with me in saying 'Yes' to what I am proposing, because saying 'No' would mean not only that I was defeated, but also that I was wrong. Thank you.

Tapescript 24

Interview with Nigel Dempster

I = Interviewer
D = Nigel Dempster

I You're by far Britain's best-known and most widely read gossip columnist. Is there a serious purpose in what you write in the *Daily Mail* or are you chiefly concerned simply to entertain your readers?

D We're basically concerned with informing our readers. Obviously if we entertain them at the same time that's an added bonus. But information is why people buy newspapers, because they want to find what's going on in places where they cannot be and they rely on me and my staff and my colleagues in the *Daily Mail* to bring them what actually happens in places of power and privilege, places where they would like to be but obviously can never get inside.

I Do most of the people whose names appear in the Mail Diary spend their time trying to avoid getting their names in the Diary or are there more people who are actually on the telephone to you trying to get you to print their names in the Mail Diary?

D The very nature of a gossip column is that people do not enjoy featuring in it because when we write a story it is not to the subject's advantage usually, because they've done something wrong, something silly, something sexual, financial misdemeanours, something along that line or treated someone very badly like a member of their staff, and they don't enjoy being in the *Daily Mail* Diary. Obviously there are people who'd like to get into gossip columns - we're not the only gossip column - those people can find somewhere like the Express, or other newspapers, which don't mind so much what they write about, or who they write about. We take the view that those who want to get in, don't, and those who don't want to get in, certainly do.

I Is gossip something people in Britain seem to enjoy more than people in other countries, as far as you can tell, is goss . . . is there a special taste for gossip in Britain?

D You've got to have the basic ingredient, which is a homogenous society, and of course we've all lived cheek by jowl with each other for nine hundred years, more or less, and therefore we all know who we are, whether it's the rich man in his castle or the poor man at his gate. We all understand who the Duke of Marlborough is, or what he represents, even though we don't know the Duke of Marlborough. And therefore we all have an interest in each other, because we can equate to any story, we can equate to stories about people who live at one end of the country, even though we live at the other end, which you can't do in vast places like America. Also we've got a very strictly structured class system, which starts with the Monarchy at the top and goes all the way down to the lower classes at the bottom. And everyone within that class system is totally

aware of where they are on that class ladder, and of course they want to climb, and to climb they need to know who's above them and who's below them.

I The Royal Family is very widely featured in the press in Britain. There seem to be stories about them in the British newspapers, especially stories about the younger and more glamorous members of the Royal Family, every day. How do you go about finding new information out about the Royals?

D There are, of course, about thirty-five members of the Royal Family if you take the oldest, the great Queen Mother, down to the youngest. And all of them are doing something every day, and if they're not, they should be. And it's very easy to find out stories because the people around them tend to tell you what's happening, so therefore you've got a filter of information coming all the way through. The Royal Family have got many staff, many people around them, from detectives, from household staff, who do gossip wherever they have time off, and stories do tend to come out. Therefore, there is a preponderance of stories about the Royal Family, and they tend usually to be highly accurate. And of course, we tend to find them amusing because they live rich and gilded lives, and they have a certain duty to the British public because the British public pays them nearly six million pounds a year reimbursing their expenses, they have a certain duty to be exposed to the British public via the Press.

I You often see much more outrageous and explicit stories about the Royal Family in foreign newspapers and magazines. Do you have any particularly extreme examples of inaccurate reporting of the Royal Family by foreign journalists?

D All reporting of the Royal Family by foreign journalists is inaccurate, and in fact it's a total invention. *France Dimanche*, which is a Sunday newspaper in France, based in Paris, has a gossip column which is one hundred per cent invention. And the Queen, who reads French, of course, extrememly well, and is fluent in French, has great fun reading it out to her family, because, in *France Dimanche* over a ten-year period, she worked out that she had abdicated thirty-two times, she'd had cancer surgery on both her breasts four hundred and thirty-two times, her mother had been banished to Scotland twenty-eight times, Lord Snowdon . . . etcetera, etcetera, etcetera. There is an amusement value as long as you start with the initial presumption that nothing is . . . is true.

UNIT 11

Tapescript 25

Edward de Bono's story of the worms

I = Interviewer
dB = Edward de Bono

I Usually we think in a straightforward, perhaps we could call it vertical way, using a certain amount of logic. Lateral thinking is a different way of thinking according to Dr de Bono, perhaps demonstrated well by one of his stories.

dB The story is of three worms who go for a walk and there's Mummy Worm, Daddy Worm, and

Baby Worm . . . and they come to a mound of sand . . . and each worm goes through the mound of sand and when they come out the Baby Worm looks back and says 'Oh that's strange, there's only two holes.'

(pause)

Now you can tell that to people and they sit around wondering and they say 'Well aren't worms hermaphrodites or maybe they went through the same holes . . .' and all sorts of things.

I That's easy . . .

dB The answer is . . . (laughs) David Brown has the answer . . . the answer is that Baby Worm couldn't count!

Tapescript 26

Interview with Tony Buzan

I = Interviewer
TB = Tony Buzan

This interview was broadcast on LBC (London Broadcasting Company) radio.

I A certain Professor Rosenweig tells us that the brain can take in ten new bits of information every second for an entire lifetime and still be not more than half full. Well that information is a little mindbending in itself. The abilities of the brain and what the job of the brain is, are discussed in a book called *The Evolving Brain* by Tony Buzan and Terence Dixon. Tony Buzan is Director of the Learning Methods Group and he told me whether our belief that the brain of a young child is more receptive than that of an adult, whether our belief that that is the case is true.

TB Historically we . . . we tend to absorb more information when we're young . . . more new information and then because we've, so to speak, learned and graduated from school or college or whatever we've been studying, we tend to assume that we don't need to take in much more. What actually happens in terms of the brain's potential is that if the brain is used properly, we can continue to learn more and more and more the older we get.

I . . . and does it reach the stage though . . . does your brain reach the stage where it is more difficult because the brain is older, to absorb new information?

TB Well that's what has been assumed . . . er . . . it can reach that stage if the brain hasn't been used . . . er . . . you know if you don't use it say for twenty years and by not using I mea . . . you don't learn any new languages, you don't read much, you don't stimulate it much, you don't ask many questions and you don't try to get many answers . . .

I You just use the information you have in order to live (unclear)

TB Yeah . . . you kind of go on automatic, if you like. If you do that for twenty years and then you suddenly say to the brain, you know, 'Now work out these problems, learn this do that' . . . and so on and so forth, it goes into shock for a little while because it literally hasn't been used to it. But if you continue to stimulate it, it will start to get better. So the only situations in which brains normally get worse are really the kind of major disease or physical damage or simply non-use.

I What are the things that er the brain is responsible for that we don't generally associate with it?

TB It seems in fact that our brain is responsible for virtually the whole lot! I mean anything you can think of that human beings do, the brain is responsible . . . is responsible for every piece of classical music that's ever been written; it's responsible for all the buildings all around the world; it's responsible for every creative thought; it's responsible for the way in which everybody moves. People used to say, for example, that the artist or the person who was good with his hands somehow wasn't brainy . . . but I mean what is it that's moving the hands? What is it that's creating that, for example, sculpture out there in space? It's the brain which is using those hands to recreate outside of itself an image that it's got inside.

I Mmm . . . it sounds as if the brain . . . er . . . is limitless because if you talk about the history of mankind, and you realize that it is only in the past few thousand years that we've come to understand anything about the brain . . . erm . . . and when you think about how many years we've got to go . . .

TB . . . Yes

I Er . . . the mind does tend to boggle a little (laughter) . . . and you think what . . . er . . . we could actually know about the brain, what we could actually do with the brain in three thousand years from now . . .

TB That's right, I mean it is the brain 'boggling' now about its own capacity.

I We've been talking about the evolution of the brain. Has it increased in size?

TB Er . . . yes it has, it's been increasing over the last little while. That's partly because of the . . . er . . . obviously . . . improvement in many of the diets. What it has improved in though, is its ability to use the different parts of itself and . . . its awareness of itself and really in terms of evolution the brain has only just started. It's a very, very new development, the human brain. Evolution's been going on for perhaps some twenty billion years and yet *Homo sapiens*, you know . . . us . . . has only been around for one and a half million, I mean it's almost nothing.

I Well . . . I suppose if it evolves to the stage where . . . I mean the head becomes considerably lar . . . larger to house this larger brain, it is already very heavy indeed, isn't it? . . . the head? It would mean possibly there would be other physical evolution to cope with it.

TB Yes . . . er . . . I mea . . . first of all, at the moment we don't need to have it any bigger . . . er . . . we've got a massive capacity in there that we're not even using but if we could perhaps imagine a time when we are using the brain generally to its full extent, there's a large possibility that it will begin to expand. That may happen in space. There've been a lot of interesting researches done . . .

I In which case the weight . . . the weight becomes less important . . .

TB Yes, and . . . and the various parts of the body will obviously change because it won't need the bones as it used to, because it'll be in a fundamentally weightless environment perhaps and in that case it may be that the brain will just continue to expand and expand . . . and it has been hypothesized that if some humans do leave the planet and they live permanently in space and breed and breed and breed and breed, that within a very few generations the creature in space will be very different from us, and may well have a much larger basic brain capacity.

I That was . . . er . . . Tony Buzan, Director of the Learning Methods Group, talking about that marvellous piece of machinery you carry around with you every day, the brain, which we are assured, is evolving.

UNIT 12

Tapescript 27

Interview with Carl Sagan

A = **Announcer**
BH = **Brian Hayes**
CS = **Dr Carl Sagan**

A This is an interview that Dr Carl Sagan gave to the LBC (London Broadcasting Company). The interviewer is Brian Hayes.

BH 'We've examined the universe in space, and seen that we live on a mote of dust, circling a humdrum star, in the remotest corner of an obscure galaxy.' Well, they're the words of Dr Carl Sagan, which put us into some kind of cosmic context. The task of communicating the history of the universe was taken on by Dr Sagan in a television series which we'll see later this year, and a book called *Cosmos*, published last week. Carl Sagan is Director of the Laboratory for Planetary Studies at Cornell University. He's been involved in the Mariner, Viking, and Voyager projects. There's been much argument recently, especially in California, about Man's origin. Was Darwin right? Do the creationists have a point? Why should we still be arguing about it?

CS Because er . . . Darwin is again disquieting. Er . . . many people who feel that there should be something special and central about human beings are unhappy about the quite compelling evidence that we are just another animal connected by many powerful lines of evidence, in an evolutionary sense, to the great apes and monkeys and the other primates. Um and er . . . they're made unhappy by this. But I think it's so much more elevating to find that we are deeply connected with all the other living things on the Earth, than to imagine that there's something particularly special. If we want to make something special about ourselves, it is within our power to do so. But the idea that we are special through some unearned grace seems to me a little peculiar.

BH The creationists, though, also now seem to be - and I don't know how it stands up, but - putting forward what they claim to be a scientific argument for a creation as it was told in the erm . . . Old Testament.

CS Er . . . they have claimed to do that, but when you look closely it turns out that er . . . nothing of the sort is being done, and their ideas are utterly bankrupt.

BH If it didn't begin when the creationists say the universe began, when and how did it?

CS Well, 'When?' is one question and 'How?' is quite another question. Er . . . there seems to be er . . . very strong, although perhaps not absolutely compelling evidence, that the universe is expanding, the more distant galaxies are running away from us er . . . faster than the nearby galaxies, and if we run this cosmic movie backwards, we find that some fifteen thousand million years ago, all the matter in the universe, and all the energy, was confined to an extremely small volume, you can imagine the galaxies touching. That event is called the Big Bang, and the key question is not just how did it happen, but whether that is the first instant in the history of the universe, because it is perfectly possible that the universe has so much matter in it, that the present expansion of the universe will one day slow down and stop, the expansion to be followed by a contraction, all the galaxies plummetting in towards each other. In which case it is perfectly possible that we live in an infinitely old universe, in which all the galaxies, stars, planets, and living organisms are ground to cosmic ashes, at each cusp in the cycle. If that is the sort of universe we live in, then there's no need to understand a creation, since it was always here. There's no beginning.

BH And is it because the human mind can't cope with that concept that we're constantly trying to find a beginning?

CS Perhaps, but we also can't co . . . cope with the concept of a creation, because I know of no plausible explanation of how that happened. There is a standard explanation, which is 'God did it', but er . . . it seems to me that logic requires that we take the next step and ask 'Where did God come from?', and somehow the theologians all blanch at that er . . . at that question, and say 'God was always here'. Well, that's fine, but why not save a step and simply say that the universe was always here ?

Tapescript 28

Desiderata

Go placidly amid the noise and haste, and remember what peace there may be in silence. As far as possible without surrender be on good terms with all persons. Speak your truth quietly and clearly and listen to others, even the dull and ignorant: they too have their story.

Avoid loud and aggressive persons, they are vexations to the spirit. If you compare yourself with others you may become vain and bitter; for always there will be greater and lesser person than yourself. Enjoy your achievements as well as your plans. Keep interested in your own career however humble; it is a real possession in the changing fortunes of time. Exercise caution in your business affairs; for the world is full of trickery. But let this not blind you to what virtue there is. Many persons strive for high ideals and everywhere life is full of heroism. Be yourself. Especially, do not feign affection. Neither be cynical about love, for in the face of all aridity and disenchantment, it is perennial as the grass. Take kindly the counsel of the years, gracefully surrendering the things of youth. Nurture strength of spirit to shield you in sudden misfortune. But do not distress yourself with imaginings. Many fears are born of fatigue and loneliness. Beyond a wholesome discipline, be gentle with yourself. You are a child of the universe no less than the trees and the stars. You have a right to be here. And whether or not it is clear to you, no doubt the universe is unfolding as it should. Therefore be at peace with God, whatever you conceive Him to be; and whatever your labors and aspirations, in the noisy confusions of life keep peace with your soul. With all its sham and drudgery and broken dreams, it is still a beautiful world. Be careful. Strive to be happy.

Acknowledgements

The publishers and authors would like to thank the following for their kind permission to use articles, extracts, or adaptations from copyright material:

Aitken & Stone Ltd.: extract from *The Murder of Roger Ackroyd* by Agatha Christie.

Geoffrey Beattie: 'Meet the burglar' from the *Guardian* of 20 October 1984.

The Bodley Head Ltd.: extract from *My Autobiography* by Charles Chaplin.

The Bodley Head Ltd. and Ed Victor Ltd.: extract from *War* by Gwynne Dyer.

Bucks & Herts Newspapers Ltd.: 'Night intruder fined £110' from the *Bucks Herald* of 14 May 1987.

Chappell Music Ltd.: 'Mad Dogs and Englishmen', written and composed by Noël Coward. © 1942 Chappell Music Limited.

Chatto & Windus: extract from *Cider with Rosie* by Laurie Lee.

The *Daily Telegraph*: 'Former judge sentenced over driving offences' from the issue of 9 May 1987.

The *Guardian*: 'Double rapist jailed for 10 years' from the issue of 12 May 1987.

The Hamlyn Publishing Group Ltd. for extracts from *My Early Life* by Winston Churchill.

Harper's Magazine: 'Goodbye Dr Spock' by James Traub. Adapted from the March 1986 issue by special permission.

The *Independent*: 'Driver jailed' from the issue of 12 May 1987.

The *Independent*: 'Tarzan of Central Park' by Alexander Chancellor from the issue of 8 October 1986.

Jonathan Cape Ltd., and Farrar, Straus and Giroux Inc.: 'Little Red Riding Hood and the Wolf' from *Revolting Rhymes* by Roald Dahl.

Laurence Pollinger Ltd. and Simon & Schuster: extract from *The Human Factor* by Graham Greene. Published by The Bodley Head Ltd. Copyright © 1978 by Graham Greene.

The *London Evening Standard*: '5 years for boy who killed a school bully' in the issue of 19 December 1986.

David Lorimer: 'On the brink of tranquillity' from the *Guardian* of 19 December 1985.

Mail Newspapers plc: 'Exposed! The fine art of Artspeak' by Jonathan Margolis from the *Daily Mail* of 22 February 1987.

Michael Joseph Ltd. and Multimedia Publications Inc.: extract from *Mindwatching* by Hans and Michael Eysenck.

Mills and Boon Ltd.: extract from *Marriage in Haste*, 1980 by Sue Peters.

Murray Pollinger: 'Parson's Pleasure' from *Kiss Kiss* by Roald Dahl, published by Michael Joseph Ltd. and Penguin Books Ltd. (abridged version by Reader's Digest).

Oxford University Press: dictionary entries from *Oxford Advanced Learner's Dictionary*, 4th edition, 1989.

Robson Books Ltd.: extracts from *How to Live to be 100 – or More: The Ultimate Diet, Sex, and Exercise Book* by George Burns.

Rupert Hart-Davis and Random House, New York: extract from *The Greatest* by Muhammad Ali.

The Scottish Health Education Group and Parents Anonymous Inc. USA: 'Children learn what they live'.

The Society of Authors: extracts from *Pygmalion* by George Bernard Shaw. Reprinted by permission of the Society of Authors on behalf of the Bernard Shaw Estate.

Syndication International (1986) Ltd.: '10 years for mob leader' from the *London Daily News* of 11 May 1987.

The Economist: extract (television statistics) from the issue of 20 December 1986.

Times Newspapers Ltd.: 'Stop being coy' by Bryan Heath from *The Sunday Times* of 29 June 1980.

Times Newspapers Ltd.: 'Test your aptitude for learning a foreign language' from *The Sunday Times* of 6 January 1985.

Polly Toynbee: 'The upper class' from the *Guardian* of 13 August 1979.

Victor Gollancz Ltd. and Curtis Brown Ltd.: extracts from *Summerhill* by A. S. Neill. Published by Victor Gollancz Ltd. and Harold Hart Publishing. Copyright © 1960 by A. S. Neill.

Viking Penguin Inc. and G. T. Sassoon: 'They' from *Collected Poems* by Siegfried Sassoon. Copyright 1918 by E. P. Dutton Co. All rights reserved.

The publishers would also like to thank the following for their permission to reproduce photographs, illustrations, and cartoons.

Chris Addams © The New Yorker Magazine Inc.
All-Action Picture Library
Ancient Art and Architecture Collection
Arcaid
Sally Artz © Reader's Digest
Nick Baker © Reader's Digest
Anthony Blake
Butlins
Quentin Blake © Jonathan Cape Ltd.
Bridgeman Art Library
Richard Bryant
Camera Press
Barbara Cartland
Colorific
Colorsport
Dominic Photography
Douglas Dickins Photo Library
Greg Evans Photo Library
Mary Evans Picture Library
Gloucester Record Archives
Ronald Grant Archive
Sally & Richard Greenhill
Hoest © Parade
Michael Holford
BBC Hulton Picture Library
Women's Journal
The Keystone Collection
The Kobal Collection
The estate of Fernand Léger, 1881–1955 ('The Red Statuette') © DACS 1989
Magnum
Ken Mahood © Punch 1981
Mansell Collection
Marks and Spencer plc
Merseyside County Museum
The estate of Joan Miró, 1893–1983 ('Harlequin's Carnival') © ADAGP (Paris); DACS (London) 1989
Mizz
Gene Myers © Good Housekeeping
Next
Private Eye
Ken Pyne © Reader's Digest
Radley College
Rex Features Ltd
Ronald Sheridans Photo Library
Science Photo Library
William Scully © Punch 1973
Sempé Cartoons © Christian Charlton
Tony Stone Worldwide
Summerhill School
The Sunday Times
Jim Thompson © King Features Syndicate
Topham Picture Library
Transworld Features Syndicate (UK) Ltd.
Trog © Reader's Digest
John Walmsley Photo Library
Zefa

Illustrations by:

Kevin Baverstock
Keith Bendis
Jacqueline Bissett
Peter Clarke
Karen Ludlow
Chris Priestley
Axel Scheffler
RDH Artists
Paul Richardson
Brian Walker
Paula Youens

Location photography by Rob Judges
Studio Photography by Mark Mason

Every effort has been made to trace the owners of copyright material used in this book, but we should be pleased to hear from any copyright holder whom we have been unable to contact.

The authors would like to thank the writers of various standard reference books, especially Randolph Quirk, Sidney Greenbaum, Geoffrey Leech, and Jan Svartvik (*A Grammar of Contemporary English*); Jake Allsop (*Cassell's Student's English Grammar*); Michael Swan: (*Practical English Usage*), and Hugh Gethin (*Grammar in Context*). We would also like to thank the people at Oxford University Press for their undying help and encouragement. Our thanks go too to Richard Carrington for his interviews with Graham Greene and the soldiers from the 1914 Christmas Truce. Finally, we would like to thank Tim Lowe, who read the manuscript and made most helpful comments.

Oxford University Press
Walton Street, Oxford OX2 6DP

Oxford New York
Athens Auckland Bangkok Bombay
Calcutta Cape Town Dar es Salaam Delhi
Florence Hong Kong Istanbul Karachi
Kuala Lumpur Madras Madrid Melbourne
Mexico City Nairobi Paris Singapore
Taipei Tokyo Toronto

and associated companies in
Berlin Ibadan

Oxford and Oxford English are trade marks
of Oxford University Press

ISBN 0 19 433563 1
© Oxford University Press 1989

First published 1989
Eleventh impression 1995

Set by Tradespools Ltd., Frome, Somerset
Printed in Hong Kong